COOKING
THE
NOUVELLE
CUISINE
IN AMERICA

COOKING THE NOUVELLE CUISINE IN AMERICA

A

Glorious Collection of Original Recipes

*Michèle Urvater
and
David Liederman*

Illustrations by Barbara Moore

Workman Publishing, New York

Library of Congress Cataloging in Publication Data
Urvater, Michèle.
Cooking the nouvelle cuisine in America.
Includes index.
1. Cookery, French.   2. Cookery, American.
I. Liederman, David, joint author.   II. Title.
TX719.U76   64.5′944   79-64785
ISBN 0-89480-111-2

Book and Cover Design: Paul Hanson

Workman Publishing Company, Inc.
1 West 39 Street
New York, New York 10018

Manufactured in the United States of America
First printing October 1979
10 9 8 7 6 5 4 3 2 1

for Michael

for Susan

1/20/2012

To Cynthia —
at this book.
Your boyfriend likes to
cat — The recipes work
well —

Fondly!

ACKNOWLEDGMENTS

Our greatest thanks go to Michael Cook who so generously helped us write the text of our cookbook. Without his
encouragement, we might never have finished. Addition-
ally we wish to thank him for the three and a half years he
spent tasting all the recipes as they were being developed.
This often led to overeating but he never abdicated his responsibility or lost his bowl.

We should also like to thank all the chefs we interviewed and who helped inspire this book, especially the
Troisgros brothers. Not only did they allow David to work
at their range for several months, but they spent time dis-
cussing with us their concept of nouvelle cuisine. Additional insight into the cuisine came from Michel Guérard,
Paul Bocuse, Jacques Pic, Palladin at Table des Cordeliers
in Condom, Bernard Loiseau in Saulieu, and Jean Pierre
Billoux in Digoin.

We are grateful to Peter Workman who had enough
faith in us to make the commitment to publish the book at
a time when no one believed nouvelle cuisine was here to
stay; to Suzanne Rafer, our editor, who had infinite pa-
tience through it all; and to Gail MacColl, who learned
more about cooking than she perhaps wanted to.

A special thanks to Adele Kaplan (David's mother)
who fed him long before he learned to cook for himself.

And finally, thanks to all the people who helped in
the testing of the recipes: Jerri Buckley, Susan Ginsberg,
Pat and John Greene, Kennan Hourwich, Pat Loughlin,
Nan Mabon, Ann Meyer, Peter Rothschild, Brenda Savard,
Robert R. Shapiro, Bert Snyder, Betty Strauss, Sone Tak-
ahara, Carol Wallace, and Rolly Woodyatt.

Introduction

THIS BOOK was written because the authors believe in the principles of the *nouvelle cuisine,* which are basically the principles of excellent, unpretentious cooking. These principles need to be de-Frenchified and demystified — to be explained, explored, and developed in the American context.

Most people are surprised to learn that they can create *at home* meals comparable to those served in the three-star restaurants of France. Some of the recipes included here are adaptations of dishes actually served in the best French nouvelle cuisine restaurants. Most, however, are original recipes created for this book. All the dishes are designed to be made by an amateur in the ordinary American kitchen with American ingredients. They have been tested by non-professional cooks and found to work.

But why on earth, you ask, should you read and practice this version of the nouvelle cuisine when you can go straight to the source and read books by Pierre and Jean Troisgros or Michel Guérard? Very simply because the authors, unlike the founders of the nouvelle cuisine movement, are familiar with both restaurant and home kitchens and with French and American ingredients.

David Liederman has known the Troisgros brothers since 1969 and has been a close observer of the development of their cuisine. He was the first American to work as a cuisinier in the Troisgros restaurant in Roanne. There he became familiar with the workings of a three-star restaurant, and learned how to make the reduced stocks which are the bases for the nouvelle cuisine sauces. He was so impressed with the intensity of the sauces, and the simplicity of their preparation once the reductions had been made, that he wanted to bring what he learned to the American cook. To do this, he founded a company, Saucier, which makes these reductions and sells them in frozen form. In this book, David describes how to make and reduce these stocks at home.

Michèle Urvater met David at the hotel and restaurant school where they both trained. She is a professional chef, a cooking teacher, and a food writer. As a teacher Michèle has seen the interest of her students in nouvelle cuisine and their misconceptions about it fostered by articles in the American press. Aware of her students' time and space restrictions—most work and have small kitchens— she developed techniques and organizational skills which would allow them to create three-star meals at home.

David and Michèle traveled to France and to Crissier in Switzerland to study nouvelle cuisine, and in the summer of 1976 they interviewed a number of chefs in the movement. These included not only luminaries such as Troisgros, Guérard, and Bocuse, but their lesser-known disciples: Loiseau, Billoux, and Palladin. Thus, they are well versed in the movement and its development.

Furthermore, no other book in English has explained the history and principles of nouvelle cuisine completely and accurately, nor truly adapted it for Americans. Today a large number of people in the United States have the interest and skills necessary to make these dishes at home. This interest manifests itself in many ways: the myriad of cookbooks published and sold, the numerous new cooking magazines, the rising sale of cooking equipment, the proliferation of cooking schools, and the celebrity of such food experts as Julia Child and James Beard.

THE EDITORS

Contents

Nouvelle Cuisine

Nouvelle Cuisine:
A History

NOUVELLE CUISINE is a phrase coined by restaurant critics Henri Gault and Christian Millau and is used as a catch-all term to describe a spirit and several new trends practiced specifically in restaurants in France over the last decade. In order to understand the new developments, it is necessary to go back in time.

It all started approximately twelve years ago, when Gault and Millau, then working for the weekly newspaper *Candide,* set out to tour and review restaurants that had three stars in *Le Guide Michelin.* They visited restaurants established by such legendary chefs as Fernand Point in Vienne and Alexandre Dumaine in Saulieu, sampling exquisite and classic meals everywhere.

At one point, they stopped for lunch at Paul Bocuse's in Collonges. He then had only two stars. They were served a superb meal of crayfish soup, *loup* (wolffish) in puff pastry, cheese, and floating island for dessert. The meal was classic and grand. It consisted of dishes which had appeared for years on three-star menus and were part of the classic Escoffier repertoire. They came back that very evening for dinner, and asked specifically for a light meal, having finished lunch at 4 o'clock. Bocuse went to the kitchen to see what he could do for them. He returned with a simple green bean salad. Unimpressed at first, they were stunned after the first bite. The beans, perfectly undercooked and crunchy, were exceptionally flavorful and had a fresh garden perfume. "It was grandiose in its simplicity," they recall. After that came a dish of slightly undercooked, moist and firm *rougets,* redolent of the sea. The formula for nouvelle cuisine was beginning to take shape.

They told Bocuse, "At noon, you cooked us a grandiose lunch. But this evening we were stunned. With the green beans and little *rougets* you have attained perfection."

Bocuse told them that if it was true simplicity they were seeking, not simplification which stems from laziness, they would have to visit the Troisgros brothers in Roanne. There, in the restaurant of Pierre and Jean Troisgros, which then had only one star, they were astonished again. That day, nouvelle cuisine emerged into the French consciousness.

Like any movement, nouvelle cuisine has its practitioners and its philosophers. As its discoverers, Gault and Millau have remained preeminent among the latter. They have spelled out its basic principles and they have worked to safeguard it from the degeneration to which all movements are prone.

Nouvelle cuisine, as it is practiced in France, was defined and codified in *Gault et Millau se mettent à table (Gault and Millau Sit Down to Eat)* published in 1976. As students and elaborators of this culinary philosophy we owe a great debt to their book and have relied on it heavily for our history and explanation of the movement.

In addition to this "sacred text" these critics have created two publications which protect the purity of the cuine and describe its continued evolution. One is the *Nouveau Guide Gault and Millau* and the other is a monthly magazine entitled *Le Nouveau Guide*.

In the book, an annual review of the better restaurants of France, Belgium, Luxemburg, and Switzerland, the authors reassure us that the nouvelle cuisine is well established. In the introduction to the 1978 guide they describe their role as "limited to following the efforts of those who practice it, to encourage its new disciples, and to chastise those who, through lack of talent, debase it." They rate restaurants on a point system, 20 being ineluctably perfect. It is a personal, not an exhaustive, list, and no one included merits fewer than 10 points. In addition, "toques" (chef's hats) embellish ratings of 13 or more points: one hat for 13 or 14; two hats for 15 or 16; three hats for 17 or 18; and four hats for 19 or 20. These hats are red, if the establishment serves the nouvelle cuisine, and black if the cooking is more classical. While Gault and Millau claim that the black hats are in no way meant to penalize restaurants so designated, it is interesting that there are no nouvelle cuisine restaurants with fewer than 13 points.

Gault and Millau use their monthly magazine as the watchdog of excellence in French food and as the advocate of the nouvelle cuisine in professional kitchens. These two roles are closely related, for, as will be seen shortly, excellence is central to this movement. The magazine publishes travel articles, and food and restaurant reviews. The food reviews rate anything from fancy food stores like Fauchon to commercially prepared products such as sorbets, wines, jams, and preserves. The restaurant reviews look for fine cooking in any style or manner. For example, a new column called "La nouvelle cuisine bourgeoise" publishes recipes developed by young chefs which are adaptations, often simplified, of classic bourgeois dishes. While the authors differentiate the nouvelle cuisine from the classical, they appreciate what is good in both and judge food on its quality, not its trendiness. They look for new dishes or imaginative combinations of foods but they will not dignify a poorly made green bean and *foie gras* salad as "nouvelle cuisine" simply because it is in the new repertory. If the string beans are fibrous and woody and the *foie gras* canned, then the dish is no more worthy of mention than a poorly executed classic *sole duglére*.

While Gault and Millau have been the staunchest and most vocal supporters of nouvelle cuisine, another source of its strength has been the publicity given to the chefs and the sharing of their recipes through their books. The publicity has not only encouraged the public to flock to their restaurants, it has also convinced many young chefs to become disciples of the movement, and to add their creative energies to its continued growth. In addition, the more famous chefs have published books in which they explain in detail how their dishes can be made at home. This openness is much more characteristic of nouvelle cuisine than of the classical school. In classical cooking, being professional was largely a question of complicated preparations, requiring a highly skilled technician, but conforming, generally, to a standard menu of hallowed dishes. In the nouvelle cuisine, the chef's creativity is as important as his technical skill, and giving away your recipes does not mean that you give away your inventiveness. Others may recreate your old dishes, but they won't be able to invent your new ones, and that is where your talent as an artist sets you above the ordinary cook.

We should be guilty of misrepresentation if we claimed that all French chefs are eager to practice this cuisine. Most regional *bistros* and restaurants continue to cook in the classical mode. And let us say right away that we appreciate this art when it is well executed, as do many enthusiasts of nouvelle cuisine. The latter was never thought of as a movement to replace or displace classical and regional cooking. Nouvelle cuisine is merely an evolution of French cooking which shows that it is alive and growing as all arts should be. In music, Beethoven and Stockhausen can be appreciated by the same audience for different qualities. So it is with the old and new cuisines.

Having described the evolution of nouvelle cuisine in France, it is high time for us to explain what it is and what it is not.

Nouvelle Cuisine:
An Explanation

A<small>S WE HAVE SAID</small> before, nouvelle cuisine is a term coined by Gault and Millau to describe a movement shifting away from classical cuisine. It was not a self-conscious, organized movement but rather something which happened and was described after the fact. As if to underscore the fact that this was no grand scheme by the leading three-star chefs of France, Pierre Troisgros in the summer of 1975 said to us "Nouvelle cuisine — I don't know what it is — some invention of the press."

For American audiences it is important to clear up one of the most common misconceptions: that it is some kind of low-calorie diet cooking. Nouvelle cuisine is *not* a diet cuisine. This confusion arose through articles in the American press that misunderstood and then misinterpreted two basic facts.

First, journalists confused nouvelle cuisine with Michel Guérard's *cuisine minceur* (cuisine of thinness). This confusion was compounded by the fact that Guérard is a prominent star of nouvelle cuisine as well, and that some of the principles and techniques of the cuisine minceur are similar to those of nouvelle cuisine. But the differences are more important than the similarities, because the products of nouvelle cuisine are definitely fattening, and only Guérard, of the new chefs, practices cuisine minceur.

Second, journalists took the lack of flour in the new sauces to mean that these sauces, and, therefore the dishes as well, must be less caloric. It is true that nouvelle cuisine sauces are not made with a *roux*, the classic butter and flour liaison, but the reason for this is gustatory, not dietetic. A sauce that is lightly reduced, then thickened with a tablespoon of *foie gras* is richer than one thickened with a *roux,* although lighter in texture and body.

Before further describing what French nouvelle cuisine is and where it is going, it might be useful to mention some of the abuses of the traditional restaurateurs which both Gault and Millau and the new chefs were reacting to. The better restaurants of France had always claimed to cook everything correctly and well, but this was simply no longer true. Much of what went on in French kitchens would have been condemned as much by Escoffier as it was by the new chefs.

To begin with, raw ingredients of an inferior quality were sometimes used, and then manipulated in some way to make them seem better or to hide their faults. Some of this was a result of the lack of quality goods available on the markets, some to the rising prices of fine ingredients. Nonetheless, it had affected the final product.

Perhaps the worst abuses in terms of ingredients involved fish. Responsibility for this goes largely to the fishmongers, who were all too ready to sell restaurants fish that were on their last fins. Chefs would then mask the fish with a strong horseradish sauce or hide it under puff pastry, which was too often store-bought.

Sauces, which are an essential part of *haute cuisine,* were being treated with cavalier contempt. They were sometimes heavily laden with flour to give them a body they did not have on their own, enabling them to stand for hours in a steam table without separating.

Egg-based sauces such as hollandaise and béarnaise might be left out in the kitchen overnight to curdle and spoil. But a chef could pull the curdled sauce together with a bit of water thrown in at the last minute, and the diner didn't know till much later that something "disagreed" with him.

More generally, restaurants were cutting corners in all kinds of preparations, like serving *quenelles* out of cans. Chefs were making old classics in a degenerate, rather than a simplified, form. *Coq au vin* used to be made with a year-old rooster which had been marinated for a day in an excellent Burgundy. But old roosters became unavailable and good Burgundy expensive.

Bouchées à la reine, which was once a chicken filling that included cock's comb and kidneys placed at the last minute in an airy puff pastry shell, had become a bland creamed chicken in a gluey sauce inside soggy pastry.

Even simple everyday procedures abounded with examples of carelessness, such as *pommes frites* which were not drained properly after frying. All this, of course, took place in poorly ventilated, dirty, greasy kitchens that had not changed much since the days George Orwell was down and out in Paris.

To top this list we must mention the shallow tricks used to impress and fool the unwary diner. Foremost among these is flambéing dishes at the table, which, with the blaze of cheap alcohol, dazzles the eyes of the innocent without hurting the food too much. Serious cooks know that flambéing may be part of preparing a dish, but that it serves little purpose at the end.

More recently, restaurateurs introduced exotic dishes, such as Peking Duck, cooking them quickly and incorrectly. The Chinese cook Peking Duck for many hours; the French achieve the same look with a last-minute glaze of honey.

With this catalogue of culinary crimes as a background, the young chefs' search for purity, simplicity, honesty, and a lost elegance in food becomes understandable. But first they had to be freed from the iron rule of Escoffier, whose word had been accepted as law for over fifty years; a law, however, more honored in form than in substance, as all those abuses show. It was Fernand Point, the great and rotund chef of the Pyramide in Vienne, who developed what Pierre Troisgros called "a personal cuisine." Point trained seven of the current three-star chefs, and showed them that they could adapt Escoffier's recipes and create some of their own while remaining true to the spirit of the classical cuisine.

It is this "personal cuisine" which evolved into what Gault and Millau called the "nouvelle cuisine." The best way to define nouvelle cuisine is to paraphrase the ten points Gault and Millau used to describe it to restaurant chefs in their book:

1. Reject unduly complicated and pretentiously overdone dishes. A good example of this might be the popular Beef Wellington. Instead of enhancing an exquisite fillet of beef with a subtle addition of *foie gras*, this dish traps in a puff pastry prison two ingredients which compete for attention, thus robbing the whole of the superb taste of each delicate part. Furthermore, in the process of baking the puff pastry to the proper degree, the insides become steamy and soggy.

2. Reduce cooking times, especially for shellfish, fish, veal, chicken, and vegetables. Rediscover the use of steaming which leaves food all its delicate flavor.

3. Cook what is available on the market and what is seasonal. For three-star chefs, this means buying produce in local markets, as these yield the freshest and best ingredients. It also means looking for the best of what is available, whether it is lobsters from Maine or *foie gras* from Israel.

4. Offer more limited menus, which makes it possible to cook all the dishes with the freshest ingredients. No restaurant can stock year round all the fresh ingredients that are needed for an exhaustive menu.

5. Abandon marinades, often used to camouflage the taste of poor quality meats.

6. Use lighter sauces made with pure reductions of stock, small doses of cream, and fresh herbs. The new chefs no longer use heavy sauces like Espagnole or Mornay.

7. Rediscover regional dishes, whose simple goodness was eclipsed by the pretentiousness of Parisian *haute cuisine*.

8. Use new and modern equipment which can aid in good cooking. An example might be a T-Fal pan, the non-sticking pan which enables the Troisgros brothers to cook their salmon without butter or oil. The French chefs are also adapting equipment from other cultures and putting it to their own use. The Moroccan *couscoussière* can be found in a French kitchen steaming calf's liver or vegetables.

9. Create dietetic dishes or dishes which are light and yet delicious, particularly those emphasizing the simple taste of the freshest ingredients. (This point was picked up by the American press to the exclusion of many of the others.)

10. Emphasize inventiveness. This means freeing yourself from the many traditional garnishes such as beans with lamb or steamed potatoes with sole. It means experimenting with new ingredients not generally used in classic dishes. For example, fresh basil, a mainstay of the Italian kitchen, is now used in nouvelle cuisine recipes. So are exotic ingredients like green peppercorns or kiwi.

In addition to these original ten points, we have noted three further developments. Most significant of these has been the emergence of the chef from the kitchen, often as the owner of the restaurant. He has become a visible personality whose opinions are widely quoted. Besides serving the ends of publicity this has had a more subtle effect on the new chefs. By putting them in closer contact with the consumers of their food, they are both more aware of their successes and more inspired to satisfy the demands of fame with new inventions.

A second development involves vegetables, which were traditionally served only as standard garnishes to classic entrées. Today they are served in more imaginative ways and combinations. For example, in 1975 we had a lamb dish at Alain Chapel's restaurant. It was garnished with succulent, tiny caramelized onions and an intensely flavored nouvelle cuisine *demi-glace* sauce made with a reduction of the onion juice. On a separate plate we had a beautifully delicious array of five vegetables: perfectly cooked green beans, a smooth carrot purée, an unusual turnip and leek purée, a potato *paillasson,* and a sweet eggplant and tomato casserole. Never before had vegetables been so elevated as to merit attention apart from the dish they accompanied. Other examples might be the Tomato Mousse served at La Paix restaurant in Chauffailles or the Eggplant and Tomato Casserole, served at Pic in Valence. Furthermore, vegetables are no longer sculptured and otherwise carved as much as they once were— now they are expected to stand up on the merit of their taste and not elegant appearance.

A third innovation has been in the presentation of food at the table. In the old days, food was elaborately arranged on a platter in the kitchen, and then brought into the dining room, often accompanied by some baroque food sculpture. At your table, the waiter might finish the sauce on a small heater, carve out your meat, put it on your plate along with some garnishes, and then cover the meat with an opaque sauce.

In nouvelle cuisine restaurants, wherever possible, "plating" is done in the kitchen, under the watchful eye of the chef. The Troisgros brothers started the custom of serving everything on oversized dinner plates, as if to frame the work of culinary art in the center. Sauces, which are now often translucent, and thinner than classic sauces, are first spooned on the plate and the meat or fish then placed on top of the sauce. Vegetables are placed in some aesthetically pleasing arrangement around this centerpiece. Or, if the chef doesn't want to detract from the pristine simplicity of the plate, he might serve the vegetables on separate plates. The art of the beautiful plate has perhaps been carried furthest by Michel Guérard. He sends the plates to the table with covers which, when dramatically removed, reveal the beauties hidden underneath.

Certain meats and fish are still carved at the table,

particularly for a dish consisting of a whole fish or fowl, or a rack of lamb. But the sauces will have been completed in the kitchen and are spooned on the plate before the meat is placed on it. This is because the sauces are no longer so thick that they stick or "drape" over the entrée.

A major thrust of the nouvelle cuisine has been the development of new sauces, or rather the adaptation and refinement of old sauces. As we have already mentioned, these new sauces achieve their rich, intense taste through the slow reduction of excellent stocks to a concentrated natural gelatin in the raw materials. The sauces are given further body by the addition of butter, *crème fraîche*, *foie gras*, or a combination of the three. Another less commonly used method of thickening a sauce is with a vegetable *coulis*. We have seen this done by Guérard and by Freddie Girardet at Crissier in Switzerland, and we have used this idea in some of our own sauces. While body and depth of color may still be important in a sauce, the sauce no longer has to cover and cling to whatever food it accompanies. Thus, it does not need a flour and butter *roux* to give it a glutinous consistency.

The reason sauces are no longer made to cling, and indeed that they are served under their accompaniment, stems from another thrust of nouvelle cuisine: the purity and excellence of its ingredients. The delicacy of a fresh fish perfectly cooked might be enhanced by a subtle sauce, but certainly should not be masked by a heavy one. A perfect *foie gras* which has been slowly baked to an exquisite state should not have to compete with brioche or aspic, so it is served plain, with a piece of toasted rough peasant bread.

A CULINARY REVOLUTION

Nouvelle cuisine is revolutionary in terms of classical French cuisine, not in terms of other cuisines. Americans, for example, have long been used to the idea of combining the sweet-sour taste of fruit with savory dishes. Cranberries and turkey or pineapple and ham are part of our culinary culture. Until very recently, this idea, and many others of foreign origin, were anathema to the French. They were unacceptable—that is, until their three-star chefs started experimenting with the forbidden combinations—then they suddenly became French and acceptable. Soon, the French had combined every fruit with every conceivable entrée. In the context of classical cooking, where apprentices had for years been told dogmatically which vegetable must garnish which meat, this freedom was indeed revolutionary.

With this freedom, the new French chefs started creating dishes almost frantically and many of these dishes barely survived the trip from the kitchen to the dining room. Others have stood the test of time, and are now standards of the nouvelle cuisine repertoire.

All this creativity can, for analytic purposes, be categorized under certain headings. Clearly the best known category is the combining of ingredients which were hitherto strangers to each other: Girardet's Scallops, Endives, and Lime; Palladin's Lobster and Sweetbreads in Aspic; and a Rabbit with Raspberries made by Jean-Pierre Billoux at La Gare in Digoin. Many chefs have created salads of greens or spinach topped with duck livers or *foie gras*. Examples of more elaborate combinations include a lobster terrine made by Bernard Loiseau who took over Dumaine's restaurant in Saulieu, and a turbot of Palladin's. The terrine consists of lobster medallions surrounded by a *mousseline* of lobster studded with flecks of cherry, carrot, and morel. The turbot is stuffed with a light purée of vegetables and tarragon, wrapped in lettuce, and steamed. This is then garnished with artichoke purée, steamed carrots, and turnips, all in a light tarragon cream sauce.

Exotic new ingredients were being introduced to the French. Most popular, perhaps, were green peppercorns, passion fruit, and the Australian kiwi. The latter has been served by Girardet with veal, passion fruit has appeared both in sorbets and soufflés, and green peppercorns have been added to poultry and game dishes.

Another innovation of nouvelle cuisine has been to undercook certain foods. The Troisgros brothers serve both a rare Sliced Breast of Duck, and a barely-cooked Salmon with Sorrel Sauce. Carried to its extreme, this has led to adaptations of *sashimi*, the Japanese dish of raw fish. Even cooked fish is undercooked so that it is still raw at the bone.

Some chefs have drawn on regional cooking for their inspiration, or their cooking has been shaped by certain regional traits. Thus, Palladin uses the goose and duck fat of his native Gascony instead of butter and oil. He roasts duck hearts stuffed with *foie gras* over a wood fire, basting them with goose fat. Alain Chapel of Mionnay, on the other hand, has taken the lowly pig's foot, and elevated it with a stuffing of truffles and *foie gras*.

Another trend has been to blend the new and the old. Classic dishes have a new ingredient added to them, like Guérard's *pot au feu* with *foie gras*. Classic preparations are applied to new ingredients, like Bocuse's Navarin of Lobster. And traditional ingredients are cooked in new ways, like Pic's *foie gras de canard* which is roasted instead of baked, and served with a light tarragon cream sauce.

Finally, new desserts have been created, though nouvelle cuisine has given this area the least attention. Guérard's desserts have probably been the most original. His famous Pear Feuilleté combines classic techniques in a new way. This consists of two slices of puff pastry, the top one encrusted with a crackling hot caramel glaze over wafer-thin pear slices lying on a *crème patissière*. Inside is a cold *crème chantilly*, whose soothing coolness surprises and delights you on your first bite. Guérard has an equally impressive, though less well known, peach dessert. This, too, is as beautiful as it is good. It consists of peeled and poached white peaches on a bed of wine *granité* topped with warm honey and a sprig of mint.

Like any movement that focuses on creativity, nouvelle cuisine has been subject to some passing fashions. Much press coverage was given in the United States to seafood being steamed in the natural moisture of seaweed. This is rarely done now in France. Similarly, one no longer sees so many small birds (squabs or pigeons) stuffed with whole vegetables, or plates of assorted vegetable purées. Currently, fruit vinegars and dry red peppercorns are the rage. Many restaurants now have on their menu something called variously *Menu Chinois, Menu Rabelais,* or *Menu Degustation,* which comprise small tastes of a number of the chef's own creations. Another change has affected the dessert cart, which contains fewer pastries and more sorbets and poached fruit. It is impossible to predict which of these innovations will be around in 10 years, but it is safe to say that some of the dishes you eat in France this year will be but a memory 10 years hence.

Nouvelle cuisine has also been guilty of some excesses, though these disappear quickly and are a small price to pay for all the good it has brought. One example we suffered recently was a quickly sautéed *foie gras* of duck served with a blueberry sauce. Not only was the jamlike sweetness of the blueberries jarring but the colors were not pleasing, as they should be in all cuisine. Another preparation that has been mishandled is the sashimi-like raw salmon; instead of being served in delicate thin slices, it is sometimes carved into thick, unappetizing, and inedible wedges.

But the worst abuses that have occurred in the name of nouvelle cuisine have not had to do with poor dishes, but with the widespread publicity given to its major stars. The rapid rise to prominence of young chefs who are imaginative and have thus captured the public's eye with the originality of some of their dishes has enabled them to bypass much of the traditional training, so that they lack a solid foundation in classic principles, and, as one young chef admitted to us, actually cannot do many of the classic dishes. This, in the end, limits their creativity.

The other danger of the publicity has been the commercialization of the movement. Some restaurants have enlarged their dining rooms and kitchens and pushed tables closer together in order to serve more dinners per sitting. Others have made two sittings per evening. Serving more dinners can affect the quality of the preparation, and crowding and rushing the diner can affect the quality of the experience. Seeing all the accoutrements of the restaurants, from plates to linen, from *pâtés* to jams, on sale in the lobby, also detracts from the graciousness of the experience. Finally, the fact that the chef may be on TV or in some foreign land on a publicity tour can affect the level of cooking in the kitchen.

But while the execution of nouvelle cuisine may suffer from its meteoric rise to fame, its principles need not, and it is the principles that we are espousing and reinterpreting.

Nouvelle Cuisine:
An American Interpretation

W<small>E ARE AMERICANS</small>, conscious of our audience, familiar with American kitchens and our native produce, and aware of how our culture differs from the French. It is in this context that we have attempted to explain the original concept of the French nouvelle cuisine, and inspired by its spirit, to create an American nouvelle cuisine.

Since the essence of the nouvelle cuisine lies in its use of the freshest of ingredients, chosen for their taste, texture, and color, we created our own recipes and adapted some French ones with the American seasonal market in mind. This meant that when the ingredients were unavailable for some well-known nouvelle cuisine dishes, such as the green bean and *foie gras* salad, we did not recreate them. To do so would be a violation of the spirit of the nouvelle cuisine. Instead, we chose to adapt a salad of smoked fish, served at Michel Guérard's Eugénie-les-Bains restaurant. Smoked fish, such as Nova Scotia salmon and sable is readily available in American markets, and perhaps even surpasses in quality the smoked fish we have had in France.

Sometimes we embroidered on nouvelle cuisine dishes not because the ingredients were unavailable but because we came up with new ideas. For instance, thoroughly enchanted by the Troisgros' Vegetable Terrine, we created our own by substituting a chicken liaison for the original pork binder. We prefer the taste and color of the chicken as a background for the vegetable mosaic.

Produce commonly available in our markets inspired some of our dishes. We have used soft shell crabs and shad roe for entrées, cranberries for a soufflé, and mangoes and limes for sorbets. We have also been influenced by the mixture of cultures in our midst. Our love of Indian food has introduced us to the tamarind, a dark, dense, slightly sour fruit which we use occasionally instead of our native lemon.

One point we must emphasize is that we created the recipes in New York City, and used the best of what was available to us. Some of these ingredients may not be available in other parts of the country, but we decided not to limit ourselves to dishes which could be made anywhere in the United States. This would have meant the elimination of many of our fish and shellfish recipes, which can only be made where these ingredients are sold fresh, not frozen. Our advice to readers is either to look for fresh local substitutes (for example Stuffed Sea Bass Steamed in Lettuce could be made with mountain trout) or to try another recipe. Since the nouvelle cuisine is a cuisine of inventiveness and of the local market, we encourage our readers to adapt these recipes to their regions—we would love to see what they come up with.

We should also warn our readers about our attitude toward frozen ingredients. We have avoided them and we recommend our readers do the same. We realize that many products are sold in this form, and are often available year round, so their use is tempting. But they do not taste like fresh ingredients, and recipes made with frozen ingredients will simply not be of the same quality. Our answer to questions like "What if we only have frozen bass available to us?" is, don't do that recipe — do another one. This is not to say that one cannot make very good meals with properly frozen ingredients, but that it is not our concern in this book.

Another point on which we are uncompromising is the manner in which we make our sauces. Part of the appeal of nouvelle cuisine is the extraordinary intensity of its sauces. The secret of this flavor lies in the fact that they are made with highly-reduced stocks which we call reductions.

There are no short cuts to this flavor. Anyone who tells you that you can achieve the same flavor by reducing canned stock or doctoring it and thickening it with a *roux* is misleading you. The truth is, you need to make excellent stocks and then reduce them, as explained in this book, and you will then be privy to the secrets of the nouvelle cuisine. Making these reductions is time-consuming but not difficult, and you can prepare them in large quantities and keep them frozen for months. We stand firm on this point because we are addressing ourselves to the large and growing number of sophisticated gourmets in this country and we feel our honesty in this matter will be respected.

Although we feel we have explained every step in every recipe so that novices can do each dish, we suspect our book will appeal especially to the ambitious cook who feels ready to recreate three-star meals at home. Thus, we hope the book will prove challenging to all good cooks and yet clear enough so that anyone interested in great food can execute the recipes if willing to put in the required time.

Cooking the Cuisine in a Restaurant Kitchen

BEFORE WE TALK about planning and organizing a three-star meal at home, we thought it might be useful to describe how a three-star restaurant actually goes about making its dishes. This may help you to understand the function of each step in your own preparation of a menu, which will be explained later.

The basic operation of all three-star restaurants is similar, with variations depending on the physical layout of the kitchen and the signature dishes that have made the restaurant famous. Obviously, a restaurant known for its poached fish will have to be set up somewhat differently from one which specializes in roast meats. On the other hand, both restaurants will have the capacity to do both kinds of cooking. And both restaurants will do their *mise en place* in a similar fashion.

The *mise en place*, the basic organizational tool of the professional kitchen, is the preparation, measuring, and setting out of all the ingredients necessary for a certain dish. This allows the chef to cook any dish ordered rapidly and without interruption. In your own kitchen this same system, adapted to your home, will allow you to cook elaborate meals in a calm frame of mind, without last-minute panics because you are out of white pepper, or you need two minced onions which you forgot to prepare.

There are five stages in the handling of food in a nouvelle cuisine restaurant: purchasing the ingredients, preparing the raw ingredients, cooking the food, plating it, and serving it. All the stages are the same in a traditional restaurant except the last two, whose order would be reversed for reasons we will explain.

PURCHASING THE FOOD

The nouvelle cuisine restaurateurs buy the best and freshest ingredients they can find. They go to the market almost every day, picking out each ingredient with care. Often the local merchants reserve the best merchandise for them because it is prestigious to say that they supply the restaurant. The restaurateurs also have an understanding with local farmers who know they will find a willing buyer in the restaurant for all their mushrooms, *fraises de bois,* and shallots. Occasionally, a farmer will appear at the kitchen door with freshly picked *giroles* or *cèpes,* and the restaurant will always purchase the entire basketful.

PREPARING THE RAW INGREDIENTS

This stage is the *mise en place.* It involves all the cleaning, cutting, and cooking of ingredients so that they are ready for the final cooking and assembly of a dish. The vegetables have to be peeled, the fish has to be boned and filleted, the stocks simmered and reduced, the herbs clipped and set aside. The object of this step is to ready the kitchen so that when the orders come in from the dining room, all the dishes can be prepared to order. At most nouvelle cuisine restaurants, the entire crew spends nearly all of their time working on the raw ingredients; cooking the food takes less than 10 percent of the total work time. There are exceptions to this, of course, such as *foie gras* and stocks, which cook for many hours at a low heat, but even these are only handled and watched for a few minutes at a time. The majority of the dishes take less than 10 minutes to cook.

In such a kitchen, and in all major professional kitchens in France, an apprentice will spend many years just preparing the raw ingredients before he graduates to actually working the range or preparing the food for final consumption. In the process of peeling case after case of fruit, of cleaning the offal from thousands of chickens, the aspiring chef acquires the manual skills necessary for working in a restaurant.

COOKING THE FOOD

Most of the dishes are cooked to order. The headwaiter comes in with orders from a particular table, and the chefs at the range gather the ingredients to make the dishes. For example, in the Troisgros restaurant if Salmon with Sorrel Sauce is ordered, the *poissonier* (fish person) will bring the thin slice of salmon to one of the sous-chefs, who will quickly fry the fish for 30 seconds per side in a greaseless T-Fal pan. Another of the sous-chefs will have made up enough sorrel sauce to last the meal. Portions of this sauce will be reheated, ladled onto a plate, and the barely cooked fish placed on top. While the dish is being put together, a waiter stands by to rush the completed dish into the dining room. The entire cooking process takes less than three minutes. If the restaurant is full, this process will be repeated hundreds of times in the course of the evening.

Work in a restaurant kitchen requires concentration and stamina. Concentration, because when the headwaiter calls out an order, each member of the crew has to note mentally whether he has to contribute anything to that order, and when that contribution will be required. If, for example, a menu is ordered with lamb chops as the second course, the butcher will have to remember to cut the chops in 30 minutes, so that the diner will get them in about one hour. Since there might be 100 people in the dining room in the course of a meal, each ordering up to three courses, this means that in a few hours, up to 300 dishes will have to be made. And since a particular table might order several different dishes for a given course, it takes a great deal of coordination to get them all out at the same time.

It should by now be clear how much stamina is needed for this job. Organizing a kitchen is not unlike choreographing a dance, with entrances and exits carefully co-ordinated, and with each performer watching for the cues that mean he is to do his particular bit.

PLATING THE FOOD

As we have already explained, an innovation of nouvelle cuisine has been to bring many of the dishes out of the kitchen on plates rather than platters. In the classical res-taurant, much effort goes into decorating a platter, from which the waiter serves you your individual plate. Beautiful as the platter may have been, the arrangement of the food on your plate, which is what you are left with, is often rather sloppy. Plating in the kitchen means that the same aesthetic care that went into decorating a platter now goes into ar-ranging the food on the plate, and this delectable display is left in front of you for your enjoyment.

SERVING THE FOOD

Clearly, this last step is the most simple one in a nouvelle cuisine restaurant. While generally it means bringing out individual plates of food, it does sometimes mean carving meat at the table. This simpler service, by dispensing with the bravura showmanship of table-side plating (which might include carving, finishing a sauce over a heater, and flambéing a dish), emphasizes the fact that it is the chef, and not the waiter, who is primarily responsible for the quality of your dinner.

This description of the work in a typical nouvelle cuisine restaurant underscores the planning and coordi-nation that goes into the making of a superior meal. But while the professional kitchen depends on the concurrent efforts of several chefs and apprentices, you will be substi-tuting the intelligent allocation of your own time over several days to achieve the same effect.

The Principles of Composing a Menu

W E GIVE MENU SUGGESTIONS with our recipes, because the secret of a great meal lies as much in the way courses complement each other as in the excellence of individual dishes. Our suggestions are meant as examples to inspire you to make up your own menus, combining recipes in this book with personal favorites.

The principles which guide the fine professional chef should also form the basis of your menu planning. Basically, a meal should consist of dishes which, from first course to last, delight the palate and the eye with interesting contrasts of taste, texture, and color. This means avoiding repetition in a menu, such as several dishes based on cream, or several foods served as a purée or mousse. For example, a cream soup followed by a fish in a tarragon cream sauce would saturate your guests with cream. Nor should these dishes be preludes to a frozen mousse *cassis*, which is again basically cream. This principle holds even if the courses are as far apart as soup and dessert.

There are, however, sensible reasons for deviating from this. For instance, a vegetable purée that is finished off with a touch of cream may follow other cream dishes, because the cream in the purée is not as noticeable a characteristic as it is in a soup or a sauce. Similarly, butter may be repeated if it is the medium in which two ingredients are sautéed, a meat and a vegetable, perhaps. However, you should avoid two dishes where the sauces are both basically butter, such as a cassoulet of fish finished with butter, and a steamed chicken and vegetable dish with *beurre blanc*.

Choose recipes which call for different cooking methods. This not only varies the textures on your menu, it also helps prevent a pile up in the kitchen. Since different cooking methods require different utensils, different areas of the stove, and different timing, you can avoid the horror of having to sauté in all your skillets at once. A steamed dish followed by one which is sautéed, then one which is roasted, and one which is cold, gives each contrasting dish an element of surprise that adds to the guests' pleasure.

The sensitive use of color can enhance a good meal. This is achieved not only through the color of the food, but also of your china. Think of the intrinsic color of the foods rather than just the overused greens of parsley or watercress. A stunning multicolored palette of vegetables can be presented on a simple white or a clear glass plate while an ivory cream fish dish can be highlighted by an oversized cobalt blue plate.

Texture is another important factor to consider. When serving an assortment of vegetables, you might have a purée and a crunchy steamed vegetable, both set against the resilient chewiness of wild rice. Texture can also be varied from course to course. You do not want to follow a puréed soup with a fish *mousseline*.

Most importantly, there is taste. Food has so many different flavors and aromas, that it is impossible to make simple generalizations about arranging tastes within a menu. This, more than the other considerations, will be most dependent on your personal preferences. Some people are crazy about dishes cooked with wine; others might prefer onion or garlic as a background. To some, a true dessert must include chocolate; others insist on fruit as an ingredient. So you will have to work out your own rules about how to vary flavors. Still, it is generally a good idea to go from the delicate to the more pungent, and to intersperse piquant dishes with milder ones, in order to rest the palate.

The above are not hard and fast rules, but rather guidelines and general principles. When you are confident in your understanding of these principles, you can set off in new directions. Instead of the standard sequence of soup, fish, main course, and dessert, you might insert a plate of different vegetable purées between the fish and meat, and serve the latter without garnishes. Or you could develop an entire seafood and fish menu, starting perhaps with cold oysters, followed by a creamed seafood stew, then a vegetable salad, and finally a baked lobster. This may strike you as unusual, and yet if you analyze it, you will see that it satisfies our principles of contrasts, and will delight seafood lovers.

You must also take into account the notions about food that your guests will bring with them. Surprise them — but don't confuse them. At a gastronomical society dinner we were once served a flavorful tomato sorbet, after a soup, fish terrine, and duck. We were interested in our fellow diners' reactions to this excellent intermezzo, since we had just created our own tomato sorbet recipe for this book. Everyone hated it without reservation. When we talked to the other guests, we discovered that their judgments were based on everything except taste. The dish had been listed on the menu simply as a "sherbet," so people expected a sweet sherbet, which is what traditionally serves as an intermezzo. It was served on a cold February night, and would have fared much better as a first course on a hot summer night. It took the place of a salad, but did not work as one. All these feelings prevented people from really tasting a dish which, in another context, would probably have pleased most of them.

All of the above is meant to help guide your thinking about menus. You must also be guided by your own limitations of time, space, and budget. If your stove has burners set close together, don't plan too many dishes which have to be made on top of the stove. On the other hand, if your oven is small or unreliable, don't depend on it for the major parts of your meal. If your refrigerator is small, you cannot store many dishes or ingredients far in advance. If you don't have time to do several recipes from the book, choose one that will stand by itself, and serve it with steamed vegetables, followed by a wonderful cheese, and perhaps a cake from your favorite pastry shop.

Composing and Planning Two Menus

THE TWO MEALS we will plan in detail are a formal winter menu and a simpler summer menu. Lest you think a timetable creates such efficiency that it allows you to be with your guests the entire evening, we should say right off that you must be prepared to be both host/hostess and chef—inevitably you will find yourself spending a good deal of time in the kitchen. We know that most people are caught between wanting to impress guests with an elaborate meal and wanting to spend time with them, but achieving both is simply not consonant with making a great meal. Careful scheduling does, however, enable you to cook a superb meal efficiently, and, by conserving your energies, gives you a more relaxed time with your guests.

When making up a menu, choose recipes that call for ingredients which are in season. If the menu you are planning is lavish, start about two weeks in advance to give yourself time to make the required reductions for the sauces, if you don't already have them on hand.

Make a schedule for the dinner courses, and a timetable for all your preparation and cooking. When working out a schedule for a meal, allow from 30 minutes to one hour for each course, leaning toward the latter if the meal is a formal one with several courses. Your timetable should include shopping, straightening up the house, buying flowers, and all the ancillary work that goes into a dinner party. Remember to allow time for heating up plates and bread, and chilling wines and plates for cold dishes. Decide when you will do the dishes that can be done entirely in advance, like pastries and cold dishes.

In planning your shopping, be sure to make adjustments in the recipes for the number you are serving.

You will, of course, want to buy the best and freshest ingredients, but this desire must be tempered by common sense. You cannot do all the marketing and preparation the day of the party (unless you have apprentices to do the latter), so you will have to buy most of your ingredients a day or two in advance. If you can order fish, meat, and produce in advance, to be delivered to you on the day of the dinner, so much the better. Otherwise, buy the last two in advance, so you only have the fish to pick up on the last day (good fishmongers get fresh fish daily, so you really should not buy it in advance). This planning is based on our own experience—both of us know the severe limitations created by working at regular jobs.

Your schedule should allow you time to finish your *mise en place* before you start cooking. Each ingredient should be cut or chopped, measured out, and placed in a separate dish or plate. This will enable you to move quickly and spend as little time as possible in the kitchen. This is also important because, as you begin to cook, you might have a couple of pans going at once, and you don't want to worry about finding an ingredient at the last minute. Cooking will become more enjoyable if you are well organized.

Since you will probably be cooking alone, you will have to work on coordinating the dishes so that they are finished at the same time. It is for this reason that we have indicated in most recipes up to what point the dish may be done in advance. Obviously, some dishes cannot be made in advance, but must be cooked and served immediately. Many dishes, however, can be either wholly or partially made in advance, and finished or reheated as the meal is actually being prepared and served. You will often be finishing a main dish and coordinating the garnishes so that they can all be served together. The pre-cooking we have been talking about is one way of doing this — make the garnish a day or two ahead, and finish or reheat it as you are doing the main dish. Another way of coordinating dishes is to cook the garnish entirely as you make the main dish, so that the garnish is finished first. Then you take the garnish off the flame, finish the main dish, and put the garnish back on the fire for 30 to 60 seconds to heat it up. This can easily be done with dishes like the caramelized onions. Should you feel that you are not being "authentic" in preparing food this way, let us remind you that even three-star kitchens will pre-cook some items and heat them up at the last minute.

FORMAL WINTER MENU

Poached Fish with Shallots and Vinegar

Julienne of Winter Root Vegetables

Squabs on a Bed of Chestnut Purée

Cheese Course with Bread

Sautéed Pears with Raspberry Sauce

Chocolate Truffles

The wine for the first two courses could be a California Chardonnay, such as David Bruce or Mondavi. For the squab and the cheese course you might serve an American Pinot Noir.

We suggest California wines because these often surpass the wines of France in the same price range. Were you to opt for French wines, both the whites and reds of Burgundy go well with such a meal. Get a white Chassagne-Montrachet for the first two courses and a Burgundy, such as Pommard or a Chateau-Neuf-du-Pape, for the squab and cheese. Whichever you choose, keep in mind that both wines for this menu should be full-bodied and stand up to the powerful flavors we have put together. With wines, it is important not to be intimidated by the old rules, but rather to trust your own tastes, to sample as many wines as you can and to enjoy wines for themselves and not for their impressive labels. If your liquor store dealer likes wines, enlist his help and get him to recommend his favorites.

Before we give you the schedule for this meal, it would be useful to know how we decided on the specific composition of this menu. We thought it more interesting to start with a fish course followed by a separate vegetable course than to start more traditionally with a soup followed by the fish. The Julienne of Winter Root Vegetables was chosen because it is light and includes vegetables appropriate to the season. Serving such a course separately frees you to present the entrée without emphasis on garnishes.

The Squabs on a Bed of Chestnut Purée was chosen because the birds are festively fitting to a formal meal. The chestnut purée has a smooth texture, in contrast to the preceding course, and the sauce is darkly dense and very different from the one accompanying the first course.

We think it appropriate to serve a cheese course with such an elaborate meal but omit this if you wish. Apples and pears are the seasonal fruit, but as we have included a purée with the main entrée, we did not want a soft dessert, such as a purée or mousse. For this reason, our pears are served in slices. The chocolate truffles are a luxurious touch, in keeping with the three-star idea of the *grand dessert*. If you wish, replace these two desserts with a choice of cakes which can be made in advance.

Below is a schedule for the two weeks leading up to the dinner and a timetable for a Saturday dinner. We will explain how we worked out this timetable, so that you will be able to do the same planning for your own menus.

SCHEDULE FOR TWO WEEKS LEADING UP TO DINNER

S	M	T	W	T	F	S
			Week I			
Plan menu, write preparation and shopping list					Shop for ingredients for weekend	Start glace de canard
			Week II			
Finish and freeze glace de canard; time each course		Shop for ingredients for chocolate truffles	Make chocolate truffles; Buy chestnuts	Shopping list for Friday; peel chestnuts	Shop; make chestnut stuffing; make chestnut purée; Roast sliced nuts for dessert; polish silver	Night of Dinner Party Set table

TIMETABLE FOR A SATURDAY DINNER

7:00   Invite guests for this time
7:45   Serve fish
8:15   Serve vegetables
9:00   Serve squabs
9:45   Serve cheese
10:30   Serve desserts
Serve coffee and liqueurs

PREPARATIONS FOR SATURDAY MORNING OR EARLY AFTERNOON

FISH COURSE: Have fish delivered or pick it up. Fillet it if you are doing that yourself. Mince the shallots for sauce; measure out the wine and vinegar for sauce, combine all, and refrigerate. Cut up butter for sauce and refrigerate. Omit vegetable garnish, as it repeats the second course.

VEGETABLE COURSE: Julienne these at latest moment in the day that is comfortable for you; wrap in plastic and refrigerate. Squeeze out the lime juice and refrigerate. Don't forget to double the recipe since you are serving this as a main course.

SQUABS: Chestnut stuffing and purée should be done the night before and refrigerated. The sauce for the squab uses the *glace de canard* reduction, which you must have on hand hand in either the freezer or refrigerator. Clean, wash, and dry the birds.

DESSERTS: Whip the cream and put it in a cheesecloth-lined sieve set over a bowl to catch any excess liquid; cover with foil so the cream does not absorb refrigerator odors; refrigerate. Measure out raspberry preserves and Grand Marnier; put in separate containers for later.

Go over table setting; bring out serving dishes or utensils you will need.

TIMETABLE FOR THE FINAL PREPARATION OF THE MEAL

5:00 Remove the squabs from the refrigerator so that they are at room temperature by the time they go into the oven.

Season the birds, stuff them, melt the butter, and place the birds in the casserole; they are now ready to be roasted.

Chill the white wine (don't do this much earlier or you will break the flavor of the wine by excess chilling).

6:00 Assemble the poaching liquid for the fish in a skillet.

Remove the chestnut purée from the refrigerator and place it in the top of a double boiler. This only has to be reheated.

Remove the *glace de canard* from freezer or refrigerator.

6:30 Guests due to arrive shortly. Note that we do not plan for food and drink before eating because we feel this would spoil appetites; you may, however, offer a Kir or light wine as an apéritif.

Remove butter from the refrigerator if you plan to serve it with bread throughout the meal.

Remove julienne of vegetables from the refrigerator; cook the vegetables and remove from the heat to reheat later.

Reduce the wine and vinegar with shallots for the fish sauce.

6:55 Remove the butter for the fish sauce from the refrigerator. Heat the oven to 425 degrees for the squabs.

7:30 Remove the cheese from the refrigerator so that it won't be too chilled later. Don't remove the cheese too early or it will melt and sweat.

7:35 Cook the fish; heat the bread if you are serving it with this course; warm the plates.

When your guests are seated, finish the sauce and serve the fish. Put the squabs in the oven to roast for 1 hour.

8:10 Remove the dirty dishes from the table.

Reheat the vegetables and heat plates for them.

Continue to baste the squabs occasionally.

Heat more bread if you need it.

Heat the chestnut purée in the double boiler.

8:35 Remove the squabs from the oven and let them rest while you prepare the sauce. Heat the plates for this course. Just before serving the squabs, remove the dirty dishes from the previous course.

9:40 Heat bread for the cheese course. It is up to you to heat bread as you need it throughout the meal.

10:00 After the cheese course, when you feel it is about time to get ready for dessert, get 2 skillets ready and peel the pears as close to the last minute as possible to preserve the flavor of pears (if you find this just frantic, peel the pears in advance and keep them in acidulated water, as suggested in the recipe).

10:20 Remove the chocolate truffles from the refrigerator. Sauté the pears.
After dessert, serve coffee and liqueurs.

If your guests arrive very late, give them 15 minutes to settle in and then adjust your schedule accordingly.

Some readers, who are themselves already highly organized in their cooking, will read this and understand right away how we arrived at this timetable. Perhaps they will even recognize their own system here. But if you are like most cooks we know, you cook by the seat of your pants. You have some kind of organization in mind, but it can be vague on some of the details, and never quite eliminates that feeling of being rushed, overworked, and sorely in need of an extra hand or two. For you, this timetable may be mysteriously complicated, and you might say, "Fine! This would help me for this menu, but how could I ever work one out myself?" To help those who are not natural list and schedule makers, we will explain in detail how we derived this one.

Timetables are basically made in reverse. First, you look at a recipe and decide approximately how long each step will take. Then, knowing when you want that dish to be ready, you put down the steps in reverse order from the time of service, taking into account that, as host, you will spend longer segments of time with your guests and shorter ones in the kitchen. We will go through this calculation for the first three courses.

First, we reproduce the recipes for the fish, vegetable, and squabs, with our estimates of how long each step will take.

POACHED FISH WITH SHALLOTS AND VINEGAR

1. Fillet the fish or have the fishmonger do it for you. Cut the fillet into 1- by 3-inch pieces, season with salt and pepper, and set aside. *30 Minutes*

2. In a saucepan mix the wine, vinegar, and shallots for the sauce and reduce over high heat until all the liquid has evaporated but the shallots remain moist. Remove from the heat and reserve. *5 Minutes*

3. In a separate skillet or pan large enough to accommodate all the fish in a single layer, mix the ingredients for the poaching liquid. Heat them until the butter is completely melted. *5 Minutes*

4. Place the fish in the poaching liquid and cover with a lid. *1 Minute*

5. Bring the liquid to a rapid boil and immediately remove the pan from the heat. The fish will continue to cook slowly while you finish the sauce. *5 Minutes*

6. While the vegetables are poaching, reheat the shallot and vinegar mixture. When hot, finish the sauce by whisking in the butter, tablespoon by tablespoon. Take care not to overheat the sauce or it will separate. The color of the sauce should remain opaque at all times. Add the optional coriander at this point. *2 Minutes*

7. Drain the fish and pat it dry with paper towels. *3 Minutes*

8. Since this dish is being served without the vegetable garnish, we have reduced the time allotted for presentation. *2 Minutes*

JULIENNE OF WINTER ROOT VEGETABLES

1. Melt the butter until very hot. Add the onion slices and sauté over medium heat for 2 minutes, or until wilted. *4-5 Minutes*

2. Add the rest of the vegetables, salt, pepper, and sugar and sauté for 1 minute. *2 Minutes*

3. Cover the skillet, lower the heat, and simmer for 5 minutes. *5 Minutes*

4. Uncover the skillet, raise the heat, add the lime juice, and evaporate all the liquid until the vegetables are slightly syrupy and glazed. Adjust the seasoning. *2 Minutes*

SQUABS ON A BED OF CHESTNUT PURÉE

1. Preheat the oven to 425 degrees.

2. With a sharp paring knife, cut the chestnuts in half and parboil them for 7 minutes in boiling water. *30 Minutes*

3. Drain the chestnuts and place them in a bowl of hot water. Remove the tough outer skin and beige inner skin, working on a few at a time, leaving the others in the water. Reserve. *25 Minutes*

4. Sauté the onions in 3 tablespoons butter until soft and tender, about 7 or 8 minutes. Add half the peeled chestnuts and sauté these along with the onions for another 5 minutes. Remove from the heat. Reserve. *10 Minutes*

5. Pull out any follicles of hair remaining on the squabs, then wash the birds very well, inside and out. Pat dry. Season well with salt and pepper. Spoon one-quarter of onion and chestnut stuffing into each bird. *10 Minutes*

6. Melt ¼ pound butter in a casserole big enough to hold the 4 birds comfortably without leaving too much room around each one. When the butter has just melted,

remove the casserole from the heat. When the butter has cooled down, roll the birds around in the melted butter to coat each one completely. *15 Minutes*

7. Place the squabs, breast side up, in the casserole on the bottom rack of the oven. Roast them, basting occasionally, for 1 hour. *1 Hour*

8. While the birds are roasting, purée the remaining chestnuts with the heavy cream in a blender or food processor. Season well with salt and pepper. Keep this warm in the top of a double boiler, over a low heat. *10-15 Minutes*

9. When the squabs are done, remove them from the oven and keep them warm on a heated platter.

10. Remove as much of the fat from the drippings as possible and transfer the drippings to a small saucepan. Add the *glace de canard* and bring this to a simmer. Whisk in 6 tablespoons of the chestnut purée. Season with salt and pepper. The sauce should have a thick consistency but be quite dark in color, and not taste very much of the chestnut purée. *10-15 Minutes*

11. To serve, place a spoonful of the warm chestnut purée in the center of each plate. Place the squab on top of the purée and spoon some of the sauce over each bird. Serve immediately. *5 Minutes*

We then look at these steps to see which are long preliminary ones we can do earlier in the day. This will include all cleaning, cutting, and measuring of ingredients, filleting the fish, making the chestnut stuffing and purée, and cleaning the birds. This leaves you with only last minute cooking and the hour-long roasting of the squabs. The next task is to put various steps on some kind of schedule.

This is best illustrated by starting with a schedule of the meal (see Table I). Next, we put in the last steps for each course (Table II). This means that for the periods indicated before you serve each of these courses, you will have to be in the kitchen — 10 minutes for the fish, 5 minutes for the vegetables, and 15 minutes for the squabs.

TABLE I

7:00 Guests due
7:45 Serve fish
8:15 Serve vegetables
9:00 Serve squabs

TABLE II

7:00 Guests arrive
7:35 Cook fish and make sauce (Steps 4–9)
7:45 Serve fish
8:10 Reheat vegetables
8:15 Serve vegetables
8:45 Take squabs out of oven, make sauce (Steps 9–11)
9:00 Serve squabs

TABLE III

6:30 Reduce wine, vinegar, and shallots for fish sauce
         Remove butter for fish sauce from refrigerator
         Remove vegetables from refrigerator, sauté and
             finish
7:00 Guests due
7:30 Preheat oven to 425 degrees for squabs
7:35 Cook fish and make sauce (steps 4–9)
7:45 Put squabs in oven
7:45 Serve fish
8:10 Reheat vegetables
8:15 Serve vegetables
8:30 Heat chestnut purée in double boiler. This takes the
             place of step 8
8:45 Take squabs out of oven, make sauce (steps 9–11)
9:00 Serve squabs

Other steps for the meal involve quick trips to the kitchen, which will be kept to a minimum by the fact that you will know exactly what your tasks are each time. The time allotted for finishing these dishes should be clear, though we might explain the fish. Steps 4 through 9 (skipping 6, which we are not doing), according to our estimates on the recipe, add up to 13 minutes, yet we only allow 10 minutes for all this. The reason is that while the fish is poaching (step 5), you can work on the sauce (step 7), so the total time is only about 10 minutes.

Now we can find time slots for the previous steps in each of these recipes (Table III). The time for the chestnut purée only involves the reheating since you cook it the day before. This is a good place, then, to go over the reasons for the times given for removing ingredients from the refrigerator as well as for reheating this purée. Large, dense masses, like a purée, take much longer to heat up than smaller ingredients like butter or vegetable juliennes. Furthermore, butter can become too runny, and even turn rancid, and vegetables can wilt, while a purée will generally stand up to a longer wait. So the purée comes out of the refrigerator at 6 o'clock giving it 2½ hours before it is heated. Then it needs half an hour in a double boiler, because the price you pay for this scorch-proof way of reheating is that it takes longer — and remember, it is a dense mass. On the other hand, the butter only needs half an hour to come to room temperature, and the julienned vegetables only a few minutes.

Can one put ingredients directly from the refrigerator on to the stove? Of course, but that increases your cooking time, so that the fish sauce, for instance, might take an extra 5 or 10 minutes. And remember, you want to be with your guests as much as possible. (Even in a professional kitchen, chefs want to be able to finish their dishes as quickly as possible, so as not to have to keep an eye on too many skillets at once. So they, too, will bring all the ingredients that won't spoil to room temperature.)

On the other hand, you don't want to take ingredients out too early. We have already explained this with the butter and the julienned vegetables. The same applies to cheese, as we explained in the timetable. A counterpart rule is, don't chill white wines too much. That is why we allow only 2½ hours for them in the refrigerator.

Then there are the somewhat more arbitrary times we have given tasks like assembling the poaching liquid for the fish. While this can be assembled at the last minute, it would make things more hectic for you, and take you away from your guests again. So we have you assemble it before your guests arrive. But it cannot be assembled too early in the day, because the butter would turn. In view of this, 6 o'clock seems a reasonable time. Similarly, we have you put the butter in the skillet for sautéing the vegetables at 6:30, just to keep your work to a minimum when your guests are there.

Now, those of you who found the timetable confusing might look it over again, to see if it doesn't begin to make more sense.

SUMMER MENU

Cold Bay Scallops with Cumin Vinaigrette

Medallions of Lamb
with Bordelaise and Port Sauce

Steamed Avocado

Lemon Almond Cake

With the scallops serve either an Alsatian Gewurtz-traminer or a California Riesling. These wines are light and refreshing on a hot summer day. With the lamb, serve a French Médoc or a California Cabernet Sauvignon from Freemark Abbey or Fetzer Vineyards.

The primary consideration in composing this menu for the summer is that both the first course and dessert can be made in advance and the main course is done on top of the stove. Thus the oven need not be on, except to warm plates, and bread if you are serving it. If, however, you have a well-ventilated kitchen, or even the luxury of an air-conditioned kitchen, this may not be an important consideration in putting together a menu and you might make a different selection.

Again, check through each recipe and note the ingredients you need, such as reductions, and plan to get them or make them in advance. See what can be done in advance and what must be done the day of the party. You should come up with a schedule and timetable that looks something like this:

SCHEDULE FOR THE WEEK

F	S	S	M.T.W.	T	F	S
Plan menu; make shopping list for Saturday; shop	Make demi-glace and bordelaise	Finish and reduce demi-glace and bordelaise	Three days off—relax	Make shopping list for Friday	Shop; order fish for Saturday; make cake; polish silver	See timetable below

TIMETABLE FOR A SATURDAY DINNER

7:30 Guests due to arrive
8:15 Serve scallops
9:00 Serve main course
10:00 Serve dessert

PREPARATIONS FOR SATURDAY MORNING
OR EARLY AFTERNOON

FIRST COURSE: Prepare scallop dish and refrigerate. Prepare garnishes for this dish (omit avocado, however, as it is featured in the main course).

MAIN COURSE: Trim lamb and finish the sauce preparation, including mincing shallots.

Set the table, arrange flowers, etc.

TIMETABLE FOR THE FINAL PREPARATION OF THE MEAL

5:00 Chill the white wine.

7:15 Remove the butter for the bread if you are serving any with the meal.

8:00 Chill the plates for the first course.
Heat the oven to heat bread.
Remove the scallops and garnish from the refrigerator to take off the excess chill.

8:15 Heat the bread while finishing and arranging the first course on plates.

8:40 Peel the avocados and rub them with lemon juice.
Finish the lamb dish.
Heat the water to steam the avocado.
Five minutes before you finish the lamb, steam the avocado.
Heat the main course plates; heat more bread if necessary.

9:45 Arrange the cake on a platter; make preparations for coffee.

The Recipe Format

I t is important before cooking from the recipes to familiarize yourself with the principles we used in establishing their format.

PREPARATION TIME: All calculations for these times are estimations based on how long it took us to execute the *mise en place* for each recipe. The calculations are *exclusive* of the time involved in making stocks, reductions, or puff pastry.

COOKING TIME: These calculations estimate the amount of time it will take to do the actual cooking for each recipe, once again, exclusive of the time involved in cooking stocks, reductions, or puff pastry. When we call for a reduction in a recipe, we are assuming it is either refrigerated or at room temperature. If you use a reduction straight from the freezer the sauce may take longer to cook.

SERVING PORTION: Most of our recipes are based on multiples of 4, rather than the more commonly used 6. If a dish can be used as either an appetizer or entrée, we have specified different portions.

SPECIAL EQUIPMENT: Only when we feel an uncommonly used piece of equipment, such as an ice cream maker, is essential to the preparation of the dish, do we list it with the recipe.

SALT AND PEPPER: Often we have indicated specific measurements for salt and pepper in the body of the recipe, but these should be considered as suggestions not requirements. Because salt and pepper are difficult to measure with exactitude, and because people generally season to their own tastes, they have not been included in each recipe's list of ingredients.

BUTTER: The butter referred to in the recipes is always "sweet" (unsalted) butter, unless otherwise specified.

● This symbol in the body of the recipe indicates that the dish may be prepared in advance up to the step in which it appears, and refrigerated for a few days. When you are ready to continue preparing the dish, the food should be taken from the refrigerator and brought back to room temperature before any further cooking. Sauces should be reheated gently, over a low heat, after they have reached room temperature.

SPICES: Unless otherwise specified, the measurements refer to dried rather than fresh ingredients.

PRESENTATION: Because the appearance of the dish is such a crucial element of the nouvelle cuisine, we have provided suggestions for arranging the food, usually on individual plates.

MENU ACCOMPANIMENT: We have given suggestions for a complete nouvelle cuisine dinner for each recipe, based on the idea of three-course meals. To plan more elaborate five to six course meals, see page 25.

Reductions

Fonds de la cuisine

THE NEW CUISINE has many subtle characteristics that distinguish it from other culinary movements that have preceded it. Perhaps the most identifiable aspect of the new cuisine is the use of highly reduced starchless stocks to make the sauces.

French food has always been identified with sauces. And reductions have always been used in French cuisine. There is a basic distinction, however, between their use in classical cuisine and in nouvelle cuisine. In classical cuisine, reductions are employed to flavor and finish already completed sauces. In the new cuisine they have taken on a much more basic role—the reductions are used as the actual base of the various sauces. Consequently, more of the reduction is used for each portion of the sauce.

French chefs of the seventeenth, eighteenth, and nineteenth centuries developed a system for making sauces that relied heavily on stocks, but instead of reducing them to a viscous consistency and using the reduced stock as the base for the sauce, they thickened the sauces with flour, arrowroot, or cornstarch. Often the thickeners would take the form of a dark or light *roux,* which is simply flour and butter cooked together. In classical cooking, whether a sauce is thickened with a *roux, béchamel,* or *velouté,* the common denominator is a finished sauce with some kind of starch in it to bind and thicken.

This is an area where the new cuisine departs from tradition. Instead of thickening sauces with starches, it thickens the reduced stocks with cream or *crème fraîche, foie gras*, reduced vegetable purées (*coulis*), or butter. The result is generally thinner than a classical sauce, but more intense. Since this intensity is achieved through the reduction of a stock, which concentrates the flavors in it, it is essential that the stock be carefully made to begin with. For this reason, we emphasize that there are no shortcuts to making a good stock. Don't believe anyone who tells you that you can make perfectly good beef stock in one hour, or that you can substitute bouillon cubes or strengthen some canned chicken stock. Well-made stock tastes good and has body because excellent ingredients have been simmered long enough that all their essential flavors have been extracted and melded into the stock.

In order to appreciate the new sauces, and to put in the time needed to make the reductions, you will have to free yourself from a couple of stereotypes associated with classical sauces: first, a sauce does not have to be thick or glutinous to taste good; and second, a sauce does not have to cover the main ingredient of a dish to enhance it. Learning to like the new sauces does not mean, however, that you must reject the old ones. It simply widens your horizons and gives you one more thing to enjoy in life.

The recipes in this book rely heavily on sauces made from reductions. This section will show you, in detail, how to make the basic stocks so crucial to these recipes. Making stock is not a particularly difficult task, and if you follow the recipes faithfully you will find that stock-making can be accomplished without too much effort on your part. Even though a *glace de viande* may take a total of 14 to 16 hours to prepare, the actual time you must pay attention to it is only a couple of hours. The rest of the time the stock is left to simmer on the stove by itself. In addition, reduced stock freezes excellently—so when the urge strikes you to make the reductions called for in this book, prepare them in large batches so that you have enough to last for several months. Remember, you can't shortcut this very important ingredient. If you want to create excellent nouvelle cuisine dishes at home you must have these reductions on hand. After you have made them a few times you will find that they are really not difficult.

Before you read any further you should run out and buy a large stockpot if you don't already own one. The recipes in this section are given in quantities perfect for a 10-quart stockpot. If you have a 20-quart pot you will have to double the recipes. In fact, we recommend you use as large a stockpot as possible so that you won't have to make reductions too often. However, we realize that large pots are awkward for many people to handle, and for many kitchens to accommodate. You may also want to consider keeping two stockpots on hand, since the reduction recipes call for a transfer of stock which will be much facilitated by having a second large pot.

The reason we recommend large stockpots is that although your final product is quite small, you have to start big. For example, approximately 16 liquid ounces of *glace de viande* began as 10 to 12 quarts of beef stock. We say approximately, because a reduction is a relative term. There is no perfect consistency for a reduction. One rule of thumb is that the reduction should lightly coat a spoon. But this is only true for reductions that have natural gelatin. *Glace de homard* (reduced lobster stock) contains no natural gelatin, so no matter how much you reduce the stock it will never be thick enough to coat a spoon.

There are two stages in the making of any reduction. The first stage is making the stock. This consists of assembling all the ingredients, doing any initial roasting or braising of the raw materials that is called for, combining all the ingredients in the stockpot, and simmering them for the recommended length of time. It is important to roast or braise the raw ingredients because the caramelization that takes place adds depth of flavor to the stock. The stock recipes in this book call for simmering times of 30 minutes to 8 hours, depending on the stock. During this time your attention should be focused on two things: that the stock maintains a constant simmer *and* that you skim the stock occasionally to remove any of the fat or scum that rises to the surface.

The second stage is the reduction of the stock. When the stock has cooked for the proper length of time, you have to remove all the cooked bones, vegetables, and *bouquet garni* , skim the remaining liquid so that all traces of fat are removed (the stock is passed through cheesecloth at this point to ensure fat removal), and then turn up the heat so that the stock is rapidly boiling and begins to reduce through evaporation. The stock must be simmered initially or it will get cloudy and develop an off taste. Once the fat has been removed from the pot it is safe to boil the stock. What happens is that in rapid boiling the fat is broken up into microscopic globules, which then incorporate themselves into the liquid and remain in suspension. However, once the bones have been removed and the fat skimmed off, this danger no longer exists.

Once you have a clear stock, you may want to boil it down as quickly as possible. The reduction process may be delayed at this point by allowing the strained stock to cool to room temperature and be either refrigerated or frozen. To continue the reduction process, place the cooled or frozen stock back in a stockpot and continue reducing as per recipe. The only thing you have to watch out for is that the boiling stock does not rise over the side of the pot. If you have removed all traces of fat this should not be a problem. After the stock has been reduced to the proper consistency, put it into appropriate containers. The reduction should always be allowed to cool, *uncovered,* to room temperature before storing. The reduction is now ready to be used, refrigerated, or frozen. If you are refrigerating or freezing the reduction, it must be placed in a *covered* container, or in ice cube trays partially wrapped in tin foil.

When you freeze the reduction, we suggest that you do it in several small containers rather than one large one. This way you can take out enough for just a few portions, and leave the rest frozen. Otherwise you would have to thaw all the reduction each time you wanted to use it. Note, however, that a well-made reduction can take thawing and refreezing quite well. The above suggestion is for your well-being, rather than the reduction's.

Glace de viande

YIELD:
4 to 5 quarts of beef stock
1 pint of *glace de viande*

PREPARATION TIME:
4 hours to roast bones
8 hours to simmer stock
2 to 4 hours to boil stock down to a reduction

EQUIPMENT:
Large pan to roast bones and vegetables
10- to 12-quart stockpot
Cheesecloth
Strainer or sieve
Skimmer or slotted spoon

4   *pounds beef marrow bones, cut into 3- to 4-inch pieces*
4   *pounds veal joint bones, such as knees, knuckles, and feet*
      (Have your butcher leave as much cartilage on these pieces
      as possible. The cartilage gives the stock its gelatinous
      characteristics.)
1   *pound peeled onions, roughly chopped into 1-inch pieces*
1   *pound carrots, roughly chopped into 1-inch pieces*
½   *pound celery, roughly chopped into 1-inch pieces*
1   *leek, roughly chopped into 1-inch pieces (optional)*
1   bouquet garni *made up of*
      6 to 8 sprigs of Italian parsley
      1 bay leaf
      14 to 18 whole black peppercorns
      1 tablespoon fresh thyme, or ¼ teaspoon dried
      2 cloves unpeeled garlic

1. Preheat the oven to 400 degrees.

2. Arrange all the bones in a roasting pan large enough to accommodate them in one layer.

3. Roast the bones in the oven for 3 hours. Remove the pan from the oven and toss the chopped vegetables on top of the bones. Add 2 cups cold water to the pan and return to the oven. Continue roasting for 1 more hour.

4. Transfer the contents of the roasting pan to a stockpot on top of the stove. Make sure you scrape out all the browned particles on the bottom of the pan into the stockpot. This will give your stock added flavor. (*Note*: The two cups of water were added to the roasting pan to make it easier to scrape the juices and brown particles into the stockpot with the bone and vegetable mixture.)●

5. Fill the stockpot with water to a point about 2 inches from the top of the pot. (*Note:* It is not crucial that the amount of water added to the pot be exactly the same each time. You are always in complete control of the reduction because you can always reduce the mixture more and thereby make it more viscous.)

6. Prepare your *bouquet garni* by enclosing all the ingredients in the piece of cheesecloth tied with a piece of string. Once this has been completed, add the bouquet garni to the pot and make sure that it is completely submerged in the water.

7. Bring all the ingredients to a slow boil over medium heat in the stockpot. As the water begins to boil, a grayish scum will rise to the surface. Lower the heat to insure that the scum does not rise over the edge. Remove the scum with a large shallow spoon. Do not be afraid to scoop out all traces of the scum and lose some of the surrounding stock. You can always replace the liquid with fresh water.

8. When the water is about to boil again, reduce the heat and simmer the stock slowly for 8 hours, skimming the scum and replacing it with fresh water every couple of hours. (*Note:* In the first hour you may have to skim the pot every 15 minutes or so.) The stock is properly simmering

when there is movement on the surface of the water in the form of tiny bubbles. If the bubbles get too large it means that the stock is boiling and you will have to reduce the heat. As the stock simmers the liquid will evaporate. Add water from time to time to maintain the level in the pot.

9. After the stock has simmered for 8 hours, turn off the heat. The object at this point is to strain all the stock through a cheesecloth-lined sieve into another stockpot or large container so that the stock can be reduced to the proper consistency. You can accomplish this in one of two ways. If you are very strong you can simply pour the stock from one pot to the next. Then discard the cooked solids. However, a safer technique is to use a large ladle and transfer the stock through the cheesecloth in smaller amounts. When most of the liquid has been removed, scoop out the remaining solids for discarding. The best way to accomplish this is with a skimmer or a slotted spoon. Just remove the solids; don't lose any of the stock in the process. This is the most unpleasant task in making a stock. Make sure the discarded solids are placed in a waterproof container because they are messy.

10. Once all the bones and vegetables are removed, pour the remaining stock through the cheesecloth into the other stockpot or container. (*Note:* If you have only one stockpot it will be necessary to wash it and then pour the reserved stock back into the pot to continue the cooking process.)

11. At this point the basic stock is ready to be used or to be stored in the refrigerator overnight. If you are storing the stock, cool it first, uncovered, to room temperature. Refrigerate, covered, overnight.● The next day remove any additional fat that has congealed on the surface. If you leave the stock at this point and don't boil it down to reduction consistency, you must bring it back to the boil every third day in order to rid it of any potential bacteria which may have accumulated.

12. If you intend to continue cooking the stock

down to the point of a *glace de viande*, return the stock to the washed pot and place it back on the heat. As the stock begins to boil it will throw off more of the grayish scum. Keep removing the scum with a large shallow spoon until the stock can be brought to a rolling boil without foaming over the top of the pot.

13. Once this has been accomplished, rapidly boil the stock until it is reduced to 1 pint of glaze, from 2 to 4 hours. When the liquid has reached this point it is *glace de viande*. Remove the syrupy liquid from the pot and let it cool, uncovered, to room temperature. Then store it, covered, in a large plastic container or in foil-covered ice cube trays in which the reduction can be easily frozen. Use one or two cubes at a time as the recipes dictate.

Demi-glace

YIELD:
4 to 5 quarts of beef and tomato stock
1 pint of *demi-glace*

PREPARATION TIME:
4 hours to roast bones
8 hours to simmer stock
2 to 4 hours to boil stock down to a reduction

EQUIPMENT:
Large pan to roast the bones and vegetables
10- to 12-quart stockpot
Cheesecloth
Strainer or sieve
Skimmer or slotted spoon

4	*pounds beef marrow bones, cut into 3- to 4-inch pieces*
4	*pounds veal joint bones, such as knees, knuckles and feet*
	(Have your butcher leave as much cartilage on these pieces as possible. The cartilage gives the stock its gelatinous characteristics.)
1	*pound peeled onions, roughly chopped into 1-inch pieces*
1	*pound carrots, roughly chopped into 1-inch pieces*
½	*pound celery, roughly chopped into 1-inch pieces*
1	*leek, roughly chopped into 1-inch pieces (optional)*
2	*pounds tomatoes, peeled, seeded, and cut into ½-inch pieces*
1	bouquet garni *made up of*
	6 to 8 sprigs of Italian parsley
	1 bay leaf
	14 to 18 whole black peppercorns
	1 tablespoon fresh thyme, or ¼ teaspoon dried
	2 cloves unpeeled garlic

1. Preheat the oven to 400 degrees.

2. Arrange all the bones in a roasting pan large enough to accommodate them in one layer.

3. Roast the bones in the oven for 3 hours. Remove the pan from the oven and add all the chopped vegetables, with the exception of the tomatoes, on top of the bones. Add two cups water to the pan. Return the pan to the oven and continue roasting for 1 more hour.

4. Transfer the contents of the roasting pan to a stockpot on top of the stove. Make sure you scrape out all the browned particles on the bottom of the pan into the stockpot. This will give your stock added flavor. (*Note:* The two cups of water were added to the roasting pan to make it easier to scrape the juices and browned particles into the stockpot with the bone and vegetable mixture.)●

5. Fill the stock pot with water to a point about 2 inches from the top of the pot. (*Note:* It is not crucial that the amount of water added to the pot be exactly the same each time. You are always in complete control of the reduction because you can always reduce the stock more and thereby make it more intense.)

6. Prepare the *bouquet garni* by enclosing all the ingredients in the piece of cheesecloth tied with a piece of string. Once this has been completed, add the *bouquet garni* to the pot and make sure that it is completely submerged in the water.

7. Bring all the ingredients to a slow boil over medium heat in the stockpot. As the water begins to boil, a grayish scum will rise to the surface. Lower the heat to insure that the scum does not rise over the edge. Remove the scum with a large shallow spoon. Do not be afraid to scoop out all traces of the scum and lose some of the surrounding stock. You can always replace the liquid with fresh water.

8. When the water is about to boil again, reduce the heat and simmer the stock for 8 hours, skimming the scum and replacing it with fresh water every couple of hours. (*Note:* In the first hour you may have to skim the pot every 15 minutes or so.) The stock is properly simmering when there is movement on the surface of the water in the form of tiny bubbles. If the bubbles get too large it means that the stock is boiling and you will have to reduce the heat. As the stock simmers the liquid will evaporate. Add water from time to time to maintain the level in the pot.

9. After the stock has simmered for 8 hours, turn off the heat. The object at this point is to strain all the stock through a cheesecloth-lined sieve into another stockpot or large container so that the stock can be reduced to the proper consistency. You can accomplish this in one of two ways. If you are strong, simply pour the stock from one pot to the next. Then discard the cooked solids. However, a safer technique is to use a large ladle and transfer the stock through the cheesecloth in smaller amounts. When most of the liquid has been removed, scoop out the remaining solids and discard them. The best way to accomplish this is with a skimmer or a slotted spoon. Just remove the solids; don't lose any of the stock in the process. This is the most unpleasant task in making a stock. Make sure the discarded solids are placed in a waterproof container because they are messy.

10. Once all the bones and vegetables are removed, pour the remaining stock through the cheesecloth into the other stockpot or container. (*Note:* If you have only one stockpot it will be necessary to wash it out and then pour the reserved stock back into the pot to continue the cooking process.)

11. At this point the basic stock is ready to be used or to be stored in the refrigerator overnight. If you are storing the stock, cool it first, uncovered, to room temperature and then refrigerate covered.● The next day remove any additional fat that has congealed on the surface. If you leave the stock at this point and don't boil it down to reduction consistency, you must bring it back to the boil every third day in order to rid it of any potential bacteria which may have accumulated.

12. If you intend to continue cooking the stock down to the point of a *demi-glace*, return the stock to a washed pot and place it back on the heat. As the stock begins to boil it will throw off more of the grayish scum. Keep removing the scum with a large shallow spoon until the stock can be brought to a rolling boil without foaming over the top of the pot.

13. Add the reserved tomatoes to the reducing stock. (The tomatoes distinguish the *demi-glace* from the *glace de viande*.) Once this has been accomplished, rapidly boil the stock, stirring the bottom of the pot every now and then so that the tomatoes do not stick and become scorched, until it is reduced to approximately 1 pint (it will lightly coat a spoon). Remove the *demi-glace* from the stockpot, making sure you scrape all the reduction from the sides and bottom of the pot, and cool it, uncovered, to room temperature. Store the *demi-glace*, covered, in a large plastic container or in foil-covered ice cube trays in which the reduction may be easily frozen. Use one or two cubes at a time as the recipes dictate.

Nouvelle cuisine bordelaise

YIELD:
1 pint of *bordelaise*

PREPARATION TIME:
4 hours to roast bones
8 hours to simmer stock
2 to 4 hours to boil stock down to a reduction

EQUIPMENT:
Large pan to roast the bones and vegetables
10- to 12-quart stockpot
Cheesecloth
Strainer or sieve
Skimmer or slotted spoon

1   *recipe* glace de viande
32   *ounces full-bodied red wine (Burgundy is good. The wine does not have to be expensive.)*
4   *ounces (½ cup) peeled and roughly chopped shallots*

    1. Refer to the *glace de viande* recipe. You should follow this recipe exactly through step 10.

    2. You should have approximately 5 quarts of reserved stock from the *glace de viande* recipe. Add the wine and chopped shallots to the stock and bring the mixture to a rolling boil. Reduce the *bordelaise* stock until approximately 1 pint remains. Like the *demi-glace* it should lightly coat a spoon. Carefully strain out the remaining pieces of shallot and allow the *bordelaise* base to cool, uncovered, to room temperature. Store the *bordelaise* base, covered, in a large plastic container or, for convenience, in foil-covered ice cube trays in which the reduction can be easily frozen and used one or two cubes at a time as the recipes dictate.

Glace de poisson

YIELD:
4 to 5 quarts of fish stock
1 pint of *glace de poisson*

PREPARATION TIME:
30 minutes to simmer stock
2 to 4 hours to boil stock down to a reduction

EQUIPMENT:
10- to 12-quart stockpot
Cheesecloth
Strainer or sieve
Skimmer or slotted spoon

7   *pounds roughly chopped flat fish carcasses (bones and heads), such as sole or flounder with gills removed*
2   *pounds peeled and quartered onions*
6   *to 8 sprigs of Italian parsley, stems removed*
2   *cups dry white wine*
1   *bay leaf*
14 *to 18 whole black peppercorns*

1.   Place all the ingredients in the stockpot and fill with water to a point about 2 inches from the top of the pot.

2.   Bring all the ingredients to a slow boil over medium heat. As the water begins to boil, a grayish scum will rise to the surface. Lower the heat to insure that the scum does not rise over the edge. Remove the scum with a large shallow spoon. Do not be afraid to scoop out all traces of the scum and lose some of the surrounding stock. You can always replace the liquid with fresh water.

3.   When the water is about to boil again, reduce the heat and simmer the stock slowly for 30 minutes, skimming and replacing the scum with fresh water every 10 minutes. The stock is properly simmering when there is movement on the surface of the water in the form of tiny bubbles. If the bubbles get too large it means that the stock is boiling and you will have to reduce the heat.

4. After the stock has simmered for 30 minutes, turn off the heat. The object at this point is to strain all the stock through a cheesecloth-lined sieve into another stock-pot or large container so that the stock can be reduced to the proper consistency. You can accomplish this in one of two ways. If you are strong, simply pour the stock through the cheesecloth from one pot to the next. Then discard the cooked solids. However, a safer technique is to use a large ladle and transfer the stock through the cheesecloth in smaller amounts. When most of the liquid has been removed, scoop out the remaining solids and discard them. The best way to accomplish this is with a skimmer or slotted spoon. Just remove the solids; don't lose any of the stock in the process. This is the most unpleasant task in making a stock. Make sure the discarded solids are placed in a water-proof container because they are messy.

5. Once the solids are removed, pour the remaining stock through the cheesecloth into the other stockpot or container. (*Note:* If you have only one stockpot it will be necessary to wash it out and then pour the reserved stock back into the pot to continue the cooking process.)

6. At this point the basic fish stock is ready to be used as a fish *fumet* or stored in the refrigerator overnight. If you are storing the stock, cool it first, uncovered, to room temperature and then refrigerate, covered.●The next day remove any additional scum that has congealed on the surface. Fish stock will last only two days in the refrigerator, however it freezes very well.

7. If you intend to continue cooking the stock down to the point of a *glace de poisson*, return the stock to the washed pot and place it back on the heat. As the stock begins to boil it will throw off more of the grayish scum.

Keep removing the scum with a large shallow spoon until the stock can be brought to a rolling boil without foaming over the top of the pot.

8. Depending on the size of your stockpot, the liquid should boil down to about 1 pint in 2 to 4 hours. (The larger the surface area of the pot the faster the stock will reduce.) When there is about 1 pint liquid remaining in the pot remove the *glace de poisson*. Make sure you scrape all the reduction from the sides and bottom of the pot. Store the *glace de poisson*, covered, in a large plastic container or in ice cube trays in which the reduction may be easily frozen. Use one or two cubes at a time as the recipes dictate. The *glace de poisson* will keep in a covered container in the refrigerator for a week to 10 days.

Glace de volaille

YIELD:
4 to 5 quarts of chicken stock
1 pint of *glace de volaille*

PREPARATION TIME:
1½ hours to roast chicken parts
3½ hours to simmer stock
2 to 4 hours to boil stock down to a reduction

EQUIPMENT:
Large roasting pan
10- to 12-quart stockpot
Cheesecloth
Strainer or sieve
Skimmer or slotted spoon

7   pounds of chicken carcasses, backs, and necks in any
        combination (For best results the pieces should be no larger
        than 2 to 3 inches.)
1   pound peeled onions, roughly chopped into 1-inch pieces
1   pound carrots, roughly chopped into 1-inch pieces
1   leek, roughly chopped into 1-inch pieces (optional)
1   bouquet garni made up of
        6 to 8 sprigs Italian parsley
        1 bay leaf
        14 to 18 whole black peppercorns
        1 tablespoon fresh thyme, or ¼ teaspoon dried
        2 cloves unpeeled garlic

  1.   Preheat the oven to 400 degrees.
  2.   Arrange all the chicken pieces in a roasting pan
large enough to accomodate them in one layer.
  3.   Roast the bones in the oven for 1 hour. Remove the pan from the oven and toss the chopped vegetables on top of the bones. Add 2 cups water to the roasting
pan and return to the oven. Continue roasting for an additional ½ hour.
  4.   Transfer the contents of the roasting pan to a
stockpot on top of the stove. Make sure you scrape out all
the browned particles on the bottom of the pan into the
stockpot. This will give your stock added flavor. (*Note:*
The two cups of water were added to the roasting pan to
make it easier to scrape the juices and browned particles
into the stockpot with the chicken and vegetables.)●
  5.   Fill the stockpot with water to a point 2 inches
from the top of the pot. (*Note:* It is not crucial that the
amount of water added to the pot be exactly the same each
time. You are always in complete control of the reduction
because you can always reduce the stock to make it more
intense and flavorful.)
  6.   Prepare the *bouquet garni* by enclosing all the
ingredients in a piece of cheesecloth tied with a piece of
string. Once this has been completed, add the *bouquet*

garni to the pot and make sure that it is completely submerged in the water.

7. Bring all the ingredients to a slow boil over medium heat in the stockpot. As the water begins to boil, the chicken fat will rise to the surface. Lower the heat to insure that the fat does not rise over the edge. Remove the fat with a large shallow spoon. Do not be afraid to scoop out all the traces of the fat and lose some of the surrounding stock. You can always replace the discarded liquid with fresh water.

8. When the stock is about to boil again, reduce the heat and simmer the stock for 3½ hours, skimming and replacing the fat with fresh water every hour. (*Note:* In the first hour you may have to skim the pot every 15 minutes or so.) The stock is properly simmering when there is movement on the surface of the water in the form of tiny bubbles. If the bubbles get too large it means that the stock is boiling and you will have to reduce the heat. As the stock simmers the liquid will evaporate. Add water from time to time to maintain the contents of the pot at the same level.

9. After the stock has simmered for 3½ hours, turn off the heat. The object at this point is to strain all the stock through a cheesecloth-lined sieve into another stockpot or large container so that the stock can be reduced to the consistency of a *glace de volaille*. You can accomplish this in one of two ways. If you are strong, simply pour the stock through a cheesecloth-lined sieve from one pot to the next. Then discard the cooked solids. However, a safer technique is to use a large ladle and transfer the stock through the cheesecloth in smaller amounts. When most of the liquid has been removed, scoop out the solids and discard them. The best way to accomplish this is with a skimmer or a large slotted spoon. Just remove the solids; don't lose any of the stock in the process. This is the most unpleasant task in making a stock. Make sure the discarded solids are placed in a waterproof container because they are messy.

10. Once all the chicken pieces and vegetables are removed, pour the remaining stock through the cheese-cloth into the other stockpot or container. (*Note:* If you have only one stockpot it will be necessary to wash it out and then pour the reserved stock back into the pot to continue the cooking process.)

11. At this point the chicken stock is ready to be used or to be stored in the refrigerator overnight. In either case you must remove any additional fat that rises to the surface.●If you leave the stock at this point and don't boil it down to reduction consistency, you must bring it back to the boil every third day in order to rid it of any potential bacteria which may accumulate. If you are storing the stock, cool it first, uncovered, to room temperature.

12. If you intend to continue cooking the stock down to the point of a *glace de volaille*, return the stock to the washed pot and place it back on the heat. As the stock begins to boil it will throw off more of the fat. Keep removing the fat with a large shallow spoon until the stock can be brought to a rolling boil without foaming over the top of the pot.

13. Depending on the size of your stockpot and the amount of stock you are making, the liquid should boil down to about 1 pint in 2 to 4 hours. (The larger the surface area of the pot, the faster the stock will reduce.) When there is about 1 pint of liquid remaining in the pot (measure if you're not sure), remove the *glace de volaille*, making sure you scrape all the reduction from the sides and bottom of the pot. Let the liquid cool, uncovered, in the refrigerator, then store the *glace de volaille*, covered, in a large plastic container or in foil-covered ice cube trays in which the reduction may be easily frozen. Use one or two cubes at a time as the recipes dictate.

Glace de canard

To make *glace de canard* follow the *glace de volaille* recipe exactly *except* substitute 7 pounds of duck carcasses, backs, and necks for the chicken pieces. Since duck pieces are harder to find than chicken it is advisable to accumulate the pieces over a period of time in your freezer. Or purchase several ducks, use the meat for one of the boneless duck recipes in the book, and use what remains to make the *glace de canard*.

Glace de homard

YIELD:
4 to 5 quarts of lobster stock
1 pint of *glace de homard*

PREPARATION TIME:
2 hours to simmer stock
2 to 4 hours to boil stock down to a reduction

EQUIPMENT:
10- to 12-quart stockpot
Cheesecloth
Strainer or sieve
Skimmer or slotted spoon

5   *pounds roughly chopped lobster carcasses (This ingredient is difficult to find. You are going to have to buy whole lobsters, remove all the meat from the tail and the claws and save the rest to make the stock. If you don't buy enough lobsters to yield 5 pounds of carcasses, accumulate all you can in the freezer until you have the right amount.)*
2   *pounds roughly chopped flat fish carcasses, such as sole or flounder, with gills removed*
6   *to 8 sprigs Italian parsley, stems removed*
2   *cups dry white wine*
1   *bay leaf*
14   *to 18 whole black peppercorns*

1. Place all the ingredients in the stockpot and fill with water to a point about 2 inches from the top of the pot.

2. Bring all the ingredients to a slow boil over medium heat in the stockpot. As the water begins to boil a grayish scum will rise to the surface. Lower the heat to insure that the scum does not rise over the edge. Remove the scum with a large shallow spoon. Do not be afraid to scoop out all traces of the scum and lose some of the surrounding stock. You can always replace the liquid with fresh water.

3. When the water is about to boil again, reduce the heat and simmer the stock slowly for 2 hours, skimming and replacing the scum with fresh water every 30 minutes. The stock is properly simmering when there is movement on the surface of the water in the form of tiny bubbles. If the bubbles get too large it means that the stock is boiling and you will have to reduce the heat.

4. After the stock has simmered for 2 hours, turn off the heat. The object at this point is to strain all the stock through a cheesecloth-lined sieve into another stockpot or large container, so that the stock can be reduced to the proper consistency. You can accomplish this in one of two ways. If you are strong, simply pour the stock through a cheesecloth-lined sieve from one pot to the next. Then discard the cooked solids. However, a safer technique is to use a large ladle and transfer the stock through the cheesecloth in smaller amounts. When most of the stock has been removed, scoop out the solids and discard them. The best way to accomplish this is with a skimmer or slotted spoon. Just remove the solids; don't lose any of the stock in the process. This is the most unpleasant task in making a stock. Make sure the discarded solids are placed in a waterproof container because they are messy.

5.   Once the solids are removed, pour the remaining stock through the cheesecloth into the other stockpot or container. (*Note:* If you have only one stockpot it will be necessary to wash it out and then pour the reserved stock back into the pot to continue the cooking process.)

6.   At this point the basic lobster stock is ready to be used or stored in the refrigerator. If you are storing the stock, cool it first, uncovered, to room temperature.● Remove any additional scum that congeals on the surface after the stock has cooled then store, covered. Lobster stock will stay fresh for only 2 to 3 days in the refrigerator, however it freezes very well.

7.   If you intend to continue cooking the stock down to the point of a *glace de homard*, return the stock to the washed pot and place it back on the heat. As the stock begins to boil it will throw off more of the grayish scum. Keep removing the scum with a large shallow spoon until the stock can be brought to a rolling boil without foaming over the top of the pot.

8.   Depending on the size of your stockpot, the stock should boil down to 1 pint in 2 to 4 hours. (The larger the surface area of the pot, the faster the stock will reduce.) When there is approximately 1 pint of liquid remaining in the pot, remove the *glace de homard*. (Since lobster does not contain any natural gelatin, the *glace de homard* will not be very thick and it will pour easily.)

9.   Store the *glace de homard* either in a large plastic container or for convenience, in ice cube trays which

may be easily frozen and used one or two cubes at a time as the recipes dictate. Remember to allow the *glace de homard* to cool, uncovered, to room temperature before storing. The *glace de homard* will keep in a covered container in the refrigerator for a week to 10 days. It is best to portion control the *glace* in foil-covered ice cube trays and freeze it, where it will last from 6 to 9 months.

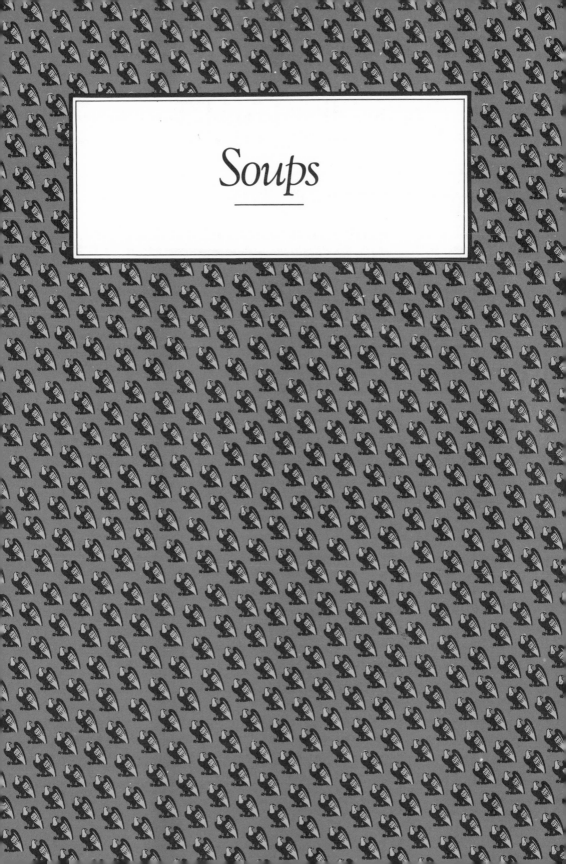

Soups

Broccoli and Apple Soup

THE FLAVOR OF the apple, although not really discernable, seems to take the sharp edge out of the broccoli and contributes a mellowness to this soup. It tastes rich without the addition of any cream, but adding a dollop of sour cream or *crème fraîche* at the end surely does not hurt. If you are planning to serve this dish cold, dust the soup with a garnish of minced mint, instead of the chives. This soup may be made up to 2 days in advance.

PREPARATION TIME:
10 minutes

COOKING TIME:
40 minutes

SERVES:
4 to 6

1   *bunch broccoli*
3   *tablespoons butter*
1   *small onion, thinly sliced*
1   *apple, peeled, cored, and roughly diced*
4   *cups chicken stock or water*
4   *tablespoons* crème fraîche *or sour cream, optional*
2   *tablespoons minced chives or parsley*
    Salt
    Freshly ground pepper

1. Trim 2 inches from the broccoli stalks and peel the outer skin with a vegetable peeler. Cut the broccoli into small dice.

2. Melt the butter in a 4-quart saucepan. Add the onion and apple, cover, and cook over low heat for 10 minutes.

3. Add the broccoli, stock or water, 1 teaspoon salt, and ½ teaspoon pepper. Bring to a boil and simmer, covered, over medium heat, for 30 minutes.

4. Remove the soup from the heat. Transfer one-third of the soup to a blender or food processor and blend thoroughly, or until smooth. Repeat in two more batches. With a large spoon, push the soup through a sieve into a clean saucepan and discard any large pieces which remain in the sieve. Reheat the soup, stirring constantly. Taste for seasoning and adjust, if necessary.

PRESENTATION

Portion out the soup into warmed soup plates or bowls and serve as is or garnished with a spoonful of *crème fraîche* or sour cream in the center. Sprinkle the *crème fraîche* with minced chives or parsley.

MENU ACCOMPANIMENT

This would be good served before a flavorful meat course, such as Medallions of Lamb with Bordelaise and Port Sauce (page 213), Sautéed Rib Lamb Chops with Rosemary and Thyme (page 215), Venison Steak with Caper Sauce (page 296), Beef Eye Round Encased in Salt (page 172), or Herbed Veal Chops with Bacon and Shallots (page 227). Obviously the vegetable garnish for your meat course should not include broccoli or any vegetable in that flavor family, such as cauliflower or turnips.

Kohlrabi Soup

THIS SOUP is extraordinarily flavorful and simple to make. The pungency of the garlic and kohlrabi dissipates with long cooking. You should use a richly flavored olive oil which will contribute to the depth of taste in this recipe. This soup is excellent cold and may be made up to 3 days in advance.

PREPARATION TIME:
20 minutes

COOKING TIME:
45 minutes

SERVES:
4

4   *to 5 kohlrabi*
2   *tablespoons butter*
1   *tablespoon olive oil*
4   *cloves garlic*
½   *teaspoon sugar*
1   *cup tomato juice, fresh or canned*
¼   *cup sour cream*
2   *tablespoons minced parsley*
     Salt
     Freshly ground pepper

1. Remove the thin stalks from the kohlrabi and peel the little knobs with a vegetable peeler. Remove the tough ends. Cut into small dice.

2. Melt the butter and olive oil in a 2- to 3-quart saucepan. Add the garlic, diced kohlrabi, and sugar. Cover the saucepan and cook over medium heat for 5 minutes. Watch that the heat is not too high or the garlic will burn and impart a bitter flavor to the soup.

3. Add the juice, 2½ cups water, 1 teaspoon salt, and ¼ teaspoon pepper. Cover, bring to a boil, and simmer gently for 40 minutes.

4. Remove the soup from the heat. Purée in batches in a food processor or blender with the sour cream. Taste for seasoning, and adjust if necessary. Reheat in a clean saucepan, stirring until the soup reaches a boil.

PRESENTATION

Serve in warmed soup plates or bowls and dust with minced parsley.

MENU ACCOMPANIMENT

See Broccoli and Apple Soup (page 72) for suggestions.

Seven-Vegetable Broth

Served hot or cold, this vegetable broth makes a refreshingly light starter, especially if you are serving a more substantial cream-based entrée. The name comes from the seven vegetables used to make the broth. You can vary them according to taste, but you must keep the tomatoes and therefore should not plan a tomato-sauced dish to follow. Be sure to chop the vegetables well so they give off all their flavor while they simmer. If the pieces are too large, the broth will have to cook for a long time. This soup may be made up to 3 days in advance.

PREPARATION TIME:
40 minutes

COOKING TIME:
2 hours and 30 minutes

SERVES:
4

4   *large carrots (about ¾ pound), minced*
4   *medium onions (about ¾ pound), minced*
2   *leeks, white part only, minced*
1   *cup fresh or canned tomatoes, peeled and seeded*
2   *stalks celery, minced*
2   *medium parsnips or parsley root (about ¼ pound), peeled and minced*
4   *sprigs parsley*
2   *cloves garlic*
10   *whole black peppercorns*
1   *bay leaf*

1   *celery knob*
½   *teaspoon sugar*
2   *teaspoons lemon juice*
2   *tablespoons fresh chives, minced, or 2 scallions, white and*
       green parts, sliced thin
     Salt
     Freshly ground pepper

1. Bring 8 cups cold water to a boil. Add all the vegetables (except for the celery knob), 1½ teaspoons salt, the peppercorns, and the bay leaf. Peel and chop the celery knob and immediately add it to the rest of the vegetables—it darkens quickly when left exposed to air.

2. Reduce the heat and simmer the broth gently, partially covered, for 2 hours. As the water level lowers, you must replace the evaporated liquid with fresh cold water, keeping the level constant throughout the 2 hours. Skim the top occasionally.

3. After 2 hours, strain the soup and discard the solids.

4. Return the strained liquid to the saucepan and over medium heat, reduce the broth until only 4 cups remain. Add the sugar and lemon juice. Taste for seasoning and adjust, if necessary.

PRESENTATION

Ladle the broth into 4 warmed soup bowls and sprinkle the chives or sliced scallions over the top.

MENU ACCOMPANIMENT

This broth goes well with just about any fish, poultry, or meat dish, although it's best not to serve it with a dish which relies heavily on tomatoes.

Black Bean Soup

T HIS SOUP may be made up to 3 days in advance, then reheated and garnished just before serving.

PREPARATION TIME:
1 hour

COOKING TIME:
2 hours and 15 minutes

SERVES:
6 to 8

½   *pound dried beans (1 generous cup)*
5   *cups chicken stock or water*
1   *ham hock*
1   *small leek, white part only, sliced*
1   *stalk celery, peeled and sliced*
1   *small carrot, sliced*
1   *small onion, sliced*
3   *cloves garlic, minced*
4   *tablespoons butter*
4   *ounces* glace de volaille, *optional if you are using the stock*
2   *scallions, julienned*
½   *green pepper*
2   *ounces (4 slices) prosciutto*
   Salt
   Freshly ground pepper

1. Place the beans in a strainer and wash them well under cold running water, removing any pebbles or debris. It is unnecessary to soak them overnight.

2. Bring the stock or water to a boil. Add the beans, 1 tablespoon salt, and the ham hock. After the liquid has come back to the boil, simmer, covered, for 2 hours, or until the beans are tender but not mushy.

3. In a skillet, over medium heat, sauté the vegetables in butter for 5 minutes, or until soft but not brown. Season with 1 teaspoon salt and ½ teaspoon pepper. (*Note:* If you are using water, add the *glace de volaille* at this time and simmer it with the vegetables for 1 minute.)

4. Remove the vegetables from the heat and blend them until smooth, using a food processor, blender, or food mill. Cover and set aside.

5. When the beans are cooked, remove and discard the ham hock. Whisk the vegetable purée into the broth. Taste for seasoning. If you find the soup too thick for your taste, add water or stock and adjust the seasoning again.

PRESENTATION

Serve in individual warmed soup bowls or plates, garnished with strips of scallion, pepper, and prosciutto.

MENU ACCOMPANIMENT

Follow this with a hearty flavored meat dish, such as Sautéed Pork Chops with Tomato and Olive Sauce (page 196), Boneless Stuffed Fresh Ham with Fruit Sauce (page 186), or Boneless Rib Roast with Roasted Garlic (page 170).

Sweet Potato Soup

THIS UNUSUAL-TASTING soup is not readily identifiable as being made from sweet potatoes. The cheese, added at the end, changes the taste without revealing the nature of the secret ingredient. This soup is also good cold. It may be made up to 3 days in advance.

PREPARATION TIME:
10 minutes

COOKING TIME:
1 hour and 10 minutes

SERVES:
4 to 6

1   *or 2 sweet potatoes (12 ounces)*
1   *quart chicken or beef stock*
½   *cup heavy cream*
½   *cup grated Swiss cheese*
    Salt
    Freshly ground pepper

1. Preheat the oven to 350 degrees.

2. Wash the potatoes, and dry them. Put the potatoes on a baking sheet and bake for 1 to 1½ hours, or until very soft.

3. When they are cool enough to handle, peel the potatoes. Blend them with some of the stock, or purée them with a food mill until very smooth. Blend in the rest of the stock and heavy cream.

4. Put the soup into a saucepan over low heat. When hot, add 1 teaspoon salt and ½ teaspoon pepper.

5. Just before serving, whisk the grated cheese into the hot soup and stir until it melts. Don't cook the soup too long after you have added the cheese, or the cheese will become stringy. Taste for seasoning and adjust, if necessary.

PRESENTATION

Serve in hot soup bowls or soup plates, and grind fresh pepper onto the center of each serving.

MENU ACCOMPANIMENT

This is an all-purpose soup which can start any meal. It is delicate enough to precede fish and veal dishes, but should not be served if you are planning a cream-based sauce as the second course.

Jerusalem Artichoke Soup

PEELING Jerusalem artichokes is a real chore, and the vegetable discolors rapidly. In order to deal with this problem we cook the soup with the peel still on. Therefore, once it has been puréed, you must pass it through a drum sieve or china cap in order to eliminate the crunchy peels and further refine the soup. This soup is good served cold with minced chives, not nutmeg. It may be made up to 4 days in advance.

PREPARATION TIME:
20 minutes

COOKING TIME:
45 minutes

SERVES:
4

1   *pound Jerusalem artichokes*
    Juice of ½ lemon
4   *tablespoons butter*
1   *leek, white part only, sliced into ½-inch pieces*
1   *carrot, sliced into ½-inch rounds*
3   *cups chicken stock or water*
½   *cup heavy cream*
    Freshly grated nutmeg
    Salt
    Freshly ground pepper

1. With a brush, scrub the Jerusalem artichokes clean under cold running water. Cut them into ¼-inch slices and toss them with the lemon juice in a bowl.

2. Melt the butter over medium heat in a 4-quart non-aluminum saucepan. When hot, add the leek, carrot, and Jerusalem artichokes with the lemon juice. Cover and cook over gentle heat for 20 minutes.

3. Add 2½ cups stock or water, 1 teaspoon salt, and ¼ teaspoon pepper. Cover and simmer for another 25 minutes.

4. When cooked, remove from the heat and purée the soup with an additional ½ cup stock or water and the cream. Pass the purée through a drum sieve. Return the soup to a clean saucepan and reheat.

Ladle the soup into warm soup plates or bowls, and generously dust each portion with freshly grated nutmeg.

MENU ACCOMPANIMENT

See the suggestions for Sweet Potato Soup (page 80).

Cold Oyster and Tamarind Soup

T HE TAMARIND, with its tart fruity pulp, is often used in Indian cooking and occasionally in dishes popular in the southern United States. It gives this summer soup its tangy taste. Best when served cold, it is perfect for a hot summer evening.

PREPARATION TIME:
1 hour
(plus 4 hours cooling time)

COOKING TIME:
5 minutes

SERVES:
4

1   dozen oysters, shucked, with liquid reserved
1   quart fish stock
½   pound shrimp, shelled and deveined
4   tablespoons fresh tomato purée (see Tomato Vinaigrette
        Sauce, page 366, through step 3)
3   tablespoons tamarind paste
4   tablespoons minced chives
    Salt
    Freshly ground pepper

1. In a saucepan, add the reserved oyster liquid to the fish stock and bring to a boil. Add the shrimp and oysters, lower the heat, and poach them for 30 seconds.

2. Using a slotted spoon, remove the shrimp and oysters from the stock. Put them in a bowl of cold water. Cover the bowl and refrigerate.

3. Whisk the tomato purée and tamarind paste into the hot stock and simmer for 5 minutes. Season with 1 teaspoon salt and ½ teaspoon pepper and remove from the heat.

4. Allow the soup to cool to room temperature. Add the drained shellfish and refrigerate for at least 4 hours, or preferably, overnight.

PRESENTATION

Serve very cold, garnished with minced chives.

MENU ACCOMPANIMENT

This soup is light enough to serve before or after most of our dishes. The tamarind flavor also makes a zesty lead-in to a selection of pork entrées.

Mussel and Saffron Soup

THIS delightful soup ages nicely and tastes even better when made the day before it is to be served. The consistency is never smooth, as the vegetables are not puréed into the body of the soup.

PREPARATION TIME:
1 hour

COOKING TIME:
1 hour

SERVES:
4 to 6

4   *tablespoons butter*
1   *large onion (½-pound), finely minced*
½   *leek, white part only, finely minced*
1   *large carrot, finely minced*
1   *clove garlic, finely minced*
1   *bay leaf*
¼   *teaspoon thyme*
1   *pound mussels*
1½ *pounds tomatoes, peeled, seeded, juiced (reserve juice,*
      see Tomato Vinaigrette Sauce, page 366, step 1),
      and roughly chopped
2¼ *cups fish stock*
½   *cup heavy cream*
½   *teaspoon saffron*
      Salt
      Freshly ground pepper

1. In a heavy 4-quart saucepan (not aluminum), melt the butter over low heat. When completely melted, add all the minced vegetables except the tomatoes, 1 tablespoon salt, ¾ teaspoon pepper, the bay leaf, and the thyme. Stew, covered, over low heat for 20 minutes, or until the vegetables reduce to a near purée. Watch that the vegetables do not scorch.

2. While the vegetables are cooking, scrub the mussels clean, pulling off their beards.

3. In a large pot, bring ½ inch of water to a boil. Drop in the mussels, cover, and steam them over high heat until they open, about 3 minutes. Drain the mussels and rinse them under cold running water. Discard any mussels that have not opened.

4. Remove the mussels from their shells, pulling off any beards you may have missed the first time. In a small bowl, place the cooked mussels in enough water just to cover so that they do not dry out. Cover the bowl and refrigerate until you are ready to use them.

5. After the vegetables have stewed, add the tomatoes and cook, uncovered, over moderate heat for another 20 minutes, or until the tomatoes have reduced to a near purée. There will still be tiny bits of vegetables and tomato, but that's what you want.

6. Add the fish stock. Bring the mixture to a boil and simmer for another 10 minutes.

7. Remove the bay leaf. Add the cream, saffron, drained, reserved mussels, and more salt and pepper, if necessary. Simmer the soup for 5 minutes, or until hot.

PRESENTATION

Serve in hot soup bowls or soup plates, and grind fresh pepper onto the center of each serving.

MENU ACCOMPANIMENT

Although fish soups often precede fish courses, be more original and follow this heady soup with a robustly flavored second course, such as Herbed Leg of Lamb with Anchovy Butter (page 200), or a poultry dish, such as Capon Stuffed with Wild Rice (page 234). As with all soups, avoid a second course with a soupy sauce.

Salads

Sautéed Summer Salad

THE SELECTION OF vegetables in this recipe are usually relegated to the salad bowl. Quickly sautéed in flavorful olive oil, they become a new and refreshing side dish.

PREPARATION TIME:
15 minutes

COOKING TIME:
3 minutes

SERVES:
4

1	*medium-sized cucumber, peeled*
1	*red pepper*
8	*radishes*
1	*ripe tomato*
1	*bunch watercress, washed and dried*
4	*romaine lettuce leaves, washed and dried*
4	*Boston lettuce leaves, washed and dried*
2	*scallions*
1	*tablespoon red wine vinegar*
¼	*teaspoon prepared mustard*
¼	*cup fresh basil leaves, minced*
4	*tablespoons green olive oil*
	Salt
	Freshly ground pepper

1. Cut the cucumber in half and scoop out the seeds with a spoon. Cut the halves into ¼- by 2-inch julienne pieces.

2. Halve the red pepper, clean out the seeds and inner membranes, and cut into ¼-inch julienne pieces.

3. Slice the radishes into ¼-inch rounds.

4. Remove the tomato core and cut the tomato into quarters. With a spoon, remove the seeds and inner pulp from each quarter. Julienne the remaining flesh into ¼-inch pieces.

5. Trim the watercress of all but 1 inch of stems.

6. Tear the lettuce leaves into large pieces.

7. Slice the scallions into thin rounds, using only about 1 inch of the green part.

8. Combine the vinegar, mustard, and basil leaves in a little dish and set aside.

9. Just before serving, heat the oil in a large skillet. Add all the vegetables and stir fry over high heat for about 45 seconds. (*Note:* When you add the vegetables, the moisture in them will cause them to sizzle in the oil and spatter a bit.)

10. Add the vinegar mixture, ½ teaspoon salt, and ¼ teaspoon pepper. Remove from the heat and stir together.

PRESENTATION

Serve either as a side dish or see below.

MENU ACCOMPANIMENT

This makes a lovely first course, before a fish and cream dish or serve it with the Herbed Leg of Lamb with Anchovy Butter (page 200), or with any of our beef recipes.

Steamed Vegetable Salad

THIS SALAD can be varied according to your taste and
the season. The important thing is to cook the vegetables so that they are crisp yet cooked through, and
to select a variety of vegetables which will present a colorful
picture on the plate.

PREPARATION TIME:
1 hour

COOKING TIME:
15 minutes

SERVES:
6 as an appetizer
4 as a main course

4   *medium celery stalks, peeled*
2   *medium carrots*
2   *zucchini, approximately 6 inches long*
1   *egg*
4   *tablespoons fresh lemon juice*
1   *teaspoon lemon rind, grated*
¼   *cup fruity olive oil, mixed with ½ cup vegetable oil*
¼   *teaspoon minced garlic*
1½ *tablespoons prepared mustard*
1   *teaspoon cumin*
    Coarse salt
    Salt
    Freshly ground pepper

1. Cut all the vegetables as evenly as possible into 3-
by ¼-inch julienne.

2. Steam each vegetable separately in a vegetable steamer over simmering, not boiling, water. The water should not touch the vegetables. The celery and zucchini should each be done after 2 minutes, and the carrots after 3 to 4 minutes. Refresh the vegetables under cold running water and dry them on paper towels. Allow the vegetables to come to room temperature. (If you do this in advance and refrigerate the vegetables, bring them back to room temperature before serving.)●

3. While the vegetables dry, prepare a mayonnaise dressing. Begin by whirring the egg in a food processor or blender. Add the lemon juice and rind. Then slowly add the oil in a steady stream of droplets. You may increase the speed at which you add the oil after ½ cup oil has been incorporated into the egg. Add the minced garlic, mustard, cumin, 1 teaspoon salt, and pepper. Taste, and adjust seasoning. (*Note:* The consistency of the mayonnaise should be quite fluid.)

PRESENTATION

On each plate, arrange 4 alternating portions of the 3 vegetables in a semi-circle. Start with the carrots, then the celery, and then the zucchini. Fill the lower half of the plate with mayonnaise. Before serving, sprinkle coarse salt on the vegetables and freshly ground pepper on the mayonnaise.

MENU ACCOMPANIMENT

Follow this salad with a dish such as the Rib Steak with Forty Cloves of Garlic (page 180), Veal Loin Laced with Peppercorns (page 220), or Capon Stuffed with Wild Rice (page 234). Because there is a mayonnaise dressing on the salad, avoid serving a dish with a creamy sauce for the next course.

Warm Asparagus
with Japanese Dressing

BEAN CURD blended into the dressing gives it a rich, thick consistency. Leftover dressing can be used with other vegetables as a change from ordinary vinaigrette recipes.

PREPARATION TIME:
20 minutes

COOKING TIME:
10 minutes

SERVES:
4

1 *clove garlic*
2 *tablespoons sesame oil*
6 *tablespoons peanut or vegetable oil*
2 *tablespoons rice vinegar*
1 *teaspoon soy sauce*
¼ *cup bean curd*
24 *asparagus*
   Salt
   Freshly ground pepper

1. Smash the garlic clove by placing the wide edge of a knife over it and giving the knife a good whack with the side of your closed fist. Cut the smashed garlic clove in half.

2. Combine the oils, vinegar, soy sauce, bean curd, half a garlic clove, 1 tablespoon water, ½ teaspoon salt, and ¼ teaspoon pepper in a blender or a food processor and blend until completely smooth. (If you find the dressing a bit too thick for your taste, thin it further with water.)●

3. Trim about 2 inches from the bottom of the asparagus spears. With a vegetable peeler, peel the stalks to within ½ inch from the bottom of the tip end.

4. Place the remaining garlic clove half with a pinch of salt in a 10-inch skillet and add cold water to a depth of about 1 inch. Bring the water to a boil. Add the asparagus spears and boil for about 3 to 4 minutes, depending on the thickness of the asparagus. They should be tender but still crunchy.Drain, and let them cool for about 1 minute. Pat them dry with paper towels.

PRESENTATION

Spoon some sauce in the center of each plate and arrange 6 asparagus spears per person on the dressing.

MENU ACCOMPANIMENT

See suggestions for Steamed Vegetable Salad (page 92).

Wilted Greens Salad

THE IDEA FOR THIS SALAD was inspired by a Japanese salad of parboiled spinach leaves coated with a spicy dressing. In this recipe the greens are served at room temperature, while the sauces are served cold.

PREPARATION TIME:
1 hour and 30 minutes

COOKING TIME:
15 minutes

SERVES:
6 as an appetizer
4 as a main course

1   *pound spinach*
16   *romaine lettuce leaves*
2   *bunches watercress*
½   *cup Tomato Vinaigrette Sauce (see page 366)*
1   *cup cream, reduced to ½ cup and cooled*
1   *tablespoon prepared mustard*
     Dash cayenne pepper
4   *teaspoons Worcestershire sauce*
     Salt
     Freshly ground pepper

    1. Bring 3 quarts salted water to a rolling boil. Plunge one-third of the spinach leaves in the water and parboil for 4 seconds. Remove the spinach leaves immediately, drain, and place them under cold running water to stop the cooking process. Return the same cooking water to a boil and repeat with two more batches of spinach. Then proceed in the same way with the romaine lettuce and watercress. Drain all 3 greens well. Squeeze out any excess moisture with your hands. Roughly chop the spinach. Set the greens aside, loosely covered with plastic wrap. (If made in advance, the lettuce leaves should be brought to room temperature before proceeding). ●

2. Combine the reduced cream, mustard, ½ teaspoon salt, ¼ teaspoon pepper, cayenne, and Worcestershire to make a second sauce. Taste, and adjust seasoning. Refrigerate for 1 hour.

PRESENTATION

Arrange a bouquet of cooked watercress, 2 rolled up romaine leaves, and a portion of spinach on the top half of a dinner plate. Salt and pepper the greens lightly. Place some mustard sauce on the bottom left half of the plate and the tomato vinaigrette on the bottom right.

MENU ACCOMPANIMENT

Serve this before any course which does not contain cream or tomato as its dominant flavor. You could also serve this salad for lunch before a cheese and fruit course.

Green Salad with Walnut Oil

THE FRENCH HAVE always used walnut oil in their salads. Rarely available before, this oil is becoming more widely used in our country. It is now obtainable in either health or gourmet food stores. In this salad, the flavor of the oil is further enhanced by the addition of pieces of roasted walnuts tossed in with the dressing.

PREPARATION TIME:
1 hour and 30 minutes

COOKING TIME:
15 minutes

SERVES:
4 to 6

12 *shelled walnuts*
6 *tablespoons walnut oil*
2 *tablespoons red wine vinegar*
1 *clove garlic*
½ *head Boston lettuce*
12 *sprigs watercress, stemmed,*
    or ½ bunch arugola, stemmed
    Salt
    Freshly ground pepper

1. Preheat the oven to 350 degrees.
2. Place the walnuts in a baking dish or on a cookie sheet and roast them for 15 minutes, or until they emit a lovely roasted aroma. Remove and cool.

3. In a bowl, combine the walnut oil, red wine vinegar, and salt and pepper to taste. Roughly chop the walnuts and add them to the oil and vinegar along with the peeled garlic clove. Let the garlic steep in the dressing for at least 1 hour, or preferably for several hours.

4. Wash the lettuce and watercress. Dry thoroughly and tear them into bite-sized pieces. Reserve in the refrigerator until serving time.

5. Just before serving, remove the garlic clove from the dressing and toss the greens with the dressing and walnuts, making sure each leaf is dressed.

PRESENTATION

Portion out each serving onto the center of a salad plate.

MENU ACCOMPANIMENT

This can be served either as an appetizer or after the main course, before the cheese course.

Piquant Chicken Liver Salad

T HE SLIGHT PIQUANCY of the sherry vinegar combined with the spice of the cloves marries well with the creamy cooked livers. Placed in the center of fresh spinach leaves it makes for a light salad, yet one that is filling enough to be served as a summer main course.

PREPARATION TIME:
45 minutes

COOKING TIME:
10 minutes

SERVES:
4

1   *pound chicken livers*
6   *tablespoons peanut oil*
4   *tablespoons minced shallots*
7   *tablespoons sherry vinegar*
    Scant ¼ teaspoon of ground cloves
3   *tablespoons olive oil*
1   *tablespoon wine vinegar*
2   *cups loosely packed spinach leaves*
    Coarse salt
    Salt
    Freshly ground pepper

1. Pick the livers over, discarding any green spots and excess fat. Wash the livers in cold water and pat them dry with paper towels. Cut the livers in half. Season lightly with salt and pepper.

2. Heat 4 tablespoons of the peanut oil in a 9-inch skillet until quite hot, but not smoking. In two batches, sauté the livers for exactly 1 minute on each side at high heat. Let them cook undisturbed so they form a slightly crusty exterior. Livers tend to spatter, so move away from the pan as they sauté, and remove the pan from the heat when turning the livers. After completing this step, remove the livers to a plate and discard the oil.

3. Add 2 fresh tablespoons of peanut oil to the pan and heat until hot. Add the shallots and sauté them over low heat for about 1 minute, scraping up any browned particles from the livers as they cook. Deglaze the pan with 6 tablespoons sherry vinegar and cook for 15 seconds more. Pour these juices into a separate little container and add the cloves, ½ teaspoon salt, and ¼ teaspoon pepper.

4. In a bowl, combine the olive oil with 1 tablespoon wine vinegar, salt, and pepper to make a light vinaigrette. Toss the spinach leaves with the vinaigrette.

5. When the livers cool to room temperature, remove them to a cutting board, discarding any juices they have exuded. Cut each liver half in half again.

PRESENTATION

On 4 dinner plates, arrange a wreath of dressed spinach leaves in a circle. Place overlapping slices of liver in a circle inside each spinach wreath. Sprinkle the sliced liver with coarse salt. In the inner circle, spoon one-quarter of the shallot and vinegar sauce. Serve at room temperature.

MENU ACCOMPANIMENT

This is good as a luncheon dish, or as a first course served before meat, poultry, game or variety meat dishes.

Cold Beef Salad

T HE DRESSING for this salad is so delicious diners have been known to eat it even after the beef runs out. To make this dressing, we use techniques of a French mayonnaise but an atypical base of Oriental ingredients. The result is a pungent yet rich sauce which goes well with the flavorful beef. The technique by which the beef is cooked is also unusual. Boiling the fillet may seem a peculiar way to cook it, but in reality this process seals in the juices just as roasting at high heat would.

PREPARATION TIME:
25 minutes

COOKING TIME:
25 minutes

SERVES:
4 as a main course

2   *star anise, or ¼ teaspoon five spice powder*
¼   *cup soy sauce*
1   *garlic clove, minced*
2   *tablespoons brown sugar*
2   *tablespoons rice vinegar*
1   *egg*
1   *tablespoon prepared mustard*
¾   *cup vegetable oil, mixed with 3 tablespoons sesame oil*
2   *pounds (net) fillet of beef in 1 piece, tied, without fat*
4   *scallions, sliced fine*
4   *pieces watercress*
     Coarse salt
     Salt
     Freshly ground white pepper

1. Place the star anise, soy sauce, minced garlic, brown sugar, and rice vinegar in a small skillet. Bring to a boil, reduce the heat, and simmer for about 1 minute, or until only ¼ cup remains. Strain out the star anise and reserve the liquid. If you're using five spice powder instead of star anise, add it now.

2. In a blender or food processor, blend the egg for 30 seconds. Add the prepared mustard and blend for 30 seconds longer. Gradually add the oil, drop by drop, until ¼ cup has been incorporated. When the mayonnaise thickens and turns white, add the rest of the oil at a faster pace. Add the reserved liquid from step 1, 1 teaspoon salt, and ¼ teaspoon white pepper. Transfer the mayonnaise to a small bowl. Cover and refrigerate while you prepare the beef.

3. Bring 3 quarts salted water to a boil. Add the beef and boil for 15 to 18 minutes (depending on whether you like it very rare or just rare). Remove the beef from the water and let it rest at room temperature for about 15 minutes. When cool, slice with the grain into ½-inch slices. Then slice across the grain into 2½- to 3-inch julienne strips. Refrigerate for 10 minutes. (*Note:* If you prepare the beef a day ahead, remember to remove it from the refrigerator 30 minutes before serving so that it is not ice cold.)

PRESENTATION

Spoon one-quarter of the sauce into the center of each chilled dinner plate. Create a crown around the sauce by surrounding it with the strips of beef. Sprinkle the meat with coarse salt, freshly ground pepper, and sliced scallions. Center a piece of watercress on the sauce.

This dish is too flavorful to be an appetizer. Serve it as a main luncheon or dinner dish. Black Bean Soup (page 78) is appropriate to serve beforehand. However, if you want to include this as part of a more extensive meal, precede or follow it with a medley of vegetable purées and sautés. Any dessert is appropriate.

Pear and Goat Cheese Salad

THE COMBINATION of sweet pear, goat cheese, and lettuce is particularly satisfying when the pear is fragrantly ripe. In order to fully appreciate the flavors, make sure you get a mouthful comprised of each ingredient when you eat this salad. This recipe is for one serving and can easily be doubled, tripled, and so on for additional eaters.

PREPARATION TIME:
15 minutes

½   *head Boston lettuce, or 1 bibb lettuce*
4   *tablespoons walnut or peanut oil*
1   *tablespoon champagne, sherry, or red wine vinegar*
½   *teaspoon prepared mustard*
4   *ounces imported French goat cheese, such as Montrachet*
1   *ripe comice pear, stemmed*
    Salt
    Freshly ground pepper

1. Wash the lettuce and dry it with paper towels.

2. In a bowl, combine the oil, vinegar, mustard, and salt and pepper to taste. Set aside.

3. Slice the goat cheese into small pieces.

4. Just before serving, cut the pear in quarters. Remove the core from each quarter and cut the quarter into ¼-inch slices.

5. Dress the lettuce with the reserved dressing.

PRESENTATION

Put the salad in a half moon pattern on the left of the plate. Garnish the upper right hand corner with slices of pear and the lower right hand corner with slices of goat cheese.

MENU ACCOMPANIMENT

This salad is too flavorful to begin a meal. Serve it only after the main entrée.

Smoked Fish Salad

T HIS SALAD is an interesting combination of tastes and textures. Inspired by similar salads eaten at restaurants in France, it is easy to prepare and beautiful to look at. The secret of this recipe is to buy excellent smoked fish and a perfectly ripe avocado.

PREPARATION TIME:
1 hour

COOKING TIME:
5 minutes

SERVES:
6 as an appetizer
4 as a main course

2 *tablespoons fresh ginger, thinly julienned*
5½ *tablespoons safflower or vegetable oil*
2 *tablespoons red wine vinegar*
½ *tablespoon lemon juice*
2 *teaspoons water-packed capers, drained*
4 *cups (1 pound) loosely packed spinach, cut into 1- by 3-inch strips*
1 *¾-pound avocado*
½ *pound smoked sturgeon, sable, or skinned whitefish, thinly sliced*
½ *pound smoked Nova Scotia salmon, thinly sliced*
Salt
Freshly ground pepper

   1. Bring 2 cups water to a boil, plunge in the ginger and boil for 2 minutes. Drain and set aside.

2. In a bowl, combine the oil, vinegar, lemon juice, capers, ¼ teaspoon salt, and ⅛ teaspoon pepper. Set this vinaigrette aside.

3. Just before serving, toss the spinach with one-half of the dressing, reserving the rest. Peel the avocado and slice it into 3- by 1-inch pieces. Toss the avocado pieces with some of the reserved dressing.

PRESENTATION

Place 1 cup of the dressed spinach in the middle of each plate. Place the pieces of smoked fish, alternating the sturgeon with the salmon, around the spinach. Place the avocado slices in a crown around the spinach. Sprinkle the ginger on the spinach and moisten the fish with the rest of the leftover vinaigrette.

MENU ACCOMPANIMENT

Good before any entrée, whether meat, fish, or fowl. Served in larger portions, this is a satisfying main course for lunch. Any of our desserts would be appropriate.

Fish and Shellfish

Halibut Steaks with Shallots and Basil

T HE TASTE OF halibut is delicate while the texture of the flesh is firm and this balance makes the halibut one of America's best eating fish. Cooking the fish in a T-fal or a Calphalon pan seals in the natural juices, without adding additional butter or oil to the sauce. You must sauté the fish over a moderately high heat or it will dry out.

PREPARATION TIME:
10 minutes

COOKING TIME:
15 minutes

SPECIAL EQUIPMENT:
10- to 12-inch non-stick skillet

SERVES:
8 as an appetizer
4 as a main course

4   *8-ounce halibut steaks*
2   *tablespoons minced shallots*
8   *tablespoons butter*
½   *cup* glace de viande *or* demi-glace
1   *tablespoon lemon juice*
2   *tablespoons minced basil, optional*
     Salt
     Freshly ground pepper

1. Lightly season the halibut steaks with salt and pepper and sauté them in a non-stick skillet over medium heat for about 3 minutes on each side.

2. In a saucepan, sauté the shallots in 2 tablespoons butter over medium heat for 2 or 3 minutes, or until they are tender.

3. Add the *glace de viande* to the shallots. When the ingredients are completely blended, whisk in the remaining butter, tablespoon by tablespoon, over low heat. Add the lemon juice. Season the sauce with ½ teaspoon salt and ¼ teaspoon pepper. Stir in the optional fresh basil.

PRESENTATION

Remove the halibut to serving plates and spoon equal amounts of the sauce over the fish.

MENU ACCOMPANIMENT

This is a hearty dish. Keep the meal light by preceding it with Steamed Vegetable Salad (page 92) or Wilted Greens Salad (page 96). You could also precede this with a soup such as Seven-Vegetable Broth (page 76) or Cold Oyster and Tamarind Soup (page 83). As a vegetable garnish, serve Sautéed Shredded Squash (page 362).

Salmon with Fresh Vegetables

THIS DISH and dishes like it were conceived with the notion of wrapping and cooking the fish and vegetables in parchment paper. The pouches are brought to the table and the diners open their individual servings, surprised by the escaping steam and lovely odors. If parchment paper is not available, substitute aluminum foil. In this case, because foil looks unattractive on a plate, the pouches should be opened in the kitchen and the salmon transferred to individual plates.

PREPARATION TIME:
1 hour

COOKING TIME:
20 minutes

SERVES:
8 as an appetizer
4 as a main course

2   *pounds whole salmon, filleted (see illustration, page 114)*
4   *tablespoons butter*
1   *medium carrot, shredded*
1   *medium stalk celery, shredded*
4   *large mushroom caps, minced*
2   *medium scallions, cut into 3-inch julienne pieces*
1   *tablespoon minced shallots*
¼   *cup heavy cream*
     Salt
     Freshly ground pepper

1. Preheat the oven to 325 degrees.

2. Butter the pieces of parchment paper and set aside.

3. Cut each salmon fillet in half, making four pieces of salmon, 1 to 2 inches thick, depending on the size of the fish. Slice each of the four pieces of salmon in half. Season with salt and pepper.

4. Melt the butter in a medium-sized skillet. When hot, add all the vegetables at once and sauté over high heat for 2 to 3 minutes. Season with ½ teaspoon salt and ¼ teaspoon pepper.

5. Add the cream to the vegetables and stir over high heat until most of the moisture has evaporated. The vegetables should remain crisp. Adjust seasonings.

6. Place a portion of salmon on each of the pieces of parchment and spread each piece of salmon with a portion of cooked vegetables. Seal each pouch.●

7. Place the pouches on a baking sheet. Bake for 10 minutes.

PRESENTATION

Transfer the pouches to warm plates. Let each diner open a pouch at the table.

MENU ACCOMPANIMENT

This is an impressive course which should be the center of attention. Either precede or follow it with an assortment of vegetables or a salad. For important occasions, this could be a second course after a soup or green salad, followed by a simple roast or a sautéed meat dish. Any dessert would be fine.

Filleting a Rounded Fish

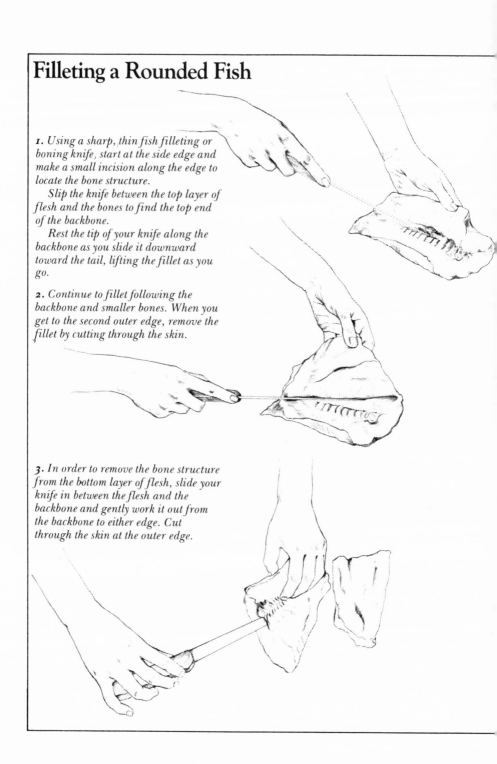

1. Using a sharp, thin fish filleting or boning knife, start at the side edge and make a small incision along the edge to locate the bone structure.

Slip the knife between the top layer of flesh and the bones to find the top end of the backbone.

Rest the tip of your knife along the backbone as you slide it downward toward the tail, lifting the fillet as you go.

2. Continue to fillet following the backbone and smaller bones. When you get to the second outer edge, remove the fillet by cutting through the skin.

3. In order to remove the bone structure from the bottom layer of flesh, slide your knife in between the flesh and the backbone and gently work it out from the backbone to either edge. Cut through the skin at the outer edge.

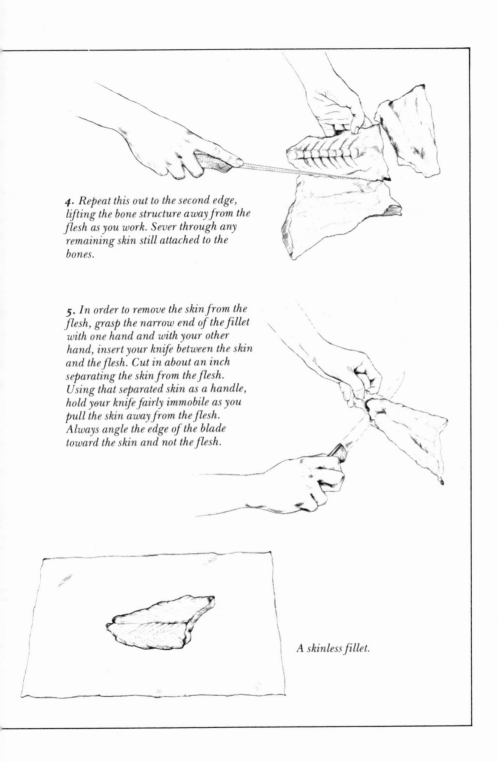

4. *Repeat this out to the second edge, lifting the bone structure away from the flesh as you work. Sever through any remaining skin still attached to the bones.*

5. *In order to remove the skin from the flesh, grasp the narrow end of the fillet with one hand and with your other hand, insert your knife between the skin and the flesh. Cut in about an inch separating the skin from the flesh. Using that separated skin as a handle, hold your knife fairly immobile as you pull the skin away from the flesh. Always angle the edge of the blade toward the skin and not the flesh.*

A skinless fillet.

Salmon Fillets with Spices and Currants

THE SAUCE for this was inspired by a medieval dish of salmon and dried fruit, an unusual combination which works extremely well. Raisins can be substituted for the currants, but the flavor is more subtle when the currants are used.

PREPARATION TIME:
45 minutes

COOKING TIME:
25 minutes

SPECIAL EQUIPMENT:
10- to 12-inch non-stick skillet

SERVES:
6 as an appetizer
4 as a main course

6   *tablespoons dried currants or raisins*
4   *tablespoons cider vinegar, mixed with 2 tablespoons water*
2½ *pounds whole salmon*
1¼ *cups heavy cream*
1   *cup fish stock*
¼   *teaspoon freshly ground nutmeg*
½   *teaspoon ground cinnamon*
6   *tablespoons butter*
    Salt
    Freshly ground pepper

1. Plump the currants by soaking them in the vinegar and water mixture.

2. While the currants soak, fillet the salmon into 4 or 6 portions (see illustrations, page 114). Season the fillets with salt and pepper.

3. Combine the cream, stock, nutmeg, cinnamon, ¾ teaspoon salt, and ¼ teaspoon pepper in a 2-quart saucepan. Bring this to a boil and simmer over moderate heat for about 10 minutes, or until the mixture is reduced to 1 cup. If you prepare this in advance, cover the sauce with buttered brown paper to prevent a skin from forming on the sauce as it cools.●

4. Preheat the oven to 250 degrees.

5. Place the non-stick skillet over moderate heat for 1 minute. Place the salmon fillets in the pan and cook for 2 minutes. With a spatula, turn the fillets over and cook them on the other side for 3 minutes more.

6. Remove the fillets to an oven-proof dish and keep them warm by placing them in the oven, covered, so they do not dry out.

7. Return the skillet to the heat and deglaze it by adding the currant and vinegar mixture. Cook until all the liquid has evaporated. Add the cream and spice mixture to the pan and heat through for another minute or so. Whisk in the butter, tablespoon by tablespoon. Adjust the seasonings. Heat the sauce briefly.

PRESENTATION

Spread equal amounts of the sauce on each heated plate. The sauce should cover the entire surface. Center 1 fillet on each plate. Serve accompanying vegetables, a garnish of shredded cucumber or squash perhaps, either along the outer edge to form a crown around the sauce, or on a separate plate.

This dish is good as a first course before a roast or sautéed meat, such as Steak with Bordelaise Sauce (page 182), or a poultry dish served with a dark and buttery sauce. Don't precede or follow this with cream sauce dishes or dishes which have a predominantly fruity flavor. For dessert, choose Lime Soufflé (page 419), Lemon Almond Cake (page 380), or Strawberry Tart (page 398).

Baked Sea Bass with Fresh Herbs

ALTHOUGH in some parts of France it is fashionable to undercook fish, we find that the texture of the uncooked fish tends to be unpleasant. It is therefore best to cook the fish until flaky at the bone.

PREPARATION TIME:
40 minutes

COOKING TIME:
1 hour

SERVES:
8 as an appetizer
4 as a main course

1   large (3-to 4-pound) sea bass, scaled and cleaned but with
        head left on
½   cup all-purpose flour seasoned with 1 teaspoon salt and ½
        teaspoon pepper
6   tablespoons butter, plus 10 tablespoons cold butter
½   cup glace de poisson
2   tablespoons minced parsley
2   tablespoons any minced fresh herb, such as basil, tarragon, or
        rosemary, or 1 ½ teaspoons of a dried herb
     Salt
     Freshly ground pepper

1. Preheat the oven to 375 degrees.

2. Coat the fish with the seasoned flour and shake off any excess flour.

3. Melt 6 tablespoons butter in a 14-inch skillet and, when melted, add the fish.

4. Sauté the fish over high heat for 2 to 3 minutes on each side until the skin begins to turn golden brown and crusty. (The butter will turn very brown but don't worry about this.)

5. Using 2 spatulas, transfer the fish to a baking dish. Pour the pan juices from the skillet over the fish.

6. Bake the fish, uncovered, for 35 to 40 minutes, or until the flesh is flaky at the bone.

7. Five minutes before the fish is done, bring the *glace de poisson* to a simmer in a 1-quart saucepan. Add the cold butter, tablespoon by tablespoon, until all is incorporated. Remove the sauce from the heat, add the parsley and herbs and season with salt and pepper. Set aside. Do not prepare the sauce in advance or the butter will separate.

8. Remove the fish from the oven and fillet into portions (see illustration, page 120).

Filleting Cooked Fish

1. Using 2 serving spoons turned bowlside down, gently lift the top fillet off the bones, beginning at either end. Remove it to the side of the dish.

2. Use 1 spoon to gently lift the center bones from the bottom fillet while the other spoon holds the fillet in place.

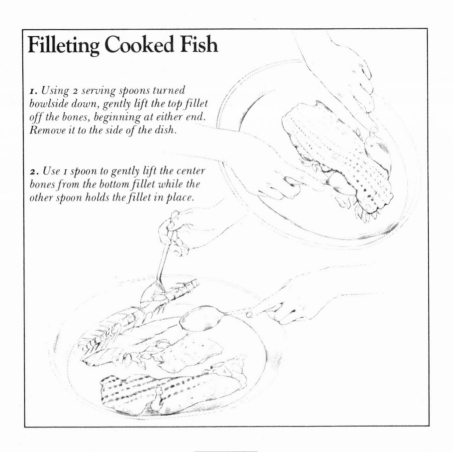

PRESENTATION

Place a portion of fish in the center of each warmed dinner plate and surround the fish with sauce.

MENU ACCOMPANIMENT

You might begin the meal with Smoked Fish Salad (page 106), or Broiled Oysters with Vegetable Julienne (page 143), or Oyster and Tamarind Soup (page 83). Follow the sea bass with a plain roast beef or veal with pan juices served with a garnish of Sautéed Summer Salad (page 90). Lemon Almond Cake (page 380), Chocolate Sweetness (page 373), or Chocolate Chip Tartlets (page 400) would be good for dessert.

Stuffed Sea Bass
Steamed in Lettuce

T HIS IS an unusual recipe and not nearly as difficult to make as it may appear. The dish may be assembled in advance and steamed at the last moment. The fish portions should be boneless, fairly thick, and squarish.

PREPARATION TIME:
40 minutes

COOKING TIME:
1 hour

SERVES:
4

10   *tablespoons butter*
6   *tablespoons minced shallots moistened with tarragon,*
       champagne, or white wine vinegar
1   *pound fresh mushrooms, minced*
8   *large Boston or romaine lettuce leaves*
4   *6-ounce portions of boneless sea bass, striped bass, cod, or*
       halibut
½   *cup* glace de poisson
4   *teaspoons tarragon, champagne, or white wine vinegar*
1   *cup heavy cream*
½   *cup packed watercress leaves, washed and dried*
       Salt
       Freshly ground pepper

   1. Melt 4 tablespoons butter in a saucepan. Add 4 tablespoons shallots and sauté over medium heat for 2 minutes. Add the mushrooms and season with 1 teaspoon salt and ½ teaspoon pepper.

2. Reduce the heat and cook for 10 to 15 minutes, or until all the liquid has evaporated and the mixture begins to dry out. Remove from the heat and set aside.

3. Parboil the lettuce leaves in 2 quarts boiling water, just until the leaves become limp. Drain and pat dry with paper towels.

4. Lightly season the fish with salt and pepper. With a sharp knife, butterfly each portion of fish by cutting through it horizontally, slipping the knife in at one side. Cut three-quarters through the middle. Spoon equal portions of the mushroom mixture on one-half of each portion of fish. Fold the other half of the fish over the stuffing.

5. Wrap each portion of stuffed fish in 2 pieces of the prepared lettuce, making sure that the lettuce forms a tight package around the fish.●

6. Gently place the packages in a vegetable steamer. Steam in a covered pot, over boiling water, for 10 to 12 minutes.

7. While the fish is steaming, prepare the sauce. Heat 2 tablespoons butter in a 9-inch skillet. Add 2 tablespoons shallots and sauté over medium heat for 2 minutes.

8. Add the *glace de poisson* and vinegar and whisk the ingredients together.

9. Add the heavy cream and watercress. Reduce the sauce over medium heat for 5 to 7 minutes.

10. Turn the heat down low and add the remaining 4 tablespoons butter bit by bit. When the butter has been incorporated into the sauce, remove the sauce from the heat immediately. Season the sauce with ½ teaspoon salt and ¼ teaspoon pepper.

PRESENTATION

Spoon equal portions of the sauce in the center of 4 heated dinner plates. Remove the fish packages from the steamer and gently pat them dry with paper towels. Put 1 package on top of each portion of sauce.

If served as a first course, this should be followed by Sautéed Rib Lamb Chops with Rosemary and Thyme (page 215), Calves Liver with Currant Glaze (page 302), or Steak with Bordelaise Sauce (page 182). If this is to be a second or main course, don't garnish it with any additional vegetables. Serve the vegetables, instead, as a first course and then follow the sea bass with a simple roast. Serve a light dessert such as Lime Soufflé (page 419), or Cranberry Soufflé (page 413).

Filleting a Flat Fish

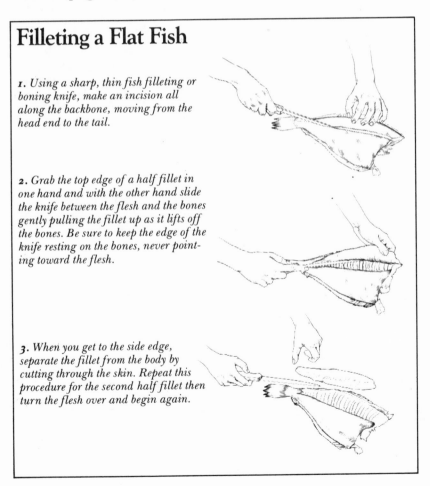

1. Using a sharp, thin fish filleting or boning knife, make an incision all along the backbone, moving from the head end to the tail.

2. Grab the top edge of a half fillet in one hand and with the other hand slide the knife between the flesh and the bones gently pulling the fillet up as it lifts off the bones. Be sure to keep the edge of the knife resting on the bones, never pointing toward the flesh.

3. When you get to the side edge, separate the fillet from the body by cutting through the skin. Repeat this procedure for the second half fillet then turn the flesh over and begin again.

Poached Fish with Shallots and Vinegar

THIS RECIPE, which uses fillets, will appeal to those who are afraid to cook a whole fish because of the problems that arise when one has to portion the cooked fish at the dinner table. The kinds of fish used here are not crucial; any combination will do. The key is to leave the skin on so the fish will not fall apart. The poaching method is foolproof. By bringing the poaching liquid to a boil and then removing the pan from the heat, the fish will cook gently and will remain moist for as long as it takes to prepare the butter sauce. The fish must be drained well before it is served—if too much of the poaching liquid comes in contact with the sauce, its intense flavor will be diluted. When choosing the fish, keep in mind the different skin colors, as a variety of hues on the plate will delight the eye.

PREPARATION TIME:

1 hour

COOKING TIME:

1 hour

SERVES:

8 as an appetizer
4 as a main course

2   *pounds fish fillets with skin left on (combine bass, salmon, red snapper, flounder, or sea trout)*
2   *tablespoons minced shallots*
6   *tablespoons champagne or white wine vinegar*
1¼   *cups dry white wine*
2   *tablespoons butter, plus 8 tablespoons cold butter*

1   tablespoon coarse salt
1   whole bay leaf
1   teaspoon dried thyme
1   cup julienned carrots
1   cup snow peas, or green bean pieces, or shelled
        fresh green peas
3   teaspoons chopped fresh coriander leaves, optional
2   medium (¾ - pound) tomatoes peeled, seeded, and chopped
     Salt
     Freshly ground pepper

1. Cut the fillets into 1- by 3-inch pieces. Season the fish with salt and pepper and set aside.

2. In a 1-quart saucepan, mix the shallots, 4 tablespoons champagne vinegar, and ¼ cup dry white wine. Reduce over high heat until all the liquid has evaporated. Be sure that the shallots remain moist. Remove from the heat and set aside.

3. In a skillet large enough to accommodate all the fish in a single layer, combine 2 tablespoons butter, the coarse salt, ¼ teaspoon pepper, the bay leaf, the thyme, 1 cup dry white wine, 2 cups water, and the remaining wine vinegar. Cook over medium heat until the butter dissolves into the liquid. ●

4. Place the fish in the poaching liquid and cover the pan.

5. Slowly bring the liquid to a boil and immediately turn off the heat under the pan. The fish will continue to cook slowly while you finish the sauce and cook the vegetable garnish. Cover the pan to keep the fish hot and moist.

6. Bring 3 quarts water mixed with 1 tablespoon salt to a boil. Place the carrots and snow peas in a strainer and submerge the strainer in the boiling water. Cook for approximately 2 minutes, or until the vegetables are barely tender. Drain and set aside.

7. While the vegetables are poaching, slowly reheat the shallot and vinegar mixture. When hot, finish the sauce by whisking in the cold butter, tablespoon by tablespoon. Take care not to overheat the sauce or it will separate. The color of the sauce should remain opaque at all times. Add the coriander.

8. Drain the fish and pat dry with paper towels.

PRESENTATION

Arrange the fish like spokes of a wheel around the center of a warmed dinner plate. Make sure to alternate the various types of fish. Heap an assortment of each of the vegetables in the center of the plate. Place the fresh tomatoes on the top. Spoon the sauce over the fish.

MENU ACCOMPANIMENT

Avoid serving this with other dishes whose sauces are finished with butter. If served as a first course, follow it with something simple, such as Beef Fillet with Pan Juices (page 168) or Veal Loin Laced with Peppercorns (page 220). If this is to be the main course, precede it with Seven-Vegetable Broth (page 76), Smoked Fish Salad (page 106), or Tomato and Basil Ice (page 318), if in season. Hot Peach and Almond Tart (page 395), Pumpkin Pie (page 405), or fresh berries are perfect for dessert.

Shad Roe with Sorrel

S HAD ROE is a great American delicacy and it should be included in any cookbook which stresses making the most out of native and fresh ingredients. Shad roe are in season for such a short time that you should treat yourself to them when available.

PREPARATION TIME:
20 minutes

COOKING TIME:
45 minutes

SERVES:
4 as an appetizer
2 as a main course

2   *pair of shad roe, each pair weighing approximately 8 ounces*
1   *cup fresh sorrel leaves*
4   *tablespoons butter*
¼   *cup* glace de poisson
¼   *cup* demi-glace
½   *cup heavy cream*
    Salt
    Freshly ground pepper

    1. Bring about 1½ cups water (or enough to cover the roe) to a boil in a shallow 9-inch skillet. With a spoon or spatula, place the roe in the water, taking care not to break the outer skin which holds them together.

    2. Lower the heat and gently poach the roe, uncovered, for about 4 minutes without turning them over.

3. Remove from the heat and let the roe cool in the water for about 10 minutes.

4. While the roe are cooling, wash the sorrel leaves and remove their stems (as you would with spinach). Chop the leaves roughly and set aside.

5. Remove the roe from the water and gently pat them dry with paper towels.

6. In a clean 9-inch skillet, heat the butter until hot, turn down the heat, and sauté the roe for approximately 6 minutes. Take care that the heat is not too high or the roe will burst. Using a spatula and a slotted spoon, turn each pair over. Season the cooked side with salt and pepper and sauté the roe for another 5 minutes. Season the second side.

7. While the roe are sautéing, make the sauce by heating the *glace de poisson* and *demi-glace* in a 7-inch skillet over medium heat. Add the heavy cream and reduce the mixture until the sauce lightly coats a spoon.

8. When the roe are done, remove them to a cutting board. Split the roe along the vertical membrane. Slice them perpendicularly to the membrane into ½ - inch thick slices.

9. Finish the sauce by adding the sorrel leaves and cooking until the leaves just wilt.

PRESENTATION

Distribute the sorrel sauce equally in the center of each of 4 warmed dinner plates. Place the sliced roe on top and serve immediately.

MENU ACCOMPANIMENT

The sauce for this dish is so rich, we would recommend serving it as a main course. To begin the meal, serve Broiled Oysters with Vegetable Julienne (page 143), or Sautéed Summer Salad (page 90), or an assortment of four vegetables. A fruit tart, or a fruit ice or sherbet would be a fitting end to this glorious meal.

Swordfish Steaks with Oranges

I N ONE OF his books Escoffier mentioned a recipe for fillets of sole with oranges. We have elaborated on this idea and made a more substantial sauce by adding the *glace de viande*. The strong flavor of the swordfish stands up to the sauce, which contains the delightful zest of oranges.

PREPARATION TIME:
45 minutes

COOKING TIME:
20 minutes

SERVES:
6 as an appetizer
4 as a main course

1½   *pounds swordfish*
4   *tablespoons softened butter, plus 4 tablespoons*
¾   *cup* glace de viande *or* demi-glace
3   *oranges, peeled and sectioned (see step 4, page 307)*
       Salt
       Freshly ground pepper

   1. Divide the swordfish steaks into 4 equal portions.
   2. Salt and pepper the swordfish while you are pre-heating the broiler.
   3. When the broiler is hot, spread each steak with 1 tablespoon softened butter and broil them for about 3 to 4 minutes on each side, or about 10 minutes for each inch of thickness. Baste the steaks with pan juices every 3 minutes or they will dry out.

4. While the steaks are broiling, combine in a sauce-pan over medium heat, the *glace de poisson* and the orange juice you have reserved from peeling the oranges. Reduce this by one-third. When the swordfish steaks are done, whisk in the remaining butter, tablespoon by tablespoon. Season with salt and pepper. Add the orange sections, and warm for 1 minute longer over very low heat or the sauce will separate.

PRESENTATION

Spoon some sauce on each of 4 plates. Place a portion of swordfish on each plate and cover with the remaining sauce and oranges. Serve immediately.

MENU ACCOMPANIMENT

Serve this as a second course with rice and a steamed vegetable, such as green beans, broccoli, or squash. Follow with a cheese course and a creamy dessert such as Frozen Mousse Cassis (page 417) or Mocha Cream (page 415). If the swordfish is to be served as a first course, avoid main courses and desserts in which fruit flavors predominate.

Sole with Chives

THIS DISH IS believed to have originated at the Trois-gros restaurant in Roanne, France. It is easily recreated because it can be made with any kind of firm white fish. Breading the fish by dipping it first in butter and then in breadcrumbs seals in the natural juices and keeps the fish from drying out. The subtle coloring of the golden fish posed on the rose and green sauce is so stunning that any additional garnish on the plate would spoil the effect.

PREPARATION TIME:
20 minutes

COOKING TIME:
15 minutes

SERVES:
6 as an appetizer
4 as a main dish

1¼ *pounds lemon sole, gray sole, or flounder, filleted*
4 *tablespoons melted butter*
1½ *cups freshly ground breadcrumbs, seasoned with ½ teaspoon salt and ½ teaspoon pepper*
½ *cup* demi-glace
¾ *cup heavy cream*
4 *tablespoons freshly snipped chives*
  Salt
  Freshly ground pepper

   1. Preheat the oven to 350 degrees.

2. Dip each fillet in the melted butter, and coat the buttered fillets on both sides with the breadcrumbs. Shake off any excess breadcrumbs.

3. Arrange the fillets in a lightly buttered oven-proof baking pan and bake the fish for 10 to 15 minutes, or until springy to the touch.

4. While the fish is baking, combine the *demi-glace* and the heavy cream in a medium skillet and bring the mixture to a boil.

5. Reduce the heat and simmer gently for 2 to 3 minutes, or until the sauce lightly coats a spoon. Season with ¾ teaspoon salt and ¼ teaspoon pepper.

PRESENTATION

Pour one-fourth of the sauce on each heated plate and spread it around so that the entire surface area of the plate is covered. Sprinkle 1 tablespoon of chives on the surface of the sauce. With a large spatula, place the fish gently in the middle of the sauce.

MENU ACCOMPANIMENT

In preceding or following courses, avoid cream and tomato. See menu suggestions for Baked Sea Bass with Fresh Herbs (page 118).

Poached Sole with Tomato and Saffron

S AFFRON IS THE world's most expensive spice but a bit of it goes a long way, and it lends incomparable flavor to fish. Not only is the taste of this dish superb, but the colors are gorgeous.

PREPARATION TIME:
30 minutes

COOKING TIME:
20 minutes

SERVES:
6 as an appetizer
4 as a main course

1½ *pounds gray or lemon sole fillets*
½ *cup* glace de homard
¼ *cup dry white wine*
2 *large bay leaves*
2 *small (¾ - pound) tomatoes, peeled, seeded, and roughly chopped*
2 *tablespoons butter*
1 *cup heavy cream*
½ *teaspoon dried saffron threads or powder*
 Salt
 Freshly ground pepper

1. Rinse the fillets and pat them dry with paper towels. Lightly salt and pepper the fillets.

2. In a large skillet, off the heat, combine for a poaching liquid the *glace de homard*, white wine, bay leaves, fresh tomatoes, and butter.

3. Place the fish in this poaching liquid and bring to a boil. Lower the heat and cover the skillet with a tight-fitting lid or with buttered aluminum foil. Tuck the ends of the foil inside the edges of the pan so that they don't burn.●

4. Simmer, covered, until the fish is springy to the touch, about 7 minutes.

5. Using a slotted spoon or spatula, remove the fish from the skillet, taking care not to break the fillets. Set aside.

6. Add the cream and saffron to the poaching liquid and reduce over high heat until the sauce is thick enough to lightly coat a spoon. Discard the bay leaf, and add ½ teaspoon salt and ¼ teaspoon pepper.

PRESENTATION

Place a portion of fish in the center of each warmed plate. Spoon some sauce around, not on, the fish.

MENU ACCOMPANIMENT

Precede this dish with Broccoli and Apple Soup (page 72) or Warm Asparagus with Japanese Dressing (page 94); accompany it with plain wild rice. For dessert, serve Chocolate Sweetness (page 373) or Upside-Down Pecan Pie (page 403).

Baked Lobster

I N THEIR RESTAURANT in Roanne, the Troisgros brothers serve this tantalizingly simple lobster dish. The warmth of the lobster meat melts the butter sauce in the shell. Keep in mind that the lobsters have to be split in half lengthwise while they are still alive, so if you are squeamish about such things, have someone on hand who isn't to help you out.

PREPARATION TIME:
45 minutes

COOKING TIME:
20 minutes

SPECIAL EQUIPMENT:
Mortar and pestle

SERVES:
4

4   *1 ¼- to 1 ½-pound lobsters*
3   *tablespoons mild vegetable oil*
8   *tablespoons softened butter*
1   *tablespoon fresh minced tarragon, or ½ teaspoon dried*
1   *teaspoon minced shallots*
2   *tablespoons minced Italian parsley*
    Salt
    Freshly ground pepper

1. Preheat the oven to 550 degrees, or as hot as it will go without being on broil.

2. Turn each lobster on its stomach and split it lengthwise down its back (see illustration). Remove and discard the small sac inside the lobster.

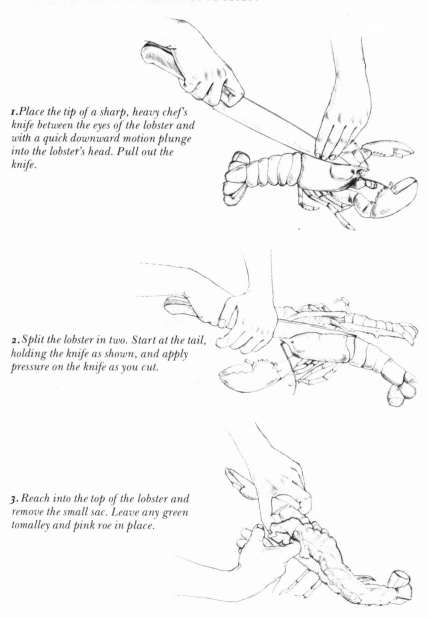

1.Place the tip of a sharp, heavy chef's knife between the eyes of the lobster and with a quick downward motion plunge into the lobster's head. Pull out the knife.

2.Split the lobster in two. Start at the tail, holding the knife as shown, and apply pressure on the knife as you cut.

3. Reach into the top of the lobster and remove the small sac. Leave any green tomalley and pink roe in place.

3. Spread the oil over the bottom of a baking pan large enough to accommodate the lobsters. Arrange the lobster halves in the baking pan on their backs so that the natural juices do not spill out.

4. Heat the baking pan with the lobsters on top of the stove until the oil begins to sizzle, about 2 to 3 minutes. Season the flesh with ½ teaspoon salt and ¼ teaspoon pepper.

5. Put the baking pan on the lowest rack, or on the floor of the oven and bake for 12 to 15 minutes, or until the lobster flesh becomes firm to the touch.

6. While the lobsters are baking, combine the butter with the tarragon, shallots, parsley, ¼ teaspoon salt, and ¼ teaspoon pepper. Mash them together with a mortar and pestle or mix them together in a food processor for a few seconds.

PRESENTATION

Place the lobster halves on warmed plates. Tear off each claw and set it alongside the lobster. Lift the tail sections up with a fork and spoon the butter mixture into the shell beneath the meat. Immediately place the tail meat on top of the butter in the shell and serve.

MENU ACCOMPANIMENT

This is somewhat lighter than our other lobster dish, so it could serve as an opener to an elegant meal. For true sumptuousness serve it before Sweetbreads with Cassis and Whole Shallots (page 304), Venison Steak with Caper Sauce (page 296), or Boned Saddle of Lamb Stuffed with Mushrooms (page 206). If you serve this as a main course, see suggestions for Shad Roe with Sorrel (page 127), but substitute a richer dessert like Chocolate Almond Cake (page 370) for the sherbet.

Lobster with Vegetables

THIS IS AN easy and delicious way to prepare lobster. The entire dish may be completed in one saucepan.

PREPARATION TIME:
45 minutes

COOKING TIME:
45 minutes

SERVES:
6 to 8 as an appetizer
4 as a main dish

	Coarse salt
3	*1 ¼- to 1 ½-pound lobsters*
4	*tablespoons butter*
½	*cup minced carrot*
¾	*cup minced onion*
3	*tablespoons minced shallots*
1	*clove garlic, minced*
1	*cup tomatoes, peeled, seeded, and chopped*
⅓	*cup Calvados or cognac*
½	*cup* glace de homard
¼	*cup* demi-glace
1½	*cups heavy cream*
3	*tablespoons* foie gras *, optional*
2	*tablespoons minced Italian parsley*
	Salt
	Freshly ground pepper

1. To a large pot three-quarters full of water, add a small handful of coarse salt. Cover and bring to a boil. Plunge the live lobsters, head first, into the boiling water. Cook them until the shells turn a bright red. This will take about 10 to 12 minutes.

2. Remove the lobsters, with tongs, from the boiling water, and either cool them at room temperature, if you are going to use them later, or under cold running water, if you are going to use them right away. The lobsters should be cool enough for you to handle.

3. To remove the meat from the lobsters, first pull off the claws, then tear the lobsters in half at the waist. Pull off the tail. Press the bottom half of the lobster's shell together to crack the shell. Break the shell off in pieces. Remove the meat. Crack the claws with a nut or lobster cracker and pull out the meat. Cut the flesh into 1-inch chunks wherever possible. Place all the meat in a bowl, cover, and reserve.

4. Melt the butter in a 10- or 12-inch skillet. Add the carrot, onion, shallots, and minced garlic, and sauté over low heat for about 5 minutes, so that they do not brown.

5. Add the tomatoes and sauté for another 5 minutes.

6. Pour the Calvados into the skillet, ignite it with a lighted match and shake the pan until the flames die out.

7. To this same skillet, add the *glace de homard*, *demi-glace* , and heavy cream. Bring this mixture to a simmer. Reduce until the sauce lightly coats a spoon. Season with ½ teaspoon salt and ¼ teaspoon pepper.

8. Add the reserved lobster chunks to the sauce and, if serving immediately, heat for 2 to 3 minutes. ●

9. If you are using the *foie gras*, add it to the lobster mixture and whisk it in until it just dissolves. Remove the skillet from the heat immediately or the *foie gras* will have a slightly sour taste.

Spoon a portion of lobster and sauce onto preheated plates. Sprinkle each portion with some parsley and serve at once.

MENU ACCOMPANIMENT

See menu accompaniment for Shad Roe with Sorrel (page 127).

Mussels in Puff Pastry

ALTHOUGH THESE ARE delicious eaten plain, they improve greatly with the addition of Tomato Vinaigrette Sauce (see the recipe on page 366).

PREPARATION TIME:
1 hour and 30 minutes (excluding pastry)

COOKING TIME:
1 hour

SERVES:
4 to 6 as an appetizer

3   pounds mussels
½   cup white wine
4   tablespoons butter
1   tablespoon minced shallots
1   tablespoon Pernod
1   tablespoon white wine vinegar
1   tablespoon minced Italian parsley
6   puff pastry rectangles (see page 388), defrosted
     Egg wash made from 1 egg beaten with 1 tablespoon water
     Salt
     Freshly ground pepper

1. Shortly before cooking the mussels, clean them with a scrub brush under cold running water. Try to remove as much as possible of the heavy beard on the sides of the mussels.

2. Place the wine and 1 cup water in a 4- or 5-quart non-aluminum heavy pot and bring to a boil.

3. Place the mussels in the boiling liquid. Cover, and steam them until they open, about 3 minutes. Drain the mussels and cool them under cold running water. Discard any unopened shells.

4. When cool enough to handle, remove the mussels from the shells and pick each one over. Where the beard is still in evidence and attached to the mussel, rip it off. Set the cleaned mussels aside.

5. Melt the butter in a small saucepan over medium heat. Add the shallots, Pernod, ½ teaspoon salt, ¼ teaspoon pepper, and vinegar, and simmer over low heat for 2 minutes.

6. Remove this mixture from the heat. Add the parsley. Add the mussels and mix them well into the butter mixture.

7. With a pastry brush, moisten the edges of each defrosted pastry rectangle with water. Place 5 or 6 mussels in the center of each rectangle and fold one corner over to the opposite corner to form a triangle. Seal the edges by pressing them together with the tines of a fork. Brush each turnover with the egg wash mixture.

8. Transfer the shaped turnovers to a baking sheet, using a spatula. Refrigerate for at least 45 minutes. ●

9. Preheat the oven to 450 degrees.

10. Put the baking sheet with the turnovers on the lowest shelf of the oven. Bake for 15 minutes. Lower the heat to 375 degrees and continue to bake for 30 minutes longer, or until the pastry is puffy and golden brown. If the turnovers are browning too quickly, cover them with a piece of aluminum foil.

PRESENTATION

Serve these on individual, heated plates.

MENU ACCOMPANIMENT

When served as an appetizer this deserves an elegant second course. Frogs' legs, venison, or any of our roast meats with two vegetable garnishes would be suitable. If fish is to be the second course, serve the Halibut Steaks with Shallots and Basil (page 110). For dessert avoid short crusts or puff pastry.

Broiled Oysters with Vegetable Julienne

AMERICA ABOUNDS with fresh oysters which are always superb when eaten simply on the half shell. This recipe enhances the natural flavor of the oysters by adding a light julienne of buttered vegetables. Easy to prepare, the results are delicious. Try to cut the vegetables the length of the oysters so that they completely cover the flesh.

PREPARATION TIME:
30 minutes

COOKING TIME:
10 minutes

SERVES:
4 as an appetizer
2 as a main course

24 *fresh oysters*
4   *tablespoons butter*
1   *tablespoon minced shallots*
1½ *stalks celery, cut into 2-inch or longer julienne pieces*
2   *medium carrots, cut into 2-inch or longer julienne pieces,*
    depending on the size of oysters
    Salt
    Freshly ground pepper

1. Shuck the oysters or have your fishmonger do it for you (in which case you must ask him to reserve half the shells).

2. Place the oysters on their shells in a broiling pan. Heat the broiler.

3. Melt the butter in a saucepan over medium heat. Add the shallots and sauté for 2 minutes, or until they are tender but not brown.

4. Add the celery and carrots and sauté for another 2 to 3 minutes or until the vegetables are soft.

5. Cover each oyster completely with some of the mixed julienned vegetables. Season with salt and pepper and broil for 3 minutes.

PRESENTATION

Remove the oysters from the broiler and arrange 6 to 12 of them on each warmed plate. The key is to serve them as quickly as possible.

MENU ACCOMPANIMENT

Serve the oysters before lobster or cream-based dishes. This nice change from oysters on the half shell would be harmonious before any meat or poultry dish.

Bay Scallops with Celery Julienne

T HE THEORY BEHIND this recipe is that foods will absorb the flavor of the liquid they are steamed over. Accordingly, the scallops and vegetables absorb the slightly sweet taste of the sauterne. In order to achieve this taste you must buy imported sauterne as the American wine is too dry.

PREPARATION TIME:
20 minutes

COOKING TIME:
10 minutes

SPECIAL EQUIPMENT:
Steamer that fits into a pot with a lid

SERVES:
6 as an appetizer
4 as a main dish

2   *cups imported French sauterne*
2   *large stalks celery, cut into 2-inch julienne pieces*
1¾ *to 2 pounds bay scallops (If sea scallops are used, cut any large ones so that they are about equal in size to the smaller ones. They will then cook evenly.)*
2   *tablespoons butter, optional*
    Salt
    White pepper

1. Off the heat, pour the wine into a saucepan and place the vegetable steamer over the liquid.

2. Place the celery in the steamer and place the scallops on top of the celery.

3. Cover the steamer, bring the sauterne to a boil, and steam the scallops for 5 to 7 minutes, or until the scallops are cooked all the way through. (Raw scallops are slightly pink. They are cooked when the insides of the scallops turn to a milky white.)

4. Remove the scallops and celery from the steamer. Sprinkle with ½ teaspoon salt and ¼ teaspoon pepper and serve right away, or transfer them to a mixing bowl and toss with the optional butter.

PRESENTATION

Scoop the scallops and celery onto warmed dessert plates. If you have tossed the scallops with butter there will be some liquid in the mixing bowl—pour this on each portion.

MENU ACCOMPANIMENT

This dish is fresh, light, and perfect as an appetizer or second course preceding any meat or poultry course.

Cold Bay Scallops with Cumin Vinaigrette

WHAT IS NEW and delightful about this dish is the combination of the Middle Eastern spice cumin with an otherwise traditional vinaigrette.

PREPARATION TIME:
30 minutes
(plus 2 hours cooling time)

COOKING TIME:
10 minutes

SERVES:
6 as an appetizer
4 as a main course

1½ *pounds bay scallops (If sea scallops are used, cut any large ones until they are about equal in size to the smaller ones. They will then cook evenly.)*
1 *tablespoon minced shallots*
1½ *teaspoons ground cumin*
¼ *teaspoon dry mustard*
6 *tablespoons olive oil*
2 *tablespoons champagne or white wine vinegar*
1 *large (1-pound) avocado*
1 *head Boston lettuce, leaves separated, or 2 to 4 small bibb lettuces, leaves separated*
2 *medium (½-pound) tomatoes, peeled and cut into wedges*
2 *tablespoons minced parsley*
 Salt
 Freshly ground pepper

1. Put a vegetable steamer in a saucepan to which you have added 2 to 2½ cups water. Bring the water to a boil, place the scallops in the steamer, cover, and steam for 3 minutes over medium heat.

2. After 3 minutes, uncover the scallops, turn them with tongs or a slotted spoon, making sure those on the bottom are now on top so that they all steam evenly. Continue steaming, covered, for another 2 minutes.

3. With a slotted spoon, remove the scallops from the heat. Place them in a bowl and leave them to cool at room temperature for 30 minutes.

4. Cover the bowl and let the scallops cool for 2 more hours in the refrigerator.

5. Combine the shallots, cumin, mustard, vinegar, ¼ teaspoon salt, and ⅛ teaspoon pepper in a mixing bowl. Beat the oil into the vinegar with a wire whisk, adding the oil in a slow steady stream of droplets as you would with a mayonnaise. (You can achieve the same emulsion by blending all the ingredients including the oil in a food processor.) If you are going to wait to use the vinaigrette, refrigerate it immediately to preserve the emulsion. ●

6. Just before serving, drain the scallops of the excess liquid that has accumulated in the bowl and toss them with all but 2 tablespoons of the vinaigrette.

7. Peel and pit the avocado and slice it into ½ -inch slices.

PRESENTATION

Place 4 or 5 leaves of lettuce on chilled serving plates. Divide the scallops into equal portions in the center of the lettuce leaves. Garnish each plate with alternating tomato wedges and avocado slices arranged in a windmill-like circle around the scallops. Sprinkle the reserved dressing on the avocado and tomatoes, and the parsley on the scallops.

This is a good main course for a lunch or summer supper. The addition of cold avocado slices and tomato wedges serves as a vegetable accompaniment. When you serve this dish as an appetizer, make sure to follow with a taste that will stand up to the powerful cumin. Pork Medallions in Fig Coulis (page 194), Herbed Veal Chops with Bacon and Shallots (page 227), or a duck dish would be perfect. For dessert, we recommend the Pink Pear with Dark Chocolate (page 433).

Sea Scallops with Chopped Fresh Tomato

THIS SCALLOP dish may be made in one skillet. The recipe calls for sea scallops because bay scallops become rubbery when cooked for the length of time required. The scallops and the sauce are so perfectly matched that a piece of French bread should be on each plate to soak up every last drop of sauce.

PREPARATION TIME:
20 minutes
(plus 2 hours cooling time)

COOKING TIME:
15 minutes

SERVES:
6 as an appetizer
4 as a main course

1½ *pounds sea scallops, at room temperature*
½ *cup all-purpose flour, seasoned with salt and white pepper*
4 *tablespoons butter*
½ *cup* demi-glace
½ *cup tomatoes peeled, seeded, and chopped*
1 *cup heavy cream*
4 *tablespoons minced Italian parsley or basil leaves*
  Salt
  White pepper

1. Dredge the scallops in the seasoned flour. Shake off any excess flour.

2. Melt the butter in a large skillet over medium heat. Add the scallops and sauté them over high heat for 2 to 3 minutes.

3. With a slotted spoon, remove the scallops to a mixing bowl and cover them. Set aside.

4. Over medium heat, add the *demi-glace* and to-matoes to the skillet in which you sautéed the scallops. Using a wooden spoon, mix with the scallop juices.

5. Add the cream, and stir the sauce with a whisk until the cream thickens slightly, about 5 minutes. Season with ¾ teaspoon salt and ½ teaspoon white pepper.

6. Return the scallops to the sauce. Do not add too much of the liquid they will have given off in the bowl or your sauce will have to simmer and reduce again, and the scallops will get tough. Heat the scallops in the sauce for about 2 minutes.

Spoon the scallops onto 4 heated dessert plates. Sprinkle each serving with the minced parsley, and serve immediately.

MENU ACCOMPANIMENT

Avoid serving with other courses which contain tomato. As a vegetable garnish, serve Sautéed Shredded Squash (page 362), Sautéed Spinach (page 352), Sautéed Asparagus (page 324), or Artichoke and Walnut Sauté (page 322). Any dessert without cream would be appropriate.

Elegant Fish Stew

THIS AMERICAN version of a delicious French fish stew has a touch of mace, which makes it even more exciting to the taste.

PREPARATION TIME:
45 minutes

COOKING TIME:
20 minutes

SERVES:
6

1   quart fish stock
1   pound cod fillets
½   pound salmon or trout fillets
½   pound sea scallops
½   pound shrimp, shelled and deveined (see page 157)
4   tablespoons butter, plus 1 tablespoon softened
8   pearl onions
2   medium carrots, cut into ½-inch dice
1   clove garlic, minced
½   pound mushrooms, cut into ½-inch pieces
2   tablespoons minced Italian parsley
1   cup heavy cream
1½ pounds tomatoes, peeled, seeded, and roughly chopped
1   bay leaf
¼   teaspoon ground mace
    Salt
    Freshly ground pepper

1. Boil the fish stock until it is reduced by half (2 cups should remain). Set aside.

2. Cut all the fish fillets in chunks approximately the size of the sea scallops and shrimp so that they all cook evenly. Salt and pepper the fish and shellfish lightly and set aside, uncovered, in the refrigerator.

3. Melt the butter in a large 14-inch skillet. Add the onions and sauté them over medium heat for 3 minutes.

4. Add the carrots and garlic to the same skillet and sauté for another 5 minutes.

5. Add the mushrooms and parsley to the skillet and mix all together. Sauté for 5 to 8 minutes, or until soft but not mushy.

6. As the vegetable mixture cooks, bring the reduced fish stock to a simmer in a 4-quart saucepan. Stir in the cream and bring the mixture back to a simmer.

7. Add the tomatoes, ¾ teaspoon salt, ¼ teaspoon pepper, the bay leaf, and the mace, and simmer over low heat for 5 minutes.

8. While the sauce is simmering and the vegetables are sautéing, steam all the fish together, covered, in a steamer for 5 minutes.

9. After the fish has been steamed, beat the softened butter into the sauce until just melted. Adjust the seasoning. Place the vegetables in a casserole. On top of the vegetables put the steamed fish and then pour the sauce over the fish.

PRESENTATION

Serve from the casserole at the table, or divide this dish into 6 small earthenware casseroles for individual servings.

MENU ACCOMPANIMENT

This is really too hearty to be served as a first course. Instead, serve as an entrée with a vegetable salad and cheese course afterwards. End with Souffléed Chocolate Cake (page 375).

Shrimp, Duck, and Spinach in Puff Pastry

ALTHOUGH this is one of the more complicated recipes in the book, the results are truly "three-star" and worth your trying at least once.

PREPARATION TIME:
1 hour and 45 minutes (excluding pastry)

COOKING TIME:
1 hour and 30 minutes

SERVES:
4

¾   *pound fresh spinach*
1   *5- to 6-pound duck*
8   *jumbo shrimp*
4   *rectangles of puff pastry (see page 388)*
     Egg wash made with 1 egg yolk mixed with 1 teaspoon water
6½   *tablespoons butter, plus 1 tablespoon softened*
     Juice of 1 lemon
3   *tablespoons red wine vinegar*
½   *cup* glace de viande
     Salt
     Freshly ground pepper

1. Roughly chop the spinach and set aside.
2. Bone out the breast and thigh meat of the duck (see page 278). You can wrap the duck carcass and thigh bones in tin foil and store them in the freezer until you have enough to make duck stock. Discard the fatty duck skin pieces; these are not appropriate in a stock pot.

3. Shell the shrimp, leaving the tails on. Devein them following the instructions in step 1 of the recipe for Shrimp in Bordelaise Sauce (page 157). ●

4. Two hours before serving, preheat the oven to 450 degrees.

5. Remove the pastry rectangles from the freezer and set them on a baking sheet. There should be 2 inches of room around each piece of pastry. Let them thaw out at room temperature for 15 minutes.

6. With a sharp knife, make decorative diagonal lines on each piece. Brush each piece with the egg wash, making sure no glaze drips down the sides of the pastry pieces or they won't rise. Put the pastry in the oven.

7. After 10 minutes turn the heat down to 350 degrees and bake the pastry for another 45 minutes. If the pieces begin to brown, cover them loosely with foil.

8. Remove the pastry from the oven and transfer it to a rack to cool. When cool enough to handle, pull each pastry in half horizontally so that you end up with half for the bottom and half for the top, very much like 2 pieces of bread for a sandwich. Set these aside until ready to assemble. ●

9. Melt 3 tablespoons butter in a 10-inch skillet. Add the duck meat and sauté over medium heat for 5 minutes on a side. Season with salt and pepper. Remove the meat to a cutting board and cover it loosely with foil to keep it warm. Reserve the skillet on the stove, off the heat.

10. In a second skillet, sauté the shrimp over high heat in 1½ tablespoons butter for about 30 seconds on each side. Season with salt and pepper and leave them in the skillet with the heat turned off.

11. Melt the remaining 2 tablespoons butter over high heat in a third skillet. Add the lemon juice. When sizzling, toss in the spinach and cook, stirring, for 30 seconds, until hot but not completely wilted. Turn off the heat and leave the spinach in the pan.

12. In the pan in which you sautéed the duck, discard any excess fat and return the pan to medium heat. When hot, deglaze it with the red wine vinegar, making sure you scrape up all of the browned particles.

13. Add the *glace de viande* and whisk together. Reduce the sauce for 2 minutes over a medium heat.

14. Whisk in the softened butter and season with salt and pepper. Keep the sauce warm on a low flame.

15. Drain the spinach. Slice the duck across the grain into ⅛-inch slices.

PRESENTATION

Place the bottom half of a pastry rectangle in the middle of a warmed dinner plate. For each serving, place a portion of spinach on the bottom half, with some of it hanging over the edges of the pastry. Place slices of thigh and breast meat on top, leaving spinach visible underneath. Place 2 shrimp on each side, head half on duck, tail on plate. Spoon some sauce on top of the duck and then cover with the decorated piece of puff pastry placed askew. This dish is *not* meant to be served piping hot.

MENU ACCOMPANIMENT

You should only serve this as an appetizer before the grandest of meals. When such an occasion arises, follow it with Veal Loin Laced with Peppercorns (page 220), or Boned Saddle of Lamb Stuffed with Mushrooms, (page 206), or Beef Fillet with Pan Juices (page 168). Served in larger portions, this is a lovely luncheon dish. Follow it with a cheese course with salad, and end with an extraordinary cake, such as David's Cake (page 377) or Chocolate Sweetness (page 373).

Shrimp in Bordelaise Sauce

T HE FRENCH are fortunate in having an abundance of crayfish which they have featured prominantly in their cuisine. Because Americans cannot easily obtain crayfish, we have created shrimp dishes in the style of the crayfish dishes found in nouvelle cuisine.

PREPARATION TIME:
1 hour and 15 minutes

COOKING TIME:
10 minutes

SERVES:
6 as an appetizer
4 as a main course

2   *pounds shrimp*
4   *tablespoons butter*
1   *clove garlic, minced*
¼   *cup* bordelaise
2   *tablespoons minced Italian parsley*
     Salt
     Freshly ground pepper

1. Remove the shell and little feet beneath the belly of each shrimp. Run the tip of a sharp knife down the entire length of the curved back of the shrimp. In so doing you will expose the large black and green intestine. Gently lift it out, in one piece if possible. Scrape out the remaining bits of the intestine with the back of your knife. Wash the shrimp under cold running water and pat them dry with paper towels.

2. Heat the butter in a large skillet and add the garlic while the butter is melting. When the butter is foaming, add the shrimp and sauté for 2 minutes over high heat, stirring occasionally with a wooden spoon.

3. Lower the heat to medium and incorporate the *bordelaise* into the shrimp and butter mixture.

4. When all the shrimp are coated with the sauce, season with ¼ teaspoon salt and ¼ teaspoon pepper.

5. Remove the pan from the heat and add the parsley. Mix it thoroughly with the shrimp.

PRESENTATION

Portion out the shrimp onto heated plates.

MENU ACCOMPANIMENT

This makes for a light course before any meat or poultry entrée. Avoid serving this before dishes where *bordelaise*, garlic, or onions dominate.

Shrimp with Tamarind Sauce

T HE NOUVELLE cuisine uses ingredients from diverse cultures to provide a singularly unique result. Tamarind, an extract of the sour-sweet fruit of the tamarind tree is a flavoring that has yet to come into widespread use in the United States. When combined with *glace de poisson*, the resulting flavor is sophisticated and tangy.

PREPARATION TIME:
1 hour and 30 minutes

COOKING TIME:
5 minutes

SERVES:
6 as an appetizer
4 as a main course

6   *tablespoons butter*
2   *tablespoons minced shallots*
½   *pound mushrooms, cut into ¼-inch slices*
½   *cup* glace de poisson
1   *tablespoon tamarind paste*
2   *pounds fresh shrimp, shelled and deveined (see p. 157)*
    Salt
    Freshly ground pepper

1. Melt the butter in a 10-inch skillet. Add the shallots and sauté over medium heat for 1 minute.

2. Add the mushrooms, ½ teaspoon salt, and ¼ teaspoon pepper and cook over high heat for 2 minutes.

3. Lower the heat to medium and add the *glace de poisson* and the tamarind. Stir all the ingredients in the pan until they are well mixed.

4. Cook the shrimp by stirring them in the sauce over medium heat for approximately 2 minutes, or until they turn pink and opaque.

PRESENTATION

Portion out the shrimp onto heated plates.

MENU ACCOMPANIMENT

Don't serve with dishes where mushrooms or tamarind dominate. This goes well before any meat or poultry entrée.

Soft Shell Crabs with Lime Sauce

THE TASTE of lime is slightly less acidic than lemon juice and more subtle when combined with the delicate flavor of a soft shell crab. In the tradition of the nouvelle cuisine, this is a quick and simple way of cooking the crabs.

PREPARATION TIME:
30 minutes

COOKING TIME:
10 minutes

SERVES:
4 as an appetizer
2 as a main course

8   medium-sized soft shell crabs, cleaned
½   cup all-purpose flour, seasoned with 1 teaspoon salt and ½
      teaspoon pepper
¼   pound butter
      Grated rind and juice of 1 lime
      Salt
      Freshly ground pepper

1. Coat the crabs with the seasoned flour and shake off any excess flour.

2. Sauté the crabs in hot butter for 4 minutes on one side; turn and sauté for about 3 minutes on the other side. (Stand a bit away from the skillet as the crabs will pop and splatter as you sauté them.)

3. Remove the crabs and keep them warm. Add the lime rind and juice, and ½ cup water to the pan. Deglaze the pan by scraping up all the browned particles with a wooden spoon and incorporating them into the lime juice. Season with ½ teaspoon salt and ½ teaspoon pepper.

PRESENTATION

Place crabs on warmed dinner plates and pour the pan juices over them. Serve 2 crabs for each main course.

MENU ACCOMPANIMENT

These are so simple that you could juxtapose any fish, meat, or poultry course before or after them. Don't serve vegetable garnishes alongside the crabs. End your meal with a refreshing Mango Ice (page 317).

Soft Shell Crabs with Lobster Sauce

S OFT SHELL crabs are delicious when simply sautéed, but they are magnificent when served with a lobster sauce. For the supreme gustatory experience, add a few tablespoons of *foie gras* to the sauce before serving.

PREPARATION TIME:
20 minutes

COOKING TIME:
15 minutes

SERVES:
4 as an appetizer
2 or 3 as a main course

8   *to 9 medium-sized soft shell crabs, cleaned*
½   *cup all-purpose flour, seasoned with 1 teaspoon salt and ¼*
      teaspoon pepper
8   *tablespoons softened butter, plus 4 tablespoons butter*
½   *cup* glace de homard
¼   *cup* demi-glace
2   *tablespoons* foie gras, *optional*
     Salt
     Freshly ground pepper

   1. Preheat the oven to 200 degrees.
   2. Coat the crabs with the seasoned flour. Shake off any excess.

3. Melt 8 tablespoons butter in a skillet large enough to accommodate the crabs in one layer without crowding them. Add the crabs, and sauté them over medium heat for 3 to 5 minutes on each side, or until they begin to turn golden brown. (Be cautious when you sauté them as the legs tend to pop and splatter. Don't be alarmed, the splattering soon subsides.)

4. Remove the crabs to an oven-proof baking dish. Set them in the oven to keep warm while you make the sauce.

5. Return the skillet to medium heat. Add the *glace de homard* and *demi-glace*. Deglaze the pan using a wooden spoon, combining the browned crab particles with the sauce.

6. When the sauce begins to bubble, remove it from the heat and whisk in the 4 tablespoons butter, tablespoon by tablespoon, until all of it is incorporated. Season with ½ teaspoon salt and ¼ teaspoon pepper. (If you are using the *foie gras*, incorporate it, off the heat, tablespoon by tablespoon after the butter, and then season the sauce with the salt and pepper.)

PRESENTATION

Spread the sauce in the center of plate. Place the crabs, centered, on the sauce.

MENU ACCOMPANIMENT

Garnish this with a steamed potato, sautéed snow peas, or spinach. Serve the Chicken Terrine (page 251) or a salad as a first course. Fine Orange Cake (page 382) is a lovely dessert with this dish.

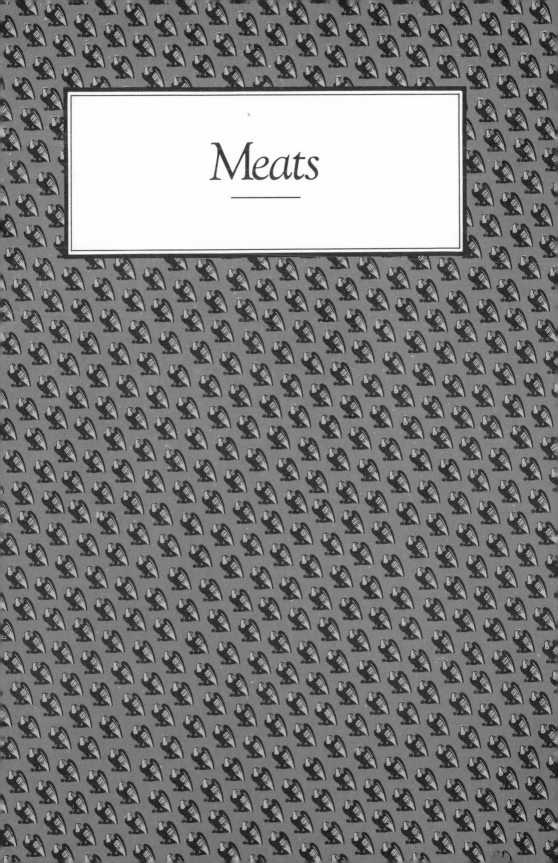

Meats

Roast Beef with Onions and Carrots

I F YOU have *glace de viande* on hand you can make an elegant sauce for a simple piece of roasted meat. The sauce will complement all cuts of roast beef.

PREPARATION TIME:
20 minutes

COOKING TIME:
1 to 2 hours,
depending on the cut of beef

SERVES:
6

2½ *pounds roasting beef (tenderloin or rib roast)*
11 *tablespoons butter*
⅓ *cup carrots, finely minced*
½ *cup onions, finely minced*
2 *tablespoons shallots, finely minced*
    (Note: The carrots, onions, and shallots should approach a purée in texture. They can be minced by hand or in a food processor.)
¾ *cup* glace de viande
    Salt
    Freshly ground pepper

   1. Preheat the oven to 450 degrees.
   2. Season the roast with salt and pepper. Put it on a rack in a roasting pan on the lowest shelf of the oven. Cook

the roast until the temperature on a meat thermometer reaches 125 degrees for rare or 135 to 140 degrees for medium.

3. When the beef is ready to come out of the oven, make the sauce. Melt 3 tablespoons butter in a 9-inch skillet. Add the carrots, onions, and shallots, and sauté over medium heat for about 5 minutes, or until the vegetables begin to get soft. Set aside.

4. Remove the roast from the oven and place it on a carving board. (*Note:* After it has been taken out of the oven, the beef needs to rest for at least 10 minutes before carving. During this period the juices of the meat are reabsorbed into the tissues, resulting in a juicier piece of beef.)

5. Discard the fat from the roasting pan. Add ½ cup water to the pan drippings and bring to a boil, while scraping the browned particles from the bottom of the roasting pan into the liquid.

6. Transfer the liquid to a saucepan and reduce by one-half.

7. Add the sautéed vegetables over medium heat. Add the *glace de viande*, and bring to a simmer.

8. Lower the heat and whisk in the remaining 8 tablespoons butter, tablespoon by tablespoon. Remove from the heat and season the sauce with salt and pepper.

PRESENTATION

Carve the beef into ¼-inch slices. Lay the sliced meat in the middle of each plate and spoon the sauce over the top. The vegetables and potatoes served with this dish should be placed on either side of the beef.

MENU ACCOMPANIMENT

Serve a soup, fish course, or light salad to start. Serve this course with any vegetable, such as Pea Purée (page 348), Floating Broccoli (page 329), or Oven-Baked Sliced Potatoes (page 347).

Beef Fillet with Pan Juices

FOR THOSE of you who have never used caul fat we suggest that you make its acquaintance immediately. Caul fat is a white lace-like fatty tissue that comes from the diaphragm area of a pig. When wrapped around a piece of meat and roasted it works to baste whatever it surrounds. After roasting, the caul fat is usually removed and discarded, however, it often dissolves completely during the cooking process. It is virtually tasteless after it has been roasted, so do not be concerned if traces of fat remain on the meat when your dish is served. The caul fat seals in the juices of the fillet and keeps the meat moist and basted while it is roasting. We have never understood people's fascination with overdone beef dishes, such as Beef Wellington, where the pastry inevitably becomes soggy and the meat has to be cooked in two stages. By simply wrapping the beef in caul fat the end result is far superior to any Wellington preparation you have ever tasted. As an added twist you may even coat the fillet with a duxelle mixture, wrap the whole beef and mushroom mixture with the caul fat and create an elegant main course.

PREPARATION TIME:
10 minutes

COOKING TIME:
30 to 40 minutes

SERVINGS:
4 to 6

½   of a whole fillet mignon, completely trimmed of all
       extraneous fat and shiny gristle, at room temperature
       (You can use a whole fillet and serve twice as many
       people.)
     Several sheets of caul fat
     Salt
     Freshly ground pepper

   1. Preheat the oven to 450 degrees.
   2. After trimming the fillet, season it with salt and
pepper and wrap the entire roast with the caul fat. (The
caul fat is rather sticky so it isn't necessary to tie the roast,
simply pat the sections of the fat together until a seal is
formed.)
   3. Roast the beef on a rack in a roasting pan. The
meat will be cooked in 30 minutes if you desire rare beef;
in 35 to 40 minutes if you prefer medium beef.
   4. Remove the meat from the oven, place it on a
carving board, and let it rest for 10 minutes.
   5. Degrease the roasting pan and discard the fat.
Deglaze the pan with 1 cup water, scraping all the browned
particles into the water.
   6. Reduce the juices by half, and season with salt
and pepper to taste.

PRESENTATION

Slice the fillet into thick 1½- to 2-inch slices. Make sure that
you remove any obvious pieces of caul fat from the surface
of the meat. Transfer the slices of beef to serving plates and
spoon the pan juices over them.

MENU ACCOMPANIMENT

To start, serve Broiled Oysters with Vegetable Julienne
(page 143), or Stuffed Sea Bass in Lettuce (page 121), or
Baked Sea Bass with Fresh Herbs (page 118). An Artichoke

and Walnut Sauté (page 322), if in season, would be a good accompaniment, or Fresh Snow Peas with Shallots and Basil (page 351). The cut of meat is elegant and sets the tone of the meal. Thus, Fine Orange Cake (page 382) or David's Cake (page 377) would end the meal on an equally elegant note.

Boneless Rib Roast with Roasted Garlic

THE CUT of meat used in this dish has been called boneless rib roast, Delmonico roast, or Newport roast. Call it what you will, this beef is delicious when roasted properly and served with a garlic-flavored sauce. Try to buy the smaller end of the rib for this recipe. This portion of the beef is more tender.

PREPARATION TIME:
10 minutes

COOKING TIME:
2 hours

SERVES:
6 to 10

1   *5- to 6-pound boneless rib roast*
     Separated, whole, unpeeled cloves of a large head of garlic
½   *cup* glace de viande
8   *tablespoons butter*
     Salt
     Freshly ground pepper

1. Preheat the oven to 450 degrees.

2. Season the roast with salt and pepper and put it in a pan with a roasting rack. Place the pan on the bottom shelf of the oven and roast the beef for 1 hour.

3. Scatter the garlic cloves in the bottom of the roasting pan and continue to cook for another half hour for rare meat. Allow an extra 15 minutes for medium and 30 minutes for well done.

4. When the roast is cooked to your taste, remove it from the oven and transfer it to a carving board. Let the roast rest for 10 to 15 minutes. (*Note:* Roasts should always rest so that the meat fibers can reabsorb the natural juices as the meat cools down.)

5. While the beef is resting, degrease the roasting pan and discard the fat. With a slotted spoon, transfer the garlic to a sieve and mash it through the sieve into the pan. The object is to get the roasted garlic flesh without the garlic skins into the pan.

6. Add ½ cup water to the pan and place it over medium heat. Using a wooden spatula, scrape the browned particles into the degreased drippings.

7. Transfer the juices into a medium-sized skillet. Add the *glace de viande* and simmer until the *glace* has incorporated itself into the sauce.

8. Turn the heat under the pan very low and whisk the butter into the sauce, tablespoon by tablespoon. Set aside.

9. Slice the meat into 1-inch thick slices.

10. After the meat has been sliced there should be a good deal of juice in the wells of your carving board. Whisk these juices into the sauce and season the sauce with salt and pepper. Reheat the sauce slightly over a low heat, so that it does not curdle.

PRESENTATION

Arrange a slice of meat on each plate and spoon a portion of the sauce over the meat.

MENU ACCOMPANIMENT

See menu accompaniments for Rib Steak with Forty Cloves
of Garlic (page 180).

Beef Eye Round Encased in Salt

THIS CENTURIES-OLD method of cooking is adapted
here to prepare an eye round of beef. The salt mold
is simple to prepare. This makes an excellent party
roast because the beef may be prepared in advance and
then baked in the oven without having to turn the meat.
The beef does not require a sauce, but should be served
with the natural juices.

PREPARATION TIME:
15 minutes

COOKING TIME:
1 hour and 15 minutes

SERVES
6

1   *3-pound boneless eye round*
4   *large garlic cloves, mashed*
3   *teaspoons fresh thyme, or 1 teaspoon dried*
8   *cups coarse salt*
3   *bay leaves*
    Freshly ground pepper

    1. Preheat the oven to 450 degrees.
    2. Wash the beef and dry it with paper towels. Rub
the mashed garlic, thyme, and pepper into the meat.

3. Mix together the salt and 2 cups water and stir until a coarse paste is formed.

4. Spoon approximately one-third of the salt paste into a roasting pan that has been lined with a double layer of aluminum foil. Press the salt down until the roast can be placed on top of it, leaving salt exposed all around the bottom of the piece of beef.

5. Press the bay leaves onto the top of the roast and use the rest of the salt mixture to completely cover the meat. The best way to do this is to work the salt onto the roast around the sides continuing until the roast is completely sealed.

6. Put the pan with the roast on the lowest shelf of the oven and bake for 30 minutes.

7. Lower the temperature to 400 degrees and continue to bake for 30 minutes more for rare and 40 minutes for well done.

8. Remove the pan from the oven after the appropriate time and let the beef rest, still encased in the salt mixture, for 5 minutes. Break away the salt shield and dust off any particles of salt still attached to the meat.

PRESENTATION

Transfer the roast to a carving board. Carve the beef into ¼-inch thick slices. Serve on plates with the natural juices of the roast. (*Note:* Do not be alarmed if the beef looks gray on the outside. The outer flesh was not exposed to any surface heat and therefore did not caramelize.)

MENU ACCOMPANIMENT

Begin your meal with a Black Bean Soup (page 78). The roast itself goes well with an accompaniment of Pea Purée (page 348) and Sweet Potato Sauté (page 363). Serve a light fruit dessert to finish off the meal.

Fillet Mignon with Fresh Ginger

T HIS RECIPE IS a favorite in the restaurants of France because the leftover tips of the whole fillets can be utilized effectively. Our version calls for 2 pounds of trimmed and cubed fillet cut from the lower part of the whole fillet. The combination of fresh ginger and the reduced cream gives the fillet a unique taste.

PREPARATION TIME:
30 minutes

COOKING TIME:
15 minutes

SERVES:
4 to 6

1   *cup heavy cream*
¼   *inch piece fresh ginger, peeled and minced*
2   *pounds trimmed fillet, cut into 1 ½-inch cubes*
4   *tablespoons butter*
½   *cup* demi-glace
2   *tablespoons minced Italian parsley*
     Salt
     Freshly ground pepper

1. Place the cream and ginger in a 2-quart saucepan and simmer over low heat until the cream is reduced by one-third. Purée the ginger and cream in a blender and set aside.

2. Season the fillet cubes lightly with salt and pepper.

3. Melt 2 tablespoons butter in a large skillet. When

the butter begins to bubble, add half of the meat to the pan and sauté over a high heat for a few minutes, stirring the beef with a wooden spoon, until the sides begin to brown. When the meat is browned, remove it to a large serving platter. Cover the meat to keep it warm and set aside.

4. Add the remaining butter to the skillet and repeat the cooking process with the remaining meat. When the fillet cubes are browned, spoon them onto the serving platter with the first batch.

5. Degrease the pan and add the *demi-glace*. Over medium heat, using a wooden spoon to scrape the bottom of the pan, incorporate the browned beef particles into the *demi-glace*.

6. Add the cream and ginger. Reduce the sauce over medium heat for 1 minute, or until it begins to thicken.

7. Season the sauce with salt and pepper to taste. Blend in any juices that have accumulated around the cooked fillet cubes.

PRESENTATION

Arrange the meat neatly on the serving platter. Pour the sauce through a strainer directly over the meat. Sprinkle the minced parsley over the entire dish and serve.

MENU ACCOMPANIMENT

Avoid cream soups or sauces before this course. Serve this dish with Steamed Avocado (page 328) and Caramelized Onions (page 342). Keep the dessert course light—any of the fruit ices or fruit purées would be lovely.

Beef Tenderloin Ragout

THIS DISH is really an elegant beef stew. It may also be prepared with chunks of chuck or top round, however it will take longer to cook and the beef pieces may be tough. The beauty of using the pieces of tenderloin is that the beef is tender to begin with. The other ingredients combine to make this ragout very tasty.

PREPARATION TIME:
1 hour and 40 minutes

COOKING TIME:
1 hour

SERVES:
6

2   *pounds beef tenderloin, trimmed and cut into 1 ½-inch pieces*
4   *tablespoons butter*
2   *tablespoons olive oil*
2   *medium onions, roughly chopped*
1   *cup red wine*
½   *cup* demi-glace, *optional (if omitted the ragout sauce will be less intense)*
½   *pound mushrooms, rinsed and sliced*
4   *large fresh artichoke hearts, cooked (see page 322)*
½   *pound snow peas, cleaned (see page 217)*
3   *teaspoons fresh thyme, or 1 teaspoon dried*
    Salt
    Freshly ground pepper

   1. Season the pieces of meat with salt and pepper.
   2. Heat the butter and oil together in a 10-inch skil-

let with high sides or a large casserole. When hot, sear the meat over high heat for about 5 minutes. Turn it to ensure that every surface browns. Lower the heat and cook the meat, uncovered, for another 5 minutes, stirring occasionally. Turn off the heat and with a slotted spoon, remove meat to a bowl. Set aside.

3. Return the skillet to medium heat. Add the onions and mushrooms and cook for an additional 15 minutes. Stir every now and then so that the onions don't stick to the pan.

4. Add in the wine, *demi-glace*, thyme, 1 teaspoon salt and ½ teaspoon pepper, and mix all the ingredients together. Simmer for 10 minutes. ●

5. Cut the artichoke hearts into 4 pieces. Add the meat and artichoke hearts to the skillet and continue cooking, covered, for 5 minutes longer.

6. Season the ragout with salt and pepper. Just before serving, toss in the snow peas and cover the pot. The snow peas will cook to the proper degree of crunch in approximately 3 to 4 minutes.

PRESENTATION

Spoon equal portions of the ragout onto dinner plates. Don't worry about the snow peas being on top of the meat and other vegetables.

MENU ACCOMPANIMENT

This dish goes well with the Oven-Baked Sliced Potatoes (page 347) and a light salad. End the meal with Penuche and Raisin Layer Cake (page 385).

Herbed Paillard of Beef

T HESE STEAKS, cooked without fat in hot skillets, have a delicious grilled flavor, but the cooking process creates a great deal of smoke. Open the windows wide for the couple of minutes it takes to execute the dish.

PREPARATION TIME:
25 minutes

COOKING TIME:
5 minutes

SERVES:
4

4   *tablespoons softened butter*
1   *minced shallot*
½   *cup loosely packed Italian parsley*
1   *cup loosely packed basil*
2   *pounds boneless rib steak, about 1 ½- to 2- inches thick*
     Salt
     Pepper

1. In a food processor, thoroughly combine the butter, shallot, parsley, basil, ½ teaspoon salt, and ¼ teaspoon pepper. Set aside.

2. Cut the steak into 4 horizontal slices, each ¼-inch thick. Cut each slice vertically, into 2 pieces.

3. Heat two 14-inch skillets over high heat for 1 minute. Add 4 steaks to each skillet and sauté for exactly 1 minute on each side. (*Note:* The amount of smoke generated is to be expected.)

PRESENTATION

Remove the steaks from the skillets and put 2 on each warmed dinner plate. Brush herbed butter on each steak and serve immediately.

MENU ACCOMPANIMENT

This course is so simple that you could serve it with any vegetable. As it calls for a butter using fresh summer herbs, concentrate on serving this with summer vegetables, such as the Artichoke and Walnut Sauté (page 322) or Sautéed Asparagus (page 324). Precede this with any soup, fish course, or salad. Any dessert would do to end the meal.

Rib Steak with Forty Cloves of Garlic

THERE IS a well-known dish called Chicken with Forty Cloves of Garlic, which is the inspiration for our steak recipe. Parboiling the garlic first rids it of its harshness.

PREPARATION TIME:
10 minutes

COOKING TIME:
15 minutes

SERVES:
4

4 *pounds rib steak, including bone*
4 *ounces garlic cloves, unpeeled*
12 *tablespoons butter*
4 *tablespoons olive oil*
1 *cup red wine*
  Salt
  Freshly ground pepper

1. Trim the steaks of all fat and season them with salt and pepper.
2. Bring 1 quart water to a boil and parboil the unpeeled garlic cloves for 10 minutes. Drain, peel, and set aside.
3. Melt 3 tablespoons butter and 2 tablespoons olive oil over high heat in each of 2 skillets. When the butter is hot, sear the steaks for 2 minutes on each side. Lower the

heat and cook for a total of 10 to 12 minutes for rare, or 15 to 17 minutes for medium. Turn the steaks occasionally as they cook. Remove them from the skillets and keep them warm on a plate loosely covered with foil.

4. Pour out all but 2 tablespoons fat in 1 of the pans. Melt 2 tablespoons butter in this skillet. Add the garlic cloves and sauté them for 1 minute over high heat, mashing the whole cloves to a rough consistency.

5. Pour the wine and whatever juices have oozed out of the steaks into the pan with the garlic and reduce this by half over high heat.

6. Turn off the heat and whisk in 4 tablespoons butter. Season with salt and pepper to taste.

PRESENTATION

Slice the steaks across the grain into ½-inch slices. Divide the meat into 4 portions and center the meat on each of the warmed dinner plates. Spoon equal portions of the sauce and garlic cloves over the meat.

MENU ACCOMPANIMENT

The flavor of this main course is obviously intense. Precede it by a light vegetable broth and serve it with any vegetable, avoiding, of course, those with a dominant onion flavor. Any dessert would be appropriate.

Steak with Bordelaise Sauce

THIS IS an easy dish to make, once the *bordelaise* is ready in your freezer. You may use any tender cut of steak for this entrée, but the sauce is so delicious it really deserves the finest piece of tenderloin.

PREPARATION TIME:
5 minutes

COOKING TIME:
15 minutes

SERVES:
4

4   *6-ounce tenderloin steaks*
10 *tablespoons butter*
½   *cup* bordelaise
    Salt
    Freshly ground pepper

1. Season the steaks with salt and pepper.

2. In a skillet large enough to hold the steaks comfortably in one layer, melt 2 tablespoons butter. (If you are using a large steak that you plan to cut into smaller pieces, you may have to use more butter.) When the butter is melted and bubbly, add the steaks and sauté over a moderate to high heat for 3 to 5 minutes on each side, depending on the thickness of the steak. Remove the steaks and keep them warm on a covered plate.

3. If there is a lot of fat in the pan, degrease it before adding the *bordelaise*. If not, just add the *bordelaise* to the pan, bring it to a boil, and scrape all the brown particles into the sauce.

4. When the sauce begins to simmer, whisk in the remaining butter, tablespoon by tablespoon, never letting the butter get too hot or the sauce will separate. Add salt and pepper to taste.

PRESENTATION

Pour a little of the sauce over the steak and the rest in a sauce dish served separately at the table.

MENU ACCOMPANIMENT

The intense flavor of this dish allows it to be preceded by just about any course. Avoid accompanying vegetables that are too rich in butter, as the *bordelaise* has much in it already. Any dessert would be fine.

Flank Steak with Fresh Tomato and Garlic Sauce

BECAUSE THERE is little fat or waste, flank steak is a relatively inexpensive cut of meat. It is delicious broiled and served with this tangy olive oil and tomato sauce.

PREPARATION TIME:
1 hours

COOKING TIME:
20 minutes

SERVES:
4 to 6

2   *pounds ripe fresh tomatoes, peeled and seeded*
1½ to 2 *pounds flank steak*
1   *tablespoon melted butter*
4   *tablespoons green olive oil*
1½ *tablespoons tarragon, white, or red wine vinegar*
1   *small clove garlic, minced*
2   *tablespoons minced parsley*
        Salt
        Freshly ground pepper

    1. Purée the tomatoes in a food processor. Remove them to a sieve placed over a bowl.

    2. With a wooden spoon, push the pulp and juice through the sieve. Discard the seeds and bits of pulp that remain.

    3. In a non-aluminum 9-inch skillet, reduce the tomato pulp over medium heat until 1½ cups remain. Remove from the heat. While the tomatoes are reducing, pre-heat the broiler. ●

4. Season the flank steak with salt and pepper. With a sharp knife, make 1-inch cuts around the outside edge of the steak at 2-inch intervals, to insure that it lies flat while broiling. Brush one side of the steak with melted butter, and broil, buttered side up, for 4 to 6 minutes, depending on how rare you like your meat. Turn the meat, brush the second side with melted butter and broil it an additional 4 to 6 minutes. Remove the meat from the broiler and let it rest, to reabsorb its juices, while you finish the sauce.

5. Transfer the reduced tomato purée to a food processor or blender. Purée with the oil, vinegar, garlic, and ¾ teaspoon salt.

PRESENTATION

Slice the steak on the diagonal into very thin slices. Spoon tomato sauce on warmed plates. Lay slices of steak in a row down the center of the sauce and sprinkle the meat and sauce with parsley, then dust with freshly ground pepper.

MENU ACCOMPANIMENT

To start, serve Jerusalem Artichoke Soup (page 81), Squash Cakes (page 358), or Steamed Vegetable Salad (page 92). Follow with the steak by itself, or with a steamed or boiled green vegetable such as green beans, zucchini, or asparagus served on a separate plate. For dessert, try homemade Vanilla (page 424) or Peach (page 422) Ice Cream.

Boneless Stuffed Fresh Ham with Fruit Sauce

T HE TEXTURES and tastes of this roast ham are absolutely glorious. Although the dish has many ingredients it is really very simple to make. The fruit sauce is closer to a condiment because it is so thick.

PREPARATION TIME:
30 minutes

COOKING TIME:
3 to 4 hours

SERVES:
10 to 12

½ *(8- to 12-pound) fresh ham with the bone removed*
1 *cup dried figs*
½ *cup dried apricots*
2 *cups fresh shelled chestnuts (see page 288)*
½ *cup dried currants or raisins*
½ *cup blanched almonds*
¾ *cup* demi-glace
8 *tablespoons butter*
   Salt
   Freshly ground pepper

1. Preheat the oven to 400 degrees.

2. Season the ham, inside and out, with pepper. Set aside.

3. Combine the fruits and nuts in a mixing bowl. Work this mixture into the cavities of the ham. Tie the ham with butchers' twine to hold it together. ●

4. Place the ham on a rack in a roasting pan. Roast the ham for 3 to 4 hours, or until the meat reaches an internal temperature of 165 degrees on a meat thermometer.

5. Remove the ham to a carving board and let it rest while you prepare the sauce.

6. Remove 1 cup stuffing from the ham and purée the mixture in a food processor.

7. In a saucepan, combine the *demi-glace* and the puréed stuffing. Whisk together over medium heat.

8. Whisk in the butter, tablespoon by tablespoon, until completely incorporated into the sauce. Remove from the heat. Season with salt and pepper.

PRESENTATION

Remove the twine from the ham. Carve the meat into ¼-inch slices. Add any juices from the carving board to the sauce, and serve it on the side.

MENU ACCOMPANIMENT

A hearty starter such as Black Bean Soup (page 78) would be appropriate. Serve a simple green salad afterward either alone, or with a cheese course. For dessert, serve a Grapefruit Sherbet (page 314) or Lime Ice (page 315) with Butter Cookies (page 407).

Pork with Cracked Peppercorns

T HE SHARP bite of the cracked peppercorns contrasts well with the rich texture and taste of the pork. A good complement to this dish is a purée of turnips, which can be made well in advance and used instead of heavy cream to thicken the sauce.

PREPARATION TIME:
10 minutes

COOKING TIME:
1 hour and 30 minutes

SERVES:
4

4 *tablespoons whole black peppercorns*
2 *pounds boned loin of pork, tied*
½ *cup* demi-glace
2 *teaspoons prepared mustard*
¼ *cup Puréed Turnips with Garlic (page 365)*
4 *tablespoons butter*
   Salt
   Freshly ground pepper

    1. Preheat the oven to 350 degrees.
    2. Wrap the peppercorns in wax paper and pound them with a mallet to crack them. Press the cracked peppercorns around the outside of the pork loin.
    3. Roast the pork, uncovered, in a roasting pan for 1½ hours, or until the juices run clear, or the meat thermometer registers 165 degrees.
    4. Remove the roast from the pan, cover it loosely with foil, and let it rest while you finish the sauce.

5. Over medium heat deglaze the pan with ½ cup water scraping all the browned particles into the sauce.

6. Transfer the juices to a skillet. Add the *demi-glace* and mustard to the juices and reduce over medium heat for about 1 minute.

7. Add to the skillet any juices the roast has given off. Add the turnip purée and reduce until the sauce coats a spoon. Add ½ teaspoon salt.

8. Taste for seasoning and whisk in the butter at the last minute, 1 tablespoon at a time. Remove from the heat immediately.

PRESENTATION

Carve the roast in ¼-inch slices. Place some slices in the center of warmed dinner plates. Spoon some sauce over each portion. Any vegetable garnishes should be placed in a semi-circle around the meat.

MENU ACCOMPANIMENT

You can highlight and intensify the sauce by serving Puréed Turnips with Garlic (page 365) as a garnish. If you want a second vegetable, serve Sautéed Grapes (page 339), Kale Simmered in Cream (page 340), sweet potatoes, or Shredded Carrots with Orange Juice (page 332). Serve a salad afterward and then a dessert of your choice.

Cold Loin of Pork with Green Peppercorn Mayonnaise

T HE LOIN in this recipe is cooked in the same manner as the Pork with Cracked Peppercorns. It is then chilled, thinly sliced, and served with a tangy green-pepper mayonnaise. The entire dish can be made up to 2 days in advance.

PREPARATION TIME:
30 minutes, plus time required to chill meat

COOKING TIME:
1 hours and 30 minutes

SERVES:
8

2   *pounds boned loin of pork, tied*
3   *egg yolks*
2   *tablespoons champagne or tarragon vinegar*
2¼ *cups olive oil*
3   *tablespoons green peppercorns packed in water, mashed*
2   *tablespoons minced Italian parsley*
     Salt
     Freshly ground white pepper

    1. Preheat the oven to 350 degrees.
    2. Roast the pork, uncovered, for 1½ hours, or until the juices run clear, or a meat thermometer registers 165 degrees.
    3. Remove the roast from the pan and let the meat reabsorb the juices for at least 15 minutes. Refrigerate the meat until chilled, 2½ hours at least.

4. Place the egg yolks in a mixing bowl, add ¼ teaspoon salt and the vinegar, and beat gently with a whisk.

5. Add the oil, drop by drop at first, and more rapidly as the yolk mixture begins to absorb the oil.

6. As soon as all the oil is absorbed, beat in 1 tablespoon boiling water to stabilize the texture of the sauce.

7. Mix in the mashed green peppercorns and adjust the seasoning with salt and pepper.

PRESENTATION

Just before serving, slice the meat as thinly as possible and serve with the sauce. Place a dollop of sauce in the center of the plate. Surround the sauce with slices of pork and sprinkle parsley over the top.

MENU ACCOMPANIMENT

If in season, precede this with Soft Shell Crabs with Lime Sauce (page 160), if not, serve Bay Scallops with Celery Julienne (page 145). Along with the pork, serve a mixed green salad with sliced ripe tomatoes. Any fresh fruit tart, such as the Hot Peach and Almond Tart (page 395) makes a lovely end to the meal.

Pork Medallions
in Pomegranate Sauce

THE LOVELY tart flavor of fresh pomegranate juice blends well with the rich flavor of the pork. Pomegranate juice is available in most health food stores, but if you can get fresh pomegranates, make your own. Squeeze them as you would oranges. If the juice seems a bit too tart, sweeten it lightly with superfine sugar.

PREPARATION TIME:
10 minutes

COOKING TIME:
20 minutes

SERVES:
4

2   *pounds pork fillets*
5   *tablespoons butter*
½   *cup* demi-glace
½   *cup pomegranate juice*
2   *tablespoons minced Italian parsley*
    Salt
    Freshly ground pepper

   1. Trim the white filament from the pork fillets and cut the fillets into cross pieces 1-inch thick. (*Note:* Don't use the tips of the fillet in this dish. Instead, freeze them for later use in a stuffing.) Season each piece lightly with salt and pepper.
   2. Melt 3 tablespoons butter in a 12-inch skillet over medium heat. When the butter is hot, add the pork

pieces and sauté them for about 5 minutes on each side. Don't overdo this step or the pork will dry out. Remove the pieces and keep them warm on a plate covered loosely with foil.

3. Deglaze the skillet with the *demi-glace* and pomegranate juice, scraping all the browned particles into the sauce. Reduce the sauce over high heat for about 2 minutes, or until it coats a spoon.

4. Whisk the remaining butter into the sauce over low heat and season with salt and a grinding of pepper.

PRESENTATION

Spoon some sauce in the center of warmed dinner plates and put the pork fillets on top. Sprinkle the sauce with minced parsley.

MENU ACCOMPANIMENT

A small portion of Sweet Potato Soup (page 80) makes a fine starter. With the medallions, serve a Cauliflower Purée with Celery (page 331) and a Julienne of Winter Root Vegetables (page 345). Almond Puff Pastry Squares (page 391), Upside-Down Pecan Pie (page 403), or Souffléed Chocolate Cake (page 375) are perfect dessert choices.

Pork Medallions in Fig Coulis

A *COULIS* REFERS to anything that has been reduced to a thick purée. In this dish, the figs are softened in port and butter and then puréed. This *coulis*, then, is used to thicken the sauce.

PREPARATION TIME:
30 minutes, plus 45 minutes marinating time

COOKING TIME:
45 minutes

SERVES:
4

4   *dried figs*
2   *tablespoons Tawny port*
7   *tablespoons butter*
2   *pounds pork fillets*
2   *tablespoons red wine vinegar*
1   *tablespoon minced shallots*
1   *cup heavy cream*
    Salt
    Freshly ground pepper

1. With a sharp knife, cut the stems off the figs and discard them. Cut each fig into 4 to 6 pieces and put them in a small bowl. Cover with the port and let them marinate for 45 minutes.

2. Place the figs, port, a pinch of salt, 1 tablespoon butter, and 2 tablespoons water in a small skillet. Cover, and simmer gently for about 20 minutes, or until figs are tender and have absorbed most of liquid. Purée the figs in a food mill or food processor with 2 additional tablespoons butter. Set aside.

3. Trim the white filament from the pork fillets and cut them into cross pieces 1-inch thick. (*Note:* Don't use the tips of the fillet in this dish. Instead, freeze them for later use in a stuffing.) Season each piece lightly with salt and pepper.

4. Melt 3 tablespoons butter in a large 12-inch skillet over medium heat. When the butter is hot, add the pork pieces and sauté them for 5 minutes on each side. Don't overdo this step or the pork will dry out. Remove the pork medallions and keep them warm on a plate loosely covered with foil.

5. Deglaze the pan with the vinegar, shallots, and 1 tablespoon butter. Scrape any browned particles into the sauce.

6. Add the heavy cream and any juices from the cooked pork. Reduce the sauce over medium heat for 1 minute.

7. Turn off the heat and whisk in the reserved fig purée. Season with salt and pepper to taste. Pass the sauce through a sieve into a small saucepan and reheat it for 1 minute.

PRESENTATION

Spoon the sauce in the center of warmed dinner plates and put the medallions of pork on top of the sauce.

MENU ACCOMPANIMENT

This is a rich dish, so keep the opening course simple. Start with Wilted Greens Salad (page 96) or Cold Bay Scallops with Cumin Vinaigrette (page 147). Sautéed Spinach (page 352) or Sautéed Shredded Squash (page 362) are excellent garnishes for the pork. Follow the meal with a Lime Soufflé (page 419) or Pumpkin Pie (page 405).

Sautéed Pork Chops with Tomato and Olive Sauce

T HE RICH flavor of the pork and the sauce is offset by the slightly acid quality of the tomatoes and by the bite from the flavor of the olive.

PREPARATION TIME:
30 minutes

COOKING TIME:
40 minutes

SERVES:
4

2	*pounds tomatoes*
2	*cups heavy cream*
4	*1 ½-inch thick center cut pork chops*
2	*tablespoons butter*
2	*tablespoons olive oil*
½	*cup* glace de viande
¼	*cup imported, pitted black olives, diced*
2	*tablespoons minced chives or scallions*
	Salt
	Freshly ground pepper

1. Peel, seed, and chop the tomatoes into large dice. Cook the tomato pulp down until it is reduced by half (see Tomato Vinaigrette Sauce, page 366). Set aside.

2. In a separate skillet, reduce the heavy cream until only 1 cup remains. Set aside. (If reduced more than 1 hour in advance of making the dish, refrigerate.) ●

3. Season the pork chops with salt and pepper. Melt the butter and oil in a large 12-inch skillet over high heat. When hot, sear the chops on both sides until brown. Lower the heat and cook the chops through for about 20 minutes in all, turning them frequently so that they do not burn. Pork chops are cooked if, when the flesh is pricked, the internal juices run clear. Remove the chops and keep them warm on a plate covered loosely with foil.

4. Degrease the skillet in which you sautéed the chops. Over medium heat, add the reduced cream, tomato pulp, and *glace de viande* and whisk together until well blended. Simmer for 2 to 3 minutes.

5. Add the olives and any juices from the chops. Season with salt and pepper.

PRESENTATION

Place a chop on a warmed dinner plate and spoon some sauce over it. Sprinkle each serving with minced chives or scallions. Serve immediately.

MENU ACCOMPANIMENT

This robust dish calls for an equally hearty appetizer. Start with Black Bean Soup (page 78) or Smoked Fish Salad (page 106). As a garnish, serve any vegetable purée, such as Puréed Turnips with Garlic (page 365) or Floating Broccoli (page 329), along with another steamed vegetable of your choice. Pink Pear with Dark Chocolate (page 433) or Cranberry Soufflé (page 413) are good desserts.

Broiled Pork Chops with Orange Sauce

A LTHOUGH BROILING pork chops can yield disastrous results when poorly done, they can taste delicious if broiled correctly. You must eat them right away or they will dry out.

PREPARATION TIME:
40 minutes

COOKING TIME:
30 minutes

SERVES:
4

1	*lemon*
4	*oranges*
4	*1-inch thick center cut pork chops*
2	*tablespoons minced shallots*
6	*tablespoons butter*
½	*cup* glace de viande
½	*cup sour cream*
	Salt
	Freshly ground pepper

1. Cut in half and squeeze the juice from the lemon and oranges. Discard the seeds but stir the pulp and juice together. Marinate the pork chops in this juice for 30 minutes in the refrigerator.

2. Pour the juice into a 10-inch skillet and reduce by one-half. Strain out the pulp and set the juice aside. ●

3. Preheat the broiler for 10 minutes. Score the fat on the pork chops at 1-inch intervals. Dry the chops and season each side with salt and pepper.

4. Broil the chops 2 inches from the heat for about 8 minutes to a side, or until the juices run clear yellow when the flesh is pricked.

5. While the chops are broiling, finish the sauce. Sauté the shallots over medium heat in 3 tablespoons butter for 2 to 3 minutes, or until soft. Add the reduced fruit juices and *glace de viande* and reduce for 2 to 3 minutes.

6. Whisk in the sour cream and reduce this, whisking all the while until only 1 cup of sauce remains. (If you stop whisking the sauce after the sour cream has been added, it will curdle.)

7. Whisk in the additional 3 tablespoons butter. Remove from the heat. Season with salt and pepper.

PRESENTATION

Spoon the sauce in the center of the warmed dinner plates and put a pork chop in the center of the sauce. Serve immediately. Serve additional vegetable garnishes to one side of the plate.

MENU ACCOMPANIMENT

Avoid a cream soup or cream-based fish or shellfish dish as a starter for this. Instead, open with Broccoli and Apple Soup (page 72) or Smoked Fish Salad (page 106). Serve Caramelized Onions (page 342) or Puréed Turnips with Garlic (page 365) with the chops. End the meal with a chocolate or other non-fruit dessert.

Herbed Leg of Lamb with Anchovy Butter

T HIS DISH is an anchovy lover's delight. The salty anchovy flavor does not overpower the lamb but goes very well with it.

PREPARATION TIME:
1 hour and 15 minutes

COOKING TIME:
1 hour and 15 minutes

SERVES:
6 to 8

1 *6-pound whole leg of lamb with the rump or aitchbone removed*
½ *cup olive oil*
1 *cup loosely packed mixed fresh herbs (such as basil, sweet marjoram, thyme, and rosemary), roughly chopped*
1 *clove garlic, unpeeled*
¼ *pound softened butter*
1 *teaspoon anchovy paste*
4 *anchovy fillets, minced*
Pinch superfine sugar
Salt
Freshly ground pepper

1. Season the lamb with salt and pepper. Place it in a roasting pan with the olive oil and half of the mixed herbs. Marinate for 1 hour, turning frequently.

2. Parboil the garlic clove for 10 minutes in 1 cup water, then drain, cool, and peel. Combine the butter, anchovy paste, anchovies, the remaining mixed herbs, sugar,

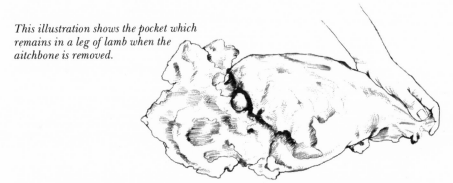

This illustration shows the pocket which remains in a leg of lamb when the aitchbone is removed.

¼ teaspoon salt and ⅛ teaspoon pepper in a bowl. Bury the peeled garlic clove in the center of the butter and refrigerate until serving time.●

3. Heat the oven to 475 degrees.

4. Remove the leg of lamb from the oil. Drain the herbs from the marinating oil and stuff them into the pockets of flesh left when the bone was removed. Tie the lamb securely. Put it on a rack in a roasting pan and roast for 1 to 1¼ hours, or until a meat thermometer registers 135 degrees.

5. Thirty minutes before the lamb comes out of the oven, take the butter from the refrigerator and remove the garlic clove. Remove the lamb from the oven and let it rest for 15 minutes.

PRESENTATION

Carve the lamb into thin slices. Place slices of lamb on warmed plates. Dab each slice with a bit of anchovy butter.

MENU ACCOMPANIMENT

The simplicity of this recipe allows for a rich appetizer, such as Eggplant Flan (page 335). Serve the lamb with Oven-Baked Sliced Potatoes (page 347) or a Sweet Potato Sauté (page 363), along with Shredded Carrots with Orange Juice (page 332) and Sautéed Spinach (page 352). Finish with a light dessert, such as Mango Ice (page 317) or Lime Ice (page 315).

Leg of Lamb with Mustard and Fresh Pineapple Sauce

T HE METHOD FOR roasting the leg of lamb in this dish is quite traditional. The sauce, however, is unusual. Pineapple is an American fruit that enrichs the simple pan sauce for the lamb. The mustard and pineapple complement each other, with the sharpness of the mustard highlighting the natural sweetness of the pineapple.

PREPARATION TIME:
20 minutes

COOKING TIME:
2 hours

SERVES:
6 to 10

1   *5- to 9-pound whole leg of lamb, with the rump or
        aitchbone removed*
2   *cups chopped fresh pineapple*
1   *tablespoon Dijon mustard*
4   *tablespoons butter*
    Salt
    Freshly ground pepper

1. Preheat the oven to 450 degrees.
2. Salt and pepper the leg of lamb on both sides.
3. Cut a piece of twine about 5 feet long and wrap the lamb in such a way that the meat is wrapped tightly together and no loose strips of meat are exposed. The easiest way to do this is to tie a slip knot around the shank of the leg and then run the twine around the loose end of the

meat several times until the end flap is secure. After each turn, tie the string to the original slip knot to secure the loop.

4. Purée the chopped pineapple in a food processor. When the pineapple is completely puréed, press the juices through a sieve into a small mixing bowl. The best way to do this is with a wooden spoon. Make sure you force as much of the juice and pulp into the bowl as possible. Set aside.●

5. Place the lamb on a roasting rack in a pan and roast at 450 degrees for 15 minutes. After 15 minutes turn down the oven temperature to 375 degrees and continue roasting for 75 to 90 minutes, or to taste. Use a meat thermometer to check internal temperature. Rare is 130 to 135 degrees; medium is 140 to 150 degrees, well-done is any temperature above that.

6. When the meat is properly cooked, remove it from the oven and place it on a slicing board to rest for at least 15 minutes.

7. Degrease the roasting pan. Add 1 cup water to the remaining pan drippings. Over medium heat, using a flat wooden spoon, scrape all the browned particles on the bottom of the pan into the water.

8. When the pan is completely clean, transfer the contents to a medium saucepan. Reduce the pan juices by half and add the puréed pineapple. Cook this mixture down by half again. The sauce should be quite thick and syrupy.

9. Add the mustard, turn the heat very low and whisk the butter into the sauce. Pour any juices that have seeped from the lamb back into the sauce. Remove from the heat and season with salt and pepper.

Carve the lamb into thin slices. Spoon portions of the sauce on each plate. Arrange the slices of lamb on the sauce. The effect you want is to completely cover the plate with the thin slices of the lamb arranged over the sauce.

MENU ACCOMPANIMENT

You can begin your meal with any fish or shellfish with a cream-based sauce such as Shad Roe with Sorrel (page 127). Most of our vegetable dishes would be a suitable accompaniment. Stay away, however, from Sautéed Grapes or Sweet Potato Sauté because of the sweetness of the pineapple in the sauce. For dessert, serve something made with chocolate.

Rack of Lamb with Anise and Sweet Garlic

COOKING THE cloves of garlic in their skins makes them tender and sweet. The quantity of garlic used seems staggering at first, but let us assure you, the flavor is quite mild. Have a butcher french the racks of lamb and be sure the chine bone is sawed through so you can carve the chops later on.

PREPARATION TIME:
25 minutes

COOKING TIME:
55 minutes

SERVES:
4

2   *racks of lamb, about 8 chops each*
     Coarse salt
2¼   *teaspoons anise seed*
2   *heads garlic, cloves separated but unpeeled*
½   *tablespoon sugar*
2   *tablespoons red wine vinegar*
     Freshly ground pepper

1. Preheat the oven to 425 degrees.

2. Season the meat with coarse salt, pepper, and 1 teaspoon of anise per rack of lamb. Place the racks of lamb without a roasting rack in one roasting pan if you have a large one, or 2 smaller ones. Strew garlic around the lamb and roast for 45 minutes for rarish lamb or 55 minutes for medium.

3. Remove the meat from the oven and place it on a carving board to rest.

4. With a slotted spoon, remove the garlic cloves from the roasting pan, and pop the flesh out of the skins into a 7-inch skillet. Add ¼ teaspoon anise seed to the same skillet, along with the sugar and vinegar.

5. Bring all of this to a boil and reduce rapidly until the sugar and liquid turn viscous and syrupy and coat the garlic. Season with salt and pepper.

Slice the racks into chops. Serve 3 to 4 lamb chops per person on warmed dinner plates.Spoon some garlic and sauce around the chops and serve.

MENU ACCOMPANIMENT

Start with Black Bean Soup (page 78), Sweet Potato Soup (page 80), or any of our vegetable salads. Serve the lamb with Cauliflower Purée with Celery (page 331) along with Shredded Carrots with Orange Juice (page 332) for contrast in texture and color. Finish with a soufflé or Lemon Almond Cake (page 380).

Boned Saddle of Lamb Stuffed with Mushrooms

THIS IS an extravagant dish, but well worth it for that special, three-star dinner.

PREPARATION TIME:
1 hour

COOKING TIME:
1 hour

SERVES:
4

7 tablespoons butter
2 tablespoons minced shallots
½ pound finely diced mushrooms
1 tablespoon Madeira
1 whole saddle of lamb, boned
½ cup demi-glace
3 tablespoons port
   Salt
   Freshly ground pepper

1. Melt 3 tablespoons butter in a small skillet over medium heat. When the butter is hot, add the shallots and sauté for 1 minute over medium heat. Add the mushrooms and continue to sauté, stirring occasionally, for 4 to 5 minutes, or until the moisture from the mushrooms has evaporated and the mushrooms begin to stick to the pan.

2. Add the Madeira. Raise the heat and cook for 1 minute more. Season with ⅛ teaspoon each of salt and pepper. Set aside.

3. Remove all traces of fat, filament, and fell from the saddle of lamb. In doing so, you will end up with 2 skinny flap-like pieces of meat, perhaps ¼ inch thick. Don't use these in the recipe, use them instead as a quick sauté or grind them for a meat loaf. You will use the two large pieces of meat, from which the thin, 1-inch in diameter fillets may become detached. If they do, don't worry. Season the meat lightly with salt and pepper.

4. Place one large piece of lamb on a board and place the fillet on top, if it has detached itself from the lamb. Spread the mushroom mixture all along these pieces. Top it with the other fillet and finally with the larger piece of lamb. You have thus created a lamb sandwich, with the mushroom filling in between.◗

5. Preheat the oven to 400 degrees.

6. Cut four 10-inch lengths of string and tie each one around the meat, at about 1-inch intervals, to secure the filling. Place the meat on a roasting rack in a roasting pan and dot the top with 2 tablespoons butter. Season with salt and pepper. Roast for 40 minutes for rare lamb or 50 minutes for medium.

7. Remove the roast from the oven and place it on a cutting board to let it rest.

8. Discard all the grease, if any, on the bottom of the roasting pan. Add ¼ cup water and the *demi-glace* to the pan. Over medium heat, with a wooden spoon, scrape all the browned particles into the sauce.

9. Transfer the sauce to a 9-inch skillet. Over medium heat, reduce the sauce until only ¾ cup remains. Add the port and reduce until only ¾ cup remains again.

10. Whisk in the remaining 2 tablespoons butter. Remove the sauce from the heat immediately. Season with salt and pepper.

PRESENTATION

Remove the string from the lamb, being careful that the pieces don't separate — you have 4 pieces of meat and filling that are barely held together. Cut the roast into 4 equal pieces. Put a piece of roast in the center of warmed dinner plates. Spoon some sauce on either side of the meat and serve.

MENU ACCOMPANIMENT

For an elegant meal, start with our unusual Tomato and Basil Ice (page 318) if in season, otherwise, Shrimp, Duck, and Spinach in Puff Pastry (page 154). Along with this dish serve only one vegetable garnish, such as Leek Purée (page 341) or Pea Purée (page 348). Follow this with a Pear and Goat Cheese Salad (page 104) and David's Cake (page 377) for dessert.

Boneless Lamb Steak with Yogurt and Mint

W E HAVE chosen to do this recipe with lamb steaks, but the same dish can be made with pan-fried loin or rib chops or with a roasted leg or rack of lamb. The point is that the sauce goes well with any cut of lamb. The secret is a sauce thickened with yogurt which has been drained of its excess water.

PREPARATION TIME:
24 to 48 hours to thicken yogurt

COOKING TIME:
10 minutes

SERVES:
4

1   *cup plain yogurt*
2   *tablespoons butter*
2   *pounds lamb steaks*
¼   *cup* demi-glace
½   *cup packed fresh mint leaves, chopped*
    Salt
    Freshly ground pepper

1. Place the yogurt in cheesecloth, then in a sieve placed over a bowl. Cover and refrigerate for 24 to 48 hours. Discard the water that has seeped to the bottom of the bowl and reserve the thickened yogurt.●

2. Melt the butter in a 12-inch skillet. When the butter turns golden, sauté the lamb over high heat for 3 to 5 minutes on a side, depending on the thickness of the lamb and how rare you want it. Season with salt and pepper. Remove the meat to a plate covered with foil to keep it warm.

3. Discard the fat from the pan. Deglaze the pan with ½ cup water and add the *demi-glace*. Whisk the browned particles into the sauce and simmer for 1 minute.

4. Turn the heat to very low and whisking constantly, stir in the yogurt.

5. Turn the heat off and add the mint and any juice the lamb has given off. Season with salt and pepper.

PRESENTATION

Slice the lamb across the grain into ¼-inch thick slices. Spoon some sauce in the center of warmed dinner plates and place the slices of lamb on top.

MENU ACCOMPANIMENT

The summer flavor of the fresh mint and the slightly exotic combination of yogurt and lamb call for an interesting starter. Cold Bay Scallops with Cumin Vinaigrette (page 147) would be appropriate. Serve the lamb as a main course along with a Pea Purée (page 348) and Sautéed Shredded Squash (page 362). Any fruit tart or pie could follow for dessert.

Medallions of Lamb with Artichoke Sauce

THE SAUCE of reduced cream, thickened with puréed fresh artichoke hearts, is so delicate that it must be served with *baby* spring lamb. Anything more pungent would destroy the flavors in the sauce. Steaming the medallions is an excellent way to keep the lamb tender.

PREPARATION TIME:
45 minutes

COOKING TIME:
1 hour and 30 minutes

SERVES:
4

1   *large or 2 small artichokes*
1   *tablespoon sour cream*
1   *tablespoon fresh lemon juice*
1½ *pounds boned loin and fillet of baby spring lamb*
1   *cup heavy cream*
1   *tomato, peeled, seeded, and chopped*
2   *tablespoons fresh chives*
    Salt
    Freshly ground white pepper

1.   Place the artichokes in a 2-quart saucepan. Cover with water and bring to a boil. Cook for 35 to 45 minutes depending on the size of the artichokes. The center of the artichokes, when pierced with a knife, should be very tender. Remove them from the water and turn them

upside down to drain off the water. Let them cool for 30 minutes.

2. When they are cool enough to handle, remove the leaves of the artichokes. With a spoon, scrape off the tender edible part of each leaf into a bowl. When you get to the center, discard the hairy choke and add the heart to the bowl (see illustration, page 322).

3. In a food processor, blend the artichoke scrapings, heart, sour cream, and lemon juice. Reserve.

4. Trim all fat, and shear the skin off the loin of lamb. Cut across the grain into 1-inch thick medallion pieces. (You should have about 16 pieces of entirely fat free lamb.) Set aside.

5. Place a vegetable steamer in a 4-quart saucepan with 2 inches of water on the bottom. Bring the water to a boil and place the lamb in the steamer. Steam, covered, for 3 to 4 minutes or until the inside of the lamb is a nice pink color.

6. In a saucepan, over medium heat, reduce the heavy cream to ¾ cup. Whisk in the artichoke purée, and the tomato. Season with ½ teaspoon salt and ¼ teaspoon pepper.

7. Reduce the sauce a bit more until you achieve the desired thickness. Add the chives and serve immediately.

PRESENTATION

Place the medallions of lamb on individually warmed dinner plates and pass the sauce separately.

MENU ACCOMPANIMENT

Because this is a delicately flavored sauce, serve something as delicate to start, perhaps Sautéed Asparagus (page 324) and Butternut Squash Purée (page 360). Follow with a salad, cheese, and Melon with Rum and Honey Sauce (page 428) for dessert.

Medallions of Lamb with Bordelaise and Port Sauce

T HE MELTINGLY tender cut of lamb used in this recipe deserves the rich, elegant sauce we have devised.

PREPARATION TIME:
15 minutes

COOKING TIME:
1 hour and 30 minutes

SERVES:
4

1½ *pounds boned loin and fillet of baby spring lamb*
    Lamb bones
¾   *cup* bordelaise
¼   *cup* demi-glace
¾   *cup port*
5   *tablespoons butter*
2   *tablespoons minced shallots*
    Salt
    Freshly ground pepper

1. Preheat the oven to 400 degrees.

2. Trim all fat and shear skin from the lamb. Cut across the grain into 1-inch thick slices (you should have about 16 medallions 2 inches in diameter.)

3. Roast the lamb bones in a baking pan for 45 minutes. With tongs, remove the bones from the fat and set aside.

4. When they are cool enough to handle, pull the bones apart and place them in a 4-quart saucepan. Combine the bones with the *bordelaise*, *demi-glace*, ½ cup port, and 1 cup water. Simmer gently for 30 minutes.

5. Remove the bones from the sauce and discard them. Degrease the sauce and transfer it to a bowl.

6. In a 10-inch skillet, melt 3 tablespoons butter. When the butter is golden, sauté the lamb medallions, 8 at a time, over fairly high heat for about 2 minutes on each side. Remove the lamb medallions from the pan and place them on a platter loosely covered with foil to keep them warm.

7. Remove all but one tablespoon of grease from the skillet. Add the shallots to the skillet and sauté them over medium heat for about 1 minute.

8. Add the reduced sauce and ¼ cup more of port to the skillet. Over high heat, rapidly reduce these juices until only about 1 cup remains. Add any juice the lamb has given off.

9. Whisk in 2 tablespoons butter, and season with salt and pepper.

PRESENTATION

Put the lamb on heated dinner plates. Spoon some sauce over the lamb and pass the rest separately.

MENU ACCOMPANIMENT

This would go well with any vegetable pureé, the Eggplant Flan (page 335), or Squash Cakes (page 358). Begin the meal with the Seven-Vegetable Broth (page 76) and end with Peach Ice Cream (page 422) or Green Tea Ice Cream (page 426).

Sautéed Rib Lamb Chops with Rosemary and Thyme

GREAT FRENCH restaurants prepare their lamb chops as simply as possible. The most important technique is to sear the outside of the chops and then reduce the heat and cook them until done. There is no sauce to speak of, just pan juices perked up with a touch of vinegar.

PREPARATION TIME:
10 minutes

COOKING TIME:
20 minutes

SERVES:
4

12 rib lamb chops, frenched
 2 teaspoons dried rosemary
 2 teaspoons dried thyme
 6 tablespoons butter
 1 tablespoon olive oil
 4 tablespoons red wine vinegar
    Salt
    Freshly ground pepper

   1. Trim the lamb chops of any extra fat. Season both sides of each chop with salt and pepper.
   2. Sprinkle both sides of the chops with dried herbs and press the seasonings into the chops.

3. Heat the butter and olive oil in two 12-inch skillets over high heat. Sear the chops for approximately 1 minute on each side.

4. Lower the heat and cook, uncovered, for 5 to 10 minutes, depending on how well you like your chops done. Turn the chops occasionally while they cook.

5. Remove the chops from the skillets and set them aside in a warm place.

6. Pour most of the fat from the skillets. Add 2 tablespoons water to each skillet and deglaze over medium heat.

7. Transfer liquid from one skillet to the other. Add the vinegar to that skillet and, over medium heat, reduce the liquid by half. Season with salt and pepper to taste.

PRESENTATION

Place chops vertically down the center of each plate. Moisten each chop with some of the pan juices. Place any vegetable garnish on either side of the lamb chops.

MENU ACCOMPANIMENT

Precede this dish with a cream soup or a fish dish with a cream-based sauce, such as Poached Sole with Tomato and Saffron (page 133). To complement this dish, you could serve wild rice or two vegetable purées. To end the meal, any chocolate dessert would be lovely.

Veal in Cider

T HE DELICATE flavor of the cucumbers, snow peas, and
cider does not overpower the flavor of the veal. The
pale colors of the two greens add another dimension
to this dish.

PREPARATION TIME:
30 minutes

COOKING TIME:
2 hours

SERVES:
4

24 *shallots in skins*
¼ *pound snow peas*
3 *8-inch cucumbers*
2 *pounds boned veal shoulder, left in large pieces*
2 *tablespoons butter*
2 *tablespoons peanut or vegetable oil*
1 *cup imported hard cider, plus 2 tablespoons*
   Bouquet garni *made up of 2 sprigs parsley, ½ teaspoon
      thyme, and 4 black peppercorns tied in cheesecloth*
¼ *cup heavy cream*
   Salt
   Freshly ground pepper

1. Peel shallots and leave them whole. (*Note:* Once a
shallot is peeled it might yield more than 1 clove, so you'll
end up with many more than 24 pieces of shallot).

2. Wash, trim, and remove the strings from the snow peas. Set aside.

3. Peel the cucumbers and slice them in two, lengthwise. Spoon out the seeds and slice them in two, lengthwise again, then cut them into ¾-inch cross pieces.

4. Cut the veal into approximately equal 2- by 2-inch pieces. They should be as equal as possible so that they cook at an even rate.

5. Melt the butter and oil in a sauteuse approximately 3 inches high and 9 inches in diameter. When the butter is very hot, begin searing the meat on all sides. Do this over high heat so that the meat takes on a brown crispy exterior. This is a messy process as the fat will splatter, but if you don't sear the meat at a high heat, it will stew and turn gray. Sear all the meat in this way. About half way through the searing process, you'll have to add another tablespoon of oil. Do not turn the heat up so high that the fat smokes and takes on a burnt taste. As the meat browns, remove it to a bowl.

6. When all the meat is seared, lower the heat and add the shallots stirring them for a few seconds.

7. Deglaze the pan by slowly adding the cider. With a flat wooden spoon or spatula, scrape all the browned particles into the cider. Season with 1 teaspoon salt.

8. Add the veal and *bouquet garni* to the pan. Cover the pan with a buttered round of brown paper, which you can cut from an ordinary paper bag, and a heavy lid. The paper helps keep the meat moist. Simmer on gentle heat for 1¼ to 1½ hours, or until the veal is very tender. (If done in advance reheat gently up to this point before proceeding to the next step.)●

9. Remove the cover and brown paper. Lay the cucumbers and snow peas on top of meat, replace the cover and steam them for 4 minutes, or until just cooked but still crunchy. Don't overdo this step or you'll end up with waterlogged cucumbers.

10. With a slotted spoon, remove the meat and vegetables to a wide sieve placed over a deep bowl to catch the juices. Discard the *bouquet garni*. Degrease the remaining liquid.

11. Add 2 tablespoons cider and the heavy cream and juices which have dripped into the bowl to the pan and reduce until only ¾ cup remains. Season with ½ teaspoon salt and ¼ teaspoon pepper. (The sauce may seem salty at this point, but this will be rectified when you add the meat and vegetables.)

PRESENTATION

Transfer the meat and vegetables to a shallow serving bowl. Over this bowl, strain the sauce through a sieve.

MENU ACCOMPANIMENT

This is light and simple to do, especially in advance, and therefore you could serve an elaborate first course such as Mussels in Puff Pastry (page 140). Souffléed Acorn Squash (page 356) would also do well as a first course, as would any shellfish or fish dish without cream in the sauce. If you keep the first course light, then indulge in a rich dessert, such as Chocolate Almond Cake (page 370) or Fine Orange Cake (page 382). If you have indulged in the puff pastry as an appetizer then stick to something light for dessert, such as Grapefruit Sherbet (page 314).

Veal Loin Laced with Peppercorns

THE VEAL is highlighted here and there by one of four kinds of peppercorns and bits of parsley. The sauce is made by deglazing the pan with sherry and vinegar and finished by whisking in butter.

PREPARATION TIME:
30 minutes

COOKING TIME:
2 hours

SERVES:
4

2   *pounds boned loin of veal*
½   *teaspoon white peppercorns*
4   *teaspoons minced parsley*
½   *teaspoon black peppercorns*
½   *teaspoon red peppercorns*
½   *teaspoon green peppercorns*
1¼   *inch thick sheet barding fat, the length and width of the veal*
¼   *cup sherry vinegar*
¼   *cup sherry*
4   *tablespoons cold butter*
     Salt
     Freshly ground pepper

1. With a larding needle or a thin-pointed knife blade make 4 incisions the length of the loin. Place all the white peppercorns and 1 teaspoon of parsley in the hollow of the needle and work it into one of the incisions. Repeat with each type of peppercorn and the same amount of parsley for each incision.

2. Preheat the oven to 350 degrees.

3. Wrap the barding fat around the loin and tie it in place with cord or string (see illustration, page 222).

4. Place the loin on a rack in a baking pan and roast for 1½ to 1¾ hours, or until the thermometer registers an internal temperature of 165 degrees.

5. Remove the meat from the roasting pan and place it on a carving board. Let the meat rest while you finish the sauce.

6. Pour out all the grease from the pan. Add ⅔ cup water to the pan. Over medium heat, scrape all the browned particles into the water with a wooden spoon or flat wooden spatula.

7. Transfer the juices to a 7-inch skillet and rapidly reduce the liquids by one-half. Add the vinegar and sherry and reduce by half again, or until you have only ½ cup liquid left.

8. Turn off the heat and whisk in the cold butter tablespoon by tablespoon. Season with salt and freshly ground pepper.

PRESENTATION

Carve the meat into ¼-inch slices. Pour the sauce on each of 4 warmed dinner plates. Place 4 pieces of veal on each plate in a 4 leaf clover arrangement. Serve additional vegetable garnishes around the sauce.

MENU ACCOMPANIMENT

A rich appetizer — Sweetbreads with Cassis and Whole Shallots (page 304) or Asparagus Spears and Hollandaise Sauce in Puff Pastry (page 325) — can precede this simple roast. Sautéed Pears with Raspberry Sauce (page 431) or Apple Purée (page 427) would be excellent for dessert.

Barding Veal

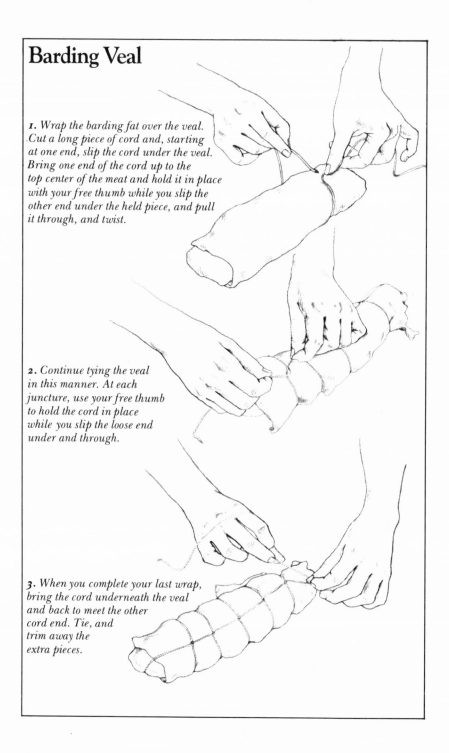

1. *Wrap the barding fat over the veal.*
Cut a long piece of cord and, starting
at one end, slip the cord under the veal.
Bring one end of the cord up to the
top center of the meat and hold it in place
with your free thumb while you slip the
other end under the held piece, and pull
it through, and twist.

2. *Continue tying the veal*
in this manner. At each
juncture, use your free thumb
to hold the cord in place
while you slip the loose end
under and through.

3. *When you complete your last wrap,*
bring the cord underneath the veal
and back to meet the other
cord end. Tie, and
trim away the
extra pieces.

Veal Loin with Capers

T HE MEAT used here is cut from a boned loin of veal. You could use the cross pieces from the fillet only, but this would be prohibitively expensive.

PREPARATION TIME:
15 minutes

COOKING TIME:
5 minutes

SERVES:
4

1½ *pounds (net) boneless loin of veal, trimmed of all fat*
8 *tablespoons butter*
1 *tablespoon capers, drained and minced*
3 *tablespoons tarragon vinegar*
  Salt
  Freshly ground pepper

1. Slice the veal into ½-inch cross slices. Pat them dry with paper towels. Season the veal slices lightly with salt and pepper.
2. Melt 3 tablespoons butter in a 12-inch skillet. When sizzling hot, add half the veal and sauté over medium to high heat for 1 to 1½ minutes per side. Don't overcook or the veal will be tough. Remove the veal to a plate and cover loosely with foil to keep it warm. Sauté the remainder of the veal in the same way.

3. Remove the skillet from the heat and discard any remaining fat. Deglaze the pan with the capers and vinegar, incorporating all of the browned drippings into the vinegar.

4. The minute this is done, turn the heat to very low. Add to the skillet any juices accumulated around the veal.

5. Whisk in the remaining butter, 1 tablespoon at a time. Remove from the heat. Season with salt and pepper.

PRESENTATION

Place the veal on warmed dinner plates and spoon a little sauce over each piece.

MENU ACCOMPANIMENT

You could start with Cold Sweetbreads with Oranges (page 307), or Bay Scallops with Celery Julienne (page 145). Serve Leak Purée (page 341) and Shredded Carrots with Orange Juice (page 332) as vegetable garnishes and Chocolate Sweetness (page 373) for dessert.

Veal and Lemon Comfit

I N THIS recipe we do not really use a sweetmeat. Instead lemon slices are simmered in honey and water until soft, then their juices are reduced until a sweet lemony essence remains which is worked into the sauce.

PREPARATION TIME:
25 minutes

COOKING TIME:
10 minutes

SERVES:
4

⅓ *cup honey*
2 *lemons sliced into ¼-inch rounds*
7 *tablespoons butter*
1½ *pounds veal scallopine, cut from the leg or rump, pounded to*
     ¼-inch thickness
2 *tablespoons minced shallots*
¼ *teaspoon minced garlic*
½ *cup* glace de viande
     Salt
     Freshly ground pepper

1. Combine the honey and ½ cup water in a 2-quart saucepan. Bring to a boil.

2. Add the lemon slices and simmer them for 10 minutes. Remove them to a plate. They will be very soft and will have lost some of their pulp.

3. Reduce the liquid that remains to ⅓ cup. Set aside.●

4. Melt 4 tablespoons butter in a 12-inch skillet. When the butter is about to turn brown, sauté one-half of the veal for about 1½ minutes per side. Sauté the rest of the veal the same way, adding more butter to the skillet if you need it. Remove the veal to a plate and cover loosely with foil to keep it warm.

5. If there is liquid in the skillet, reduce it until it begins to sizzle and the pan is nearly dry. Add the shallots and garlic and sauté for 15 seconds over medium high heat.

6. Add the reserved honey-lemon syrup and stir for 15 seconds. Add the *glace de viande* and reduce the sauce for a couple of minutes, until the sauce begins to look syrupy. Add the lemon slices and any juices the veal has given off. Season the sauce with ½ teaspoon salt and ¼ teaspoon pepper.

7. Turn off the heat and whisk in the remaining butter, tablespoon by tablespoon. Taste, and adjust the seasoning.

PRESENTATION

Divide the meat among 4 warmed dinner plates. Spoon a portion of the sauce and lemon slices on each piece and serve immediately.

MENU ACCOMPANIMENT

Because of the strong fruity and sweet flavor of this dish, stay away from other sweet garnishes, such as Sautéed Grapes (page 339). Serve baked wild rice on the side. Precede this with Wilted Greens Salad (page 96) or a plate of vegetables. A first course of fish might be Salmon with Fresh Vegetables (page 112). Avoid citrus fruit flavor in your dessert.

Herbed Veal Chops with Bacon and Shallots

T HE VEAL, bacon, shallots, and herbs all contribute their flavors and aromas to each other in the parchment paper packages.

PREPARATION TIME:
20 minutes

COOKING TIME:
15 minutes

SERVES:
4

4 *¾-inch thick loin veal chops*
3 *tablespoons butter*
2 *ounces sliced bacon, cut into 1-inch pieces*
3 *tablespoons minced shallots*
   Juice of ½ lime
1 *cup loosely packed fresh herbs (a combination of tarragon, mint, basil, and parsley or a combination of your own choosing) chopped after they are measured*
   Salt
   Freshly ground pepper

1. Lightly salt and pepper the veal chops.
2. Melt the butter in a 12- to 14-inch skillet. When sizzling, sauté the chops over high heat for 2 minutes on each side. Turn off the heat, remove the chops from the pan to a plate, and return the skillet to the heat.
3. Add the bacon to the skillet and sauté over medium heat for 1 minute, using a flat wooden spatula to

scrape up all the browned particles from the bottom of the pan.

4. Add the minced shallots and continue cooking for 2 minutes longer.

5. Add in the lime juice and stir all the ingredients together with the spatula. Add to the skillet juices from the reserved veal. Add the chopped herbs and immediately turn off heat. Continue to stir the herbs into the bacon and shallots mixture, until well blended.

6. Preheat the oven to 400 degrees.

7. Place each chop in the center of a standard piece of parchment paper (10 by 15 inches). Spoon one-fourth of the bacon and herb mixture on top of each chop and spread it evenly over the entire surface. Bring the long sides of the paper up so that they meet in the middle. Fold the joined edges over twice. Fold the sides onto themselves then tuck them under the veal package.

8. Place the packages on a baking sheet and bake for 15 minutes.

PRESENTATION

Either place packages on individual plates and let each diner open his own or cut each package open with a knife and place each chop on the center of a warmed dinner plate. Spoon any juices from the packages and the baking sheet over the meat.

MENU ACCOMPANIMENT

Start with a cream soup, Wilted Greens Salad (page 96), Steamed Vegetable Salad (page 92), or Piquant Chicken Liver Salad (page 100). If you want a fish course, start with Sole with Chives (page 131) or Salmon Fillets with Spices and Currants (page 116). Serve Sautéed Spinach (page 352) or Sautéed Asparagus (page 324) as a garnish. Finish with Apple Purée (page 427) or Pumpkin Pie (page 405).

Veal Packets Stuffed with Fresh Vegetable Julienne

I TALIAN AND French dishes include many versions of veal scallopine stuffed and rolled into little packets, then sautéed, and served with a light sauce. In our version, the stuffing is a julienne of freshly sautéed vegetables and the sauce is a reduction of cream with minced watercress leaves. Although rich, the dish is surprisingly light.

PREPARATION TIME:

40 minutes

COOKING TIME:

15 minutes

SERVES:

4

8   *tablespoons butter*
3   *carrots, cut into ⅛- by 2-inch julienne pieces*
3   *leeks, white part only, cut into ⅛- by 2-inch julienne*
        pieces
2   *ounces mushrooms, thinly sliced*
2   *bunches watercress, leaves only*
1   *cup heavy cream*
8   *3-ounce pieces veal scallopine*
     Salt
     Freshly ground pepper

1. In a 12-inch skillet, melt 4 tablespoons butter. Just before it turns brown, add the carrots, leeks, and mushrooms, and sauté over high heat for 1 minute or so.
2. Turn down the heat, cover the skillet, and cook

the vegetables gently for 5 minutes, or until they soften but do not turn brown.

3. Remove the cover and add ½ cup of the watercress leaves and sauté for another 30 seconds. Season with ¼ teaspoon salt and ¼ teaspoon pepper. Remove ½ cup vegetables to one dish and the remaining vegetables to another. Set aside.

4. Bring 1 quart water to a boil. Plunge the remaining watercress leaves into the water and parboil for 10 seconds. Drain, then refresh under cold running water. Using your hands, squeeze out the excess moisture. Mince and reserve the leaves.

5. In a 9-inch skillet, reduce the heavy cream until only ¾ cup remains. Transfer the reduced cream to a bowl.

6. Lightly salt and pepper the veal scallopine. Place a small portion of vegetables in each piece (using up all but the ½ cup reserved for garnish.) Roll up the veal pieces and fasten each with a toothpick.●

7. Just before sautéing, place the reserved ½ cup vegetables in a small covered saucepan, on a burner, but do not turn on the heat. Also get ready on a burner, and with the heat off, the 9-inch skillet with a sieve placed over it.

8. Melt the remaining butter in the 12-inch skillet. Just before the butter browns, add the veal packets and sauté them for about 2 minutes, turning frequently so each side takes on color.

9. Lower the heat, cover the skillet and cook the packets gently for about 5 minutes, or until they are cooked through. Remove the packets and keep them warm on a foil-covered plate.

10. Remove the fat from the skillet and return it to the heat. Deglaze the skillet with ¼ cup water, scraping up all the browned particles.

11. Add the reduced cream and bring it to a boil. Season with ½ teaspoon salt and ¼ teaspoon pepper. Remove from the heat.

12. Warm the reserved ½ cup of vegetables gently over low heat.

13. Strain the cream sauce through the sieve and into the skillet you have ready on the burner. Bring the sauce to a boil and whisk in the reserved watercress leaves. Add any accumulated veal juices. Remove from the heat. Taste, and adjust the seasonings.

PRESENTATION

Place 2 packets per person on warmed dinner plates. Spoon the sauce around the packets and strew the vegetable garnish attractively on the meat and sauce.

MENU ACCOMPANIMENT

Start with either Piquant Chicken Liver Salad (page 100) or Smoked Fish Salad (page 106). Don't accompany this course with other vegetables. You may serve a dish of Floating Broccoli (page 329) afterwards. Veal Packets can be followed by any dessert.

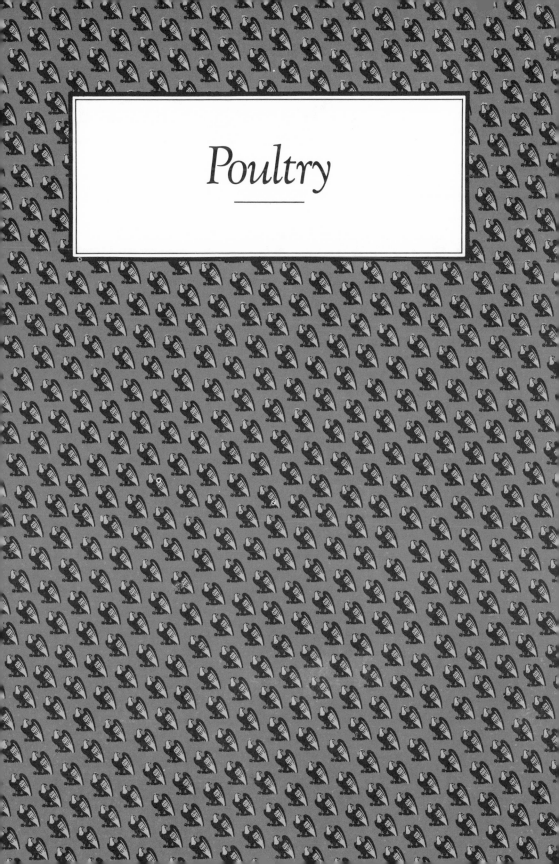

Poultry

Capon Stuffed with Wild Rice

C APON, although juicier than chicken, needs some help to bring out its flavor. In this case, the truffles and the vinegar are used to perfume the flesh.

PREPARATION TIME:
2 hours

COOKING TIME:
1 hour and 45 minutes

SERVES:
8

1   *recipe Baked Wild Rice with Onions, Carrots, and*
     Mushrooms (page 344), using the mushroom stems
     instead of whole mushrooms
6   *whole large mushroom caps*
7   *tablespoons butter*
1   *6-pound capon*
1   *fresh or canned truffle (if in the can, reserve the juice)*
2   *tablespoons champagne or white wine vinegar*
2   *tablespoons sliced scallions*
     Parsley or watercress for garnish
     Salt
     Freshly ground pepper

   1. Bake the wild rice, substituting the stems for the mushroom caps. If there is any liquid left once the rice is cooked, drain it off and reserve it for later. Set the rice aside.
   2. Sauté the whole mushroom caps in 2 tablespoons butter until cooked but still crunchy. Set aside.

3. Bone the capon, starting at the backbone. Just bone out the rib cage, leaving in the drumstick and the thigh bone. Leave in the wings from the elbows up. Wash and pat dry; salt and pepper the insides.

Follow the procedure for Boning a Duck on page 278, steps 2 through 6. Once the breast meat has been disconnected from the breastbone, pull the entire rib cage up toward the neck bone area and sever the carcass from the flesh.

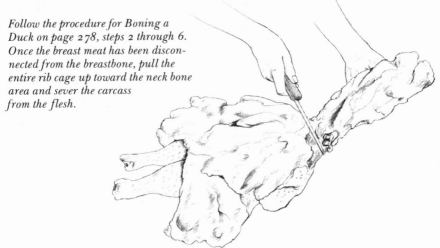

4. Slice the truffle into paper thin slices and wedge them, here and there, around the legs and breast, under the skin and on top of the flesh.

5. Preheat the oven to 425 degrees.

Remove any remaining small bones from the neck area at this point. After stuffing, sew the flaps of the capon breast together.

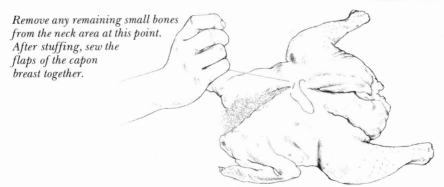

6. Place the wild rice in the center of the capon, put a row of sautéed mushroom caps down the center of this, and bring the loose flaps over, overlapping slightly. Sew the flaps together. Essentially, the rice is now taking the place of the rib cage and gives body to the capon.

7. Place the capon on a rack, in a 9- by 13-inch baking or roasting pan. (If you are preparing this in advance refrigerate at this point and remove it a half hour before roasting.)●

8. Melt 3 tablespoons butter and mix the melted butter with the reserved truffle juice and wild rice liquid if there is any. Season with ½ teaspoon salt and ¼ teaspoon pepper.

9. Baste the capon with these juices and bake, on the lowest shelf of the oven, for 1½ hours, or until the juices of the bird, when pricked, run clear yellow.

10. Remove the capon from the pan to a platter and let it rest as you make the sauce.

11. Strain out the juices from the roasting pan into a saucepan and degrease them if there is a lot of fat. Add the vinegar and reduce this over medium heat for 1 minute, or until the vinegar flavor has mellowed a bit.

12. Whisk in 2 tablespoons butter. Add the scallions and remove the sauce from the heat. Taste, and adjust the seasoning.

PRESENTATION

Remove the string from the capon and bring the capon to the table on a platter garnished with parsley or watercress. At the table, serve the capon by first cutting off the drumstick and wing and then slicing the breast, and scooping out and serving the rice with it. Moisten the capon with some pan juices.

MENU ACCOMPANIMENT

Serve with any of the vegetable purées; Butternut Squash would be the most colorful (page 360). Garnish this with Sautéed Grapes (page 339) and Shredded Carrots with Orange Juice (page 332). Black Bean Soup (page 78) would be a good starter on a winter day. Any dessert would go well.

Chicken with Garlic Sauce

T HE PERFECT roast chicken is perhaps one of the greatest of all dishes. Many people from all over the world eat chicken every day but few take the time and care to roast a chicken properly. Once you have mastered this recipe you will have discovered a taste treat with few rivals.

PREPARATION TIME:
30 minutes

COOKING TIME:
60 to 75 minutes

SERVES:
4

1	*3- to 4-pound chicken*
7	*tablespoons butter*
3	*teaspoons fresh thyme, chopped, or ¾ teaspoon dried*
3	*teaspoons fresh sage, chopped, or ¾ teaspoon dried*
15	*cloves garlic*
½	*cup* glace de volaille *or* glace de viande
¼	*cup water*
	Salt
	Freshly ground pepper

1. Preheat the oven to 450 degrees.

2. Wash the chicken inside and out and pat dry with paper towels. Season all over with salt and pepper.

3. Truss the chicken, following the illustrations (page 238). Place the chicken in a roasting pan just slightly larger than the bird.

4. Melt 3 tablespoons butter in a small saucepan, add 2 teaspoons fresh thyme and 2 teaspoons fresh sage (or

Trussing a Chicken

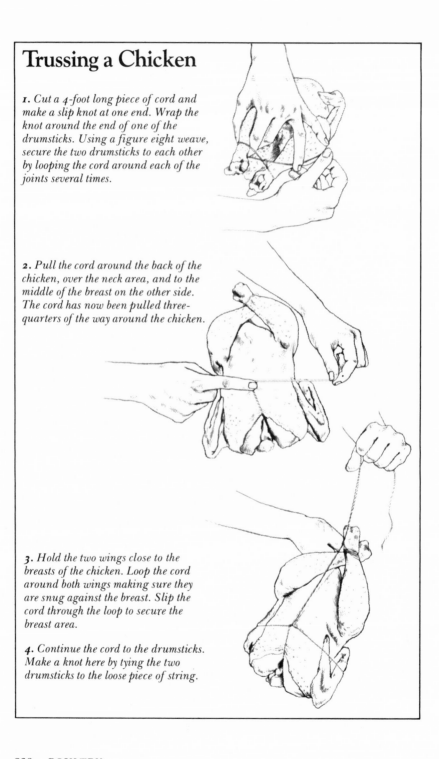

1. Cut a 4-foot long piece of cord and make a slip knot at one end. Wrap the knot around the end of one of the drumsticks. Using a figure eight weave, secure the two drumsticks to each other by looping the cord around each of the joints several times.

2. Pull the cord around the back of the chicken, over the neck area, and to the middle of the breast on the other side. The cord has now been pulled three-quarters of the way around the chicken.

3. Hold the two wings close to the breasts of the chicken. Loop the cord around both wings making sure they are snug against the breast. Slip the cord through the loop to secure the breast area.

4. Continue the cord to the drumsticks. Make a knot here by tying the two drumsticks to the loose piece of string.

¾ teaspoon of each, dried) and brush the butter mixture over the entire surface of the chicken.

5. Roast the chicken on the bottom shelf of the hot oven. Baste every 20 minutes. The chicken is cooked if the juices run clear, not bloody, when the bird is pricked in the meatiest part of the thigh. This should take 60 to 75 minutes depending on the size of the bird.

6. While the chicken is roasting, place the peeled garlic in a small saucepan of boiling water. Cook, covered, for 20 minutes. Remove, drain, and mash the garlic through a sieve. Set aside. Discard the garlic skins that remain in the sieve.

7. Remove the chicken from the oven, and transfer it to a platter where it will rest while you are making the sauce.

8. In a small saucepan, bring the *glace de volaille* to a simmer and add the mashed garlic. Whisk together.

9. Deglaze the roasting pan with ¼ cup water. Add these pan drippings and any juices the chicken may have exuded while resting to the sauce. Over low heat, whisk the remaining butter, tablespoon by tablespoon to the sauce. Remove from the heat. Season with salt and pepper.

PRESENTATION

Remove the trussing string from the chicken. Transfer the sauce to a sauceboat. Sprinkle the chicken with the remaining fresh herbs, and bring it to the table where you will carve it and portion it out.

MENU ACCOMPANIMENT

Start with the Jerusalem Artichoke (page 81) or Kohlrabi (page 74) soup. Oven-Baked Sliced Potatoes (page 347) or Sweet Potato Sauté (page 363) could be vegetable garnishes served with this main course. Fruit tarts or Apple Purée (page 427) would make a lovely finish.

Chicken in Spinach Broth with Fresh Vegetables

T HIS IS similar to a classic boiled chicken dinner. The difference is that crunchy green beans, carrots, and cauliflower are added at the end and the broth is mixed with a light spinach and cream purée to give it a beautiful color and a richer taste.

PREPARATION TIME:
30 minutes

COOKING TIME:
2 hours

SERVES:
4

1	*4-pound chicken*
1	*pound onions, roughly chopped*
2	*carrots, roughly chopped*
3	*bay leaves*
1	*teaspoon whole black peppercorns*
6	*sprigs Italian parsley*
¼	*cup white wine, tarragon, or cider vinegar*
1	*quart chicken stock*
	Coarse salt
½	*pound spinach, stemmed*
½	*cup heavy cream*
1	*carrot, cut into ⅛- by 2-julienne pieces*
¾	*pound cauliflower flowerets*
½	*pound green beans, trimmed and cut into 2-inch lengths*
	Salt
	Freshly ground pepper

1. Wash the chicken inside and out, and place it, whole, with the onions, carrots, bay leaves, peppercorns, parsley, vinegar, stock, and 1 tablespoon coarse salt in an 8-quart stock pot or casserole. Barely cover the chicken with water.

2. Bring to a boil, then reduce the heat and poach the chicken at a gentle simmer for 1 hour. Skim off any scum that rises to the top.

3. After it is poached, remove the chicken from its poaching liquid. Strain the broth through a cheesecloth-lined sieve, making sure you catch it all. Return the broth to the pot and boil it over high heat until it is reduced to 1½ quarts in all.

4. While the broth is reducing, remove the skin from the chicken (except for the wings) and discard. Cut the chicken into the following serving pieces: 2 legs, 2 thighs, 2 wings, and 2 breast pieces (you may remove the breast bone if you like). Set aside.

5. In a blender or food processor, purée the spinach with the cream. (If you are using a blender, this might not be enough liquid so wait until the broth has properly reduced and use some of it to help purée the spinach.)

6. After the broth has been reduced, add in the julienned carrots, cauliflower, and green beans and simmer them for 5 to 10 minutes, until cooked but still crunchy.

7. Add the spinach and cream purée and the chicken pieces and heat through for another 5 minutes. Taste, and adjust the seasoning.

PRESENTATION

Place the broth, chicken, and vegetables in a large soup tureen and bring this to the table. In each soup plate ladle some broth, place a couple of chicken pieces in the center, and spoon the vegetables over the chicken.

If you want to serve something before this course, try Warm Asparagus with Japanese Dressing (page 94) or Piquant Chicken Liver Salad (page 100) served without the spinach. If you want to serve something after this course, try the Pear and Goat Cheese Salad (page 104). For dessert, a rich cake such as Fine Orange Cake (page 382) or Chocolate Almond Cake (page 370) would be perfect.

Chicken with Vegetables

T HE CHICKEN and vegetables are simmered separately, then combined at the end and simmered together only for a brief time. In this way the vegetables retain their crunch and distinct flavor. This dish tastes even better the second day.

PREPARATION TIME:
45 minutes

COOKING TIME:
1 hours and 30 minutes

SERVES:
4

2   *artichokes*
8   *tablespoons butter*
¼   *cup olive oil*
1   *3- to 3 ½- pound chicken, cut into 8 pieces*
¼   *cup flour, seasoned with ½ teaspoon salt and ¼ teaspoon freshly ground pepper*

1   pound onions, roughly chopped
4   cloves garlic, minced
2   pounds ripe tomatoes, peeled, seeded, and roughly chopped
4   bay leaves
2   teaspoons fresh thyme, or ½ teaspoon dried
2   teaspoons fresh rosemary, or ½ teaspoon dried
2   cups red wine
½   cup pitted black imported olives
1   large carrot, thinly sliced
¾   pound small mushrooms, stemmed
½   cup glace de volaille, optional
2   tablespoons minced Italian parsley
    Salt
    Freshly ground pepper

1. In a 6-quart saucepan, bring 2 quarts water to a boil. Drop in the whole artichokes and boil them covered for 30 minutes, or until nearly cooked. Drain from the liquid and cool upside down for 30 minutes.

2. When cool enough to handle, remove the leaves (and serve separately), remove the chokes (see illustration, page 322), and thinly slice the parboiled hearts. Set aside.

3. Wash the chicken pieces and pat them dry with paper towels.

4. Melt 4 tablespoons butter and the oil in a 10-inch skillet over medium heat. While this is getting hot, dip each piece of chicken into the seasoned flour and shake off any excess. Place each piece of floured chicken, skin side down, in the hot fat and sauté for 10 minutes, or until golden brown, turning every once in a while so that the pieces do not stick.

5. Remove the browned pieces of chicken to a platter. If the fat is badly burned at this point, discard it and melt 3 tablespoons butter with 1 tablespoon oil before proceeding to the next step.

6. Add onions and garlic to the fat remaining in the skillet and mix them in with a wooden spoon, scraping up any browned particles on the bottom of the pan into the onions. Turn heat down to very low, cover, and simmer for 10 minutes.

7. Remove the cover, add the tomatoes and bay leaves, and simmer, uncovered, for another 10 minutes.

8. Add 1 tablespoon salt, ½ teaspoon pepper, thyme, rosemary, and wine and reduce the liquid over medium heat for 10 minutes.

9. Add the chicken pieces to this sauce and simmer uncovered, the liquid reducing all the while, thickening the sauce.

10. While the chicken is simmering, melt the remaining 4 tablespoons butter in a separate skillet. Add the sliced artichoke hearts and olives and sauté these for 3 minutes. Remove them with a slotted spoon and add them to the simmering chicken.

11. In the same skillet, in the remaining fat, sauté the carrots and mushrooms over fairly high heat for about 2 minutes. Remove them to the simmering chicken.

12. Add the *glace de volaille* at this point, if you wish. Continue to simmer the chicken, uncovered, for another 15 minutes.

PRESENTATION

Portion out some chicken and vegetables in the center of 4 warmed dinner plates. Sprinkle parsley over each portion.

MENU ACCOMPANIMENT

This is a wonderful main course which only needs boiled rice, boiled potatoes, or plain buttered pasta to complete the meal. A perfect starter would be Broccoli and Apple (page 72), Black Bean (page 78), or Mussel and Saffron (page 85) soup. For dessert, serve Mocha Cream (page 415), Frozen Mousse Cassis (page 417), or Pineapple Gratin (page 430), along with Butter Cookies (page 407).

Chicken in Fresh Tomato and Vinegar Sauce

A FEW years back, *poulet au vinaigre*, which inspired this recipe, was all the rage in France. It is a simple recipe which does not call for expensive ingredients.

PREPARATION TIME:
1 hours and 20 minutes

COOKING TIME:
1 hour

SERVES:
4

1   *3-pound chicken, cut into 8 pieces*
3   *tablespoons butter*
3   *tablespoons oil*
5   *cloves garlic, unpeeled*
½   *cup red wine vinegar*
3   *pounds fresh ripe tomatoes, peeled, seeded, and reduced to 1 cup of purée, or 4 pounds canned Italian plum tomatoes, seeded and reduced to 1 cup purée (see page 366)*
½   *cup red wine*
1   *cup packed Italian parsley leaves*
    Watercress or Italian parsley for garnish
    Salt
    Freshly ground pepper

1. Wash the chicken pieces and pat them dry with paper towels. Salt and pepper each piece lightly.

2. In a 12- to 14-inch skillet, melt the butter and oil over medium heat. When hot, add the garlic cloves, along with the thigh and drumstick pieces of the chicken. Sear them in the hot fat for 3 minutes on each side. Add the breast and wing pieces and sear those as well, over high heat, until golden brown, about 3 minutes on each side.

3. Remove the breast and wing pieces from the skillet. Continue to sauté the leg and thigh pieces over fairly high heat so that the flesh continues to brown as it cooks.

4. After 10 minutes, add the reserved breast and wing pieces. Cover and continue to cook, over gentle heat, for another 15 minutes or until the juices of the chicken run clear when the thigh piece is pricked.

5. Remove the chicken to a platter, and keep it warm, loosely covered with foil.

6. Remove the burnt particles from the skillet and discard. Remove all but 1 tablespoon of the fat (if the fat is burnt, replace it with 1 tablespoon fresh butter). Mash the garlic against the sides of the skillet. The skins should come off easily; discard them.

7. Add the vinegar, tomato purée, and wine, and bring this mixture to a boil. Reduce it over high heat until only 1 cup remains, mashing the garlic into the sauce. Season with 1 teaspoon salt and ¼ teaspoon pepper. ●

8. Return the chicken pieces to the sauce. Add the parsley and heat the chicken for about 5 minutes, turning the pieces to ensure that they are coated with the sauce.

PRESENTATION

Place the chicken pieces on a warm platter, garnished with watercress or more parsley, or serve individual portions surrounded by the vegetable garnish on heated dinner plates.

Begin the meal with Spinach Soufflé (page 354) or Sautéed Summer Salad (page 90). Perfect side dishes in terms of contrasts of tastes and textures would be the Oven-Baked Sliced Potatoes (page 347) and Leek Purée (page 341). Finish with a Hot Peach and Almond Tart (page 395).

Sautéed Chicken Breasts

LIGHT and very simple to make, this chicken dish makes an excellent first course for an elaborate formal meal. It is also delicious as a summertime entrée.

PREPARATION TIME:
30 minutes

COOKING TIME:
10 minutes

SERVES:
6

6   *chicken breast halves, boned and skinned*
7   *tablespoons butter*
    Juice of 1 large lemon
½   *cup* bordelaise
    Salt
    Freshly ground pepper

1. Preheat the oven to 250 degrees.

2. Slice the chicken breast halves in half horizontally. Season lightly with salt and pepper.

3. Melt 2 tablespoons butter in a 10-inch skillet. Sauté one-third of the chicken pieces over moderate heat for 1½ minutes on each side. Transfer the cooked pieces to a baking dish and keep them warm, covered, in the oven.

4. Add 2 more tablespoons butter to the same skillet and sauté the second third of the chicken. Remove the sautéed chicken to the oven. Cook the last third of the chicken in the same manner.

5. Deglaze the pan with the lemon juice and *bordelaise*. Reduce this sauce for 2 minutes. Season with 1 teaspoon salt and ¼ teaspoon pepper and swirl in the remaining butter.

PRESENTATION

Place the chicken pieces down the center of each warmed dinner plate and pour the sauce over them. Surround the chicken with any accompanying vegetables.

MENU ACCOMPANIMENT

Precede this dish with either a cream soup or a fish dish such as Poached Sole with Tomato and Saffron (page 133) or Shad Roe with Sorrel (page 127). Fennel Purée (page 337) or Sautéed Grapes (page 339) would make an interesting vegetable garnish. Serve any dessert that is not primarily composed of cream, if cream is a main ingredient in the first course.

Chicken and Sautéed Apples in Puff Pastry

ONE OF THE areas that nouvelle cuisine is experimenting with involves combining meats and fruits. There is no sauce for this recipe because the apples in the filling provide enough moisture.

PREPARATION TIME:
1 hour

COOKING TIME:
45 minutes

SERVES:
4

4   rectangles of puff pastry (see page 388)
1   egg, beaten with 1 teaspoon water
8   tablespoons butter
3   large shallots, minced
2   medium onions, roughly diced
2   baking apples, peeled, cored, and sliced into ½-inch pieces
1   pound fresh spinach, stemmed
1   tablespoon red wine vinegar
4   chicken breast halves, skinned and boned
    Salt
    Freshly ground pepper

1. Preheat the oven to 425 degrees.

2. Place the puff pastry rectangles on a baking sheet, which has been buttered or lined with parchment paper, and brush the surface of each piece with the egg wash.

3. Bake the pastry for 10 minutes at 425 degrees. Lower the oven temperature to 350 degrees and continue baking for 25 minutes, or until the pastry is nut brown and crisp to the touch.

4. While the pastry is baking, melt 6 tablespoons butter over medium heat in a large skillet. Sauté the shallots for 1 minute, add the onions and sauté over low heat for an additional 5 minutes. Add the apples and cook for 15 more minutes. Add the spinach and sauté for 3 minutes. Once you've added the spinach, rapidly mix all the ingredients together with a wooden spoon. At the last moment add 1 tablespoon vinegar. Season the mixture with salt and pepper to taste and set aside. ●

5. Remove the pastry from the oven when it has finished baking. Split each piece in half by carefully pulling the top piece off the bottom with your fingers. Try to do this with a light touch or the fragile pastry will break apart, and into many pieces.

6. Split each breast half in half horizontally, so that you have 8 pieces of chicken. Lightly season the chicken breasts with salt and pepper.

7. Melt 2 tablespoons of butter in a 12-inch skillet and sauté the breasts over fairly high heat for 3 minutes per side. Remove the breasts from the pan and pat dry on each side with paper towels. Set aside.

PRESENTATION

Place the bottom half of the pastry on a heated dinner plate and rest the top half on the side of the plate while you finish the filling. Quickly reheat the spinach and apple mixture and spoon it on the bottom piece of pastry. Place pieces of chicken breast on top and cover with the top half of the puff pastry. Serve immediately.

Serve this as a first course only if you are serving an elaborate "three-star" meal. Squash Cakes (page 358) or Souffléed Acorn Squash (page 356) could be a second course followed by a simple seafood dish, such as Lobster with Vegetables (page 138) or Soft Shell Crabs with Lime Sauce (page 160). End this meal with Chocolate-Dipped Strawberries (page 435) and Butter Cookies (page 407). If you are serving this as a main course, follow it with a vegetable salad and a more substantial dessert, such as Souffléed Chocolate Cake (page 375).

Chicken Terrine

THIS WAS inspired by one of the most original recipes offered in the Troisgros brothers' three-star restaurant in Roanne, France. Pierre Troisgros, the creator, modestly dismissed the dish as a *fantasie*. It is lovely, refreshing, and absolutely gorgeous-looking. In this version, the original pork binder is replaced by a chicken binder which lends a lighter color to the background, thereby enhancing the vegetable mosaic. The terrine can be made up to 5 days in advance.

PREPARATION TIME:
1 hour and 30 minutes
(plus 3 hours cooling time)

COOKING TIME:
1 hour and 15 minutes

SPECIAL EQUIPMENT:
8- by 4-inch loaf pan

SERVES:
8
_____

½   *pound carrots*
1   *pound trimmed green beans*
3   *tablespoons minced shallots*
1½ *tablespoons butter*
½   *cup black olives, pitted*
1   *pound chicken breasts, skinned and boned*
½   *cup vegetable oil*
4   *tablespoons champagne or white wine vinegar*
1   *egg*
      Double recipe for Tomato Vinaigrette Sauce (see page 366)
      Salt
      Freshly ground pepper

1. Cut the carrots into strips, about ¼ inch wide, the length of the whole carrots. Keep the green beans whole.

2. Parboil the carrots in salted water to cover for 5 minutes or until cooked but still crunchy. Drain, and refresh carrots under cold water to stop the cooking process.

3. Parboil the green beans in salted water to cover for 5 to 7 minutes or until cooked but still crunchy. Drain and refresh in cold water. Now trim the carrot strips so that they are about the same length as the green beans. Set aside.

4. Sauté the shallots in the butter over medium high heat until soft but not brown. Set aside.

5. Cut the raw chicken into 2-inch pieces and little by little blend it in a food processor with the oil, vinegar, 1½ teaspoons salt, ¼ teaspoon pepper, shallots, and egg until very smooth. (If you don't have a food processor this texture may be achieved by passing the chicken breasts through the medium blade of a meat grinder then mixing the ingredients together in a mortar and pestle and then passing the mixture through a fine meshed sieve.) This will be the binder.

6. Divide the chicken mixture into three bowls. In one of these bowls, add the carrots, in another the green beans. The third bowl should contain just the binder. Using your hands, mix the vegetables into the chicken mixture in each bowl, making sure they are completely coated.

7. Preheat the oven to 350 degrees.

8. In a buttered 8- by 4-inch bread loaf pan, place enough of the binder (from the third bowl) to coat the bottom. This should be covered with a layer of carrot mixture, keeping the carrots in as straight a line as possible. Next comes a layer of green bean mixture, keeping the green beans as straight as possible. Using a spatula, layer some plain chicken binder on top of the green beans—just enough to barely coat them—and then place a row of black olives down the center. Being careful not to disrupt the carrots or beans, push the olives into the bottom layers of vegetables so that the mixture stays flat. Coat this layer of olives with a paper-thin layer of chicken binder. Then repeat the green bean layer topped by the carrot layer and finally by a layer of chicken binder, which should entirely cover the vegetables. Cover the top with buttered brown paper pressing the paper directly on the top of the terrine.

9. Gently tap the loaf pan on the counter a few times to eliminate air bubbles. Then place it in a larger pan filled with enough hot water to reach three-quarters of the way up the sides of the loaf pan. Place in the oven and bake for 1 hour.

10. Remove the pan from the oven. Let the terrine rest for another hour, until it is a little cooler. Leave the foil cover on.

11. After the terrine has cooled, drain off any excess water that has collected on top of the terrine. Run a sharp knife between the terrine and the pan to loosen then carefully turn it upside down onto a board. The terrine should come out quite easily. Pat it dry with paper towels. Wrap it in plastic wrap and then in foil and let it cool in a refrigerator 3 hours or overnight.

PRESENTATION

Place one-quarter of the Tomato Vinaigrette Sauce on each chilled dessert or dinner plate. Place 2 or 3 thin slices of the chicken terrine in a pretty pattern on top and serve.

MENU ACCOMPANIMENT

This makes a terrific first course for any dish except our chicken dishes. If you are to serve this as a main course, serve it with spinach salad, and follow with a rich dessert, such as Upside-Down Pecan Pie (page 403) or Chocolate Sweetness (page 373).

Stuffed Chicken Legs

T HE STUFFING replaces the bone in the thigh, plumping up the chicken when it steams. The effect of the vegetables bursting onto the dinner plates when you cut into the chicken is tantalizing.

PREPARATION TIME:
1 hour and 45 minutes

COOKING TIME:
35 to 40 minutes

1   *carrot, cut into ¼-inch dice*
1   *stalk celery, peeled and cut into ¼-inch dice*
10 *green beans, cut into ¼-inch pieces*
1   *leek, white part only, cut into ¼-inch pieces*
2   *minced shallots*
6   *tablespoons butter*
¼   *teaspoon thyme*
2   *tablespoons minced Italian parsley*
4   *chicken legs*
1   *cup white wine*
½   *cup* glace de volaille
1   *cup heavy cream*
1   *cup packed watercress leaves*
2   *tablespoons minced fresh chives, optional*
     Salt
     Freshly ground pepper

1. Melt 4 tablespoons butter in a small saucepan. When hot, add the carrot, celery, green beans, leek, and shallots, cover and stew, over gentle heat, for 25 to 30 minutes, or until soft but not brown. Add ¼ teaspoon salt, ¼ teaspoon pepper, thyme, and parsley. Cool to room temperature while preparing the chicken legs.

2. Using a sharp boning knife, cut the tendons around upper thigh bone and rip the bone out, leaving the lower bone in chicken leg. (See illustrations, page 257.)

3. Loosen the flesh, with your fingers, around the bone still in the leg so that you can fit some stuffing in it.

4. With your fingers, force some stuffing in the lower part of the chicken leg, around the bone, and place some in the boneless upper thigh area. With a needle and thread, sew up each leg so that it is entirely closed and all the stuffing is secured inside the legs.

5. Place a steamer in a 4-quart saucepan. Add the wine and enough water to bring the liquid level just beneath the bottom of the steamer. Bring the wine and water to a boil. Place the stuffed chicken legs in the steamer. Cover the pot and steam for 35 minutes. Turn off the heat and keep the lid on the pot.

6. Combine the *glace de volaille* and the cream over medium heat in a 9-inch skillet. Reduce for 2 minutes, or until the sauce lightly coats a spoon. Add the watercress leaves, ½ teaspoon salt, and ¼ teaspoon pepper and simmer 1 minute more.

7. Whisk in 2 tablespoons softened butter and the chives, and taste for seasoning.

PRESENTATION

Place 1 chicken leg in the center of each warmed dinner plate. Remove the thread. Spoon some sauce over each portion.

MENU ACCOMPANIMENT

Start with the Jerusalem Artichoke (page 81) or Kohlrabi (page 74) soup. Oven-Baked Sliced Potatoes (page 347) or Sweet Potato Sauté (page 363) could be served with this course. Any other vegetable except for those dominant in onion flavor could be a second vegetable garnish and Sautéed Grapes (page 339) a third. Pink Pear with Dark Chocolate (page 433) would make a lovely finish.

Boning a Chicken Thigh

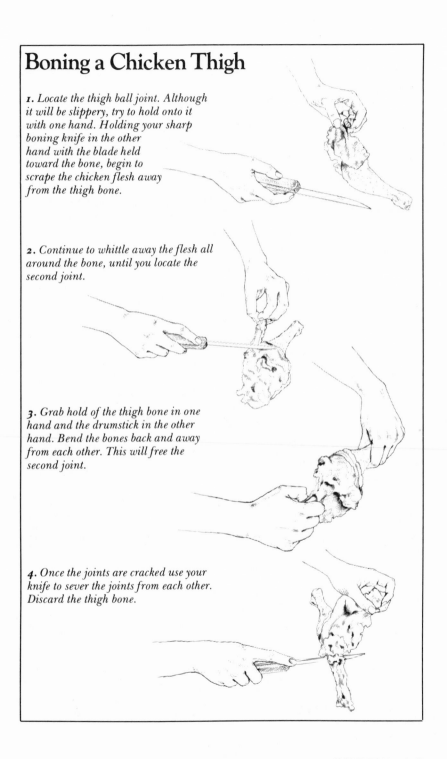

1. *Locate the thigh ball joint. Although it will be slippery, try to hold onto it with one hand. Holding your sharp boning knife in the other hand with the blade held toward the bone, begin to scrape the chicken flesh away from the thigh bone.*

2. *Continue to whittle away the flesh all around the bone, until you locate the second joint.*

3. *Grab hold of the thigh bone in one hand and the drumstick in the other hand. Bend the bones back and away from each other. This will free the second joint.*

4. *Once the joints are cracked use your knife to sever the joints from each other. Discard the thigh bone.*

Pecan-Breaded Chicken Breasts with Mustard Sauce

THE PECANS add an exquisite taste and texture to the chicken breasts and make this a very rich dish, so the sauce is really meant to just moisten the chicken and not saturate it. Serve with a plain vegetable that will make a nice contrast to the luxurious taste of the chicken.

PREPARATION TIME:

35 minutes

COOKING TIME:

10 to 20 minues

SERVES:

4

2	*whole chicken breasts, skinned, boned, and cut in half*
10	*tablespoons butter*
3	*tablespoons Dijon mustard*
5	*to 6 ounces ground pecans*
2	*tablespoons safflower oil*
⅔	*cup sour cream*
	Salt
	Freshly ground pepper

1. Between 2 pieces of wax paper, lightly flatten the chicken breasts with a meat pounder. Season the chicken with salt and pepper.

2. Melt 6 tablespoons butter in a small saucepan over medium heat. Remove from the heat and whisk in 2 tablespoons mustard.

3. Dip each piece of chicken into the butter and mustard mixture and heavily coat each with the ground pecans by patting them on with your hands. •

4. Preheat the oven to 200 degrees.

5. Melt 4 tablespoons butter in a 12- to 14-inch skillet. Stir in the oil. When hot, sauté as many pieces of chicken at a time as you can without crowding them. Sauté for about 3 minutes on each side. Remove to a baking dish and place in the oven to keep warm. Continue cooking the chicken pieces until all are done. (This, of course, can be done in half the time if you have 2 large skillets; use 4 tablespoons of butter and 2 tablespoons of oil in each skillet.)

6. Discard the butter and oil. If you find that the pecans that are left in the skillet are too burnt, discard them; otherwise spoon them onto the chicken while it is being kept warm in the oven.

7. Deglaze the pan with the sour cream, scraping up all the browned particles.

8. Whisk the remaining tablespoon mustard, 1 teaspoon salt and ¼ teaspoon pepper into the sauce. The sauce should retain a strong mustardy flavor. Remove it from the heat.

PRESENTATION

Place a dollop of the sour cream sauce in the middle of warmed dinner plates and cover it completely with a portion of chicken. Only a small portion of sauce should accompany each piece so as not to overpower the chicken. It should not be visible on the plate and, thus, will be a surprise to the diner when he or she discovers it.

MENU ACCOMPANIMENT

Start with the Cold Oyster and Tamarind (page 83) or Broccoli and Apple (page 72) soup. Serve either the Pumpkin (page 349), Leek (page 341), or Butternut Squash (page 360) purée as one vegetable garnish, along with steamed green beans, zucchini, or asparagus. For dessert, serve either the Souffléed Chocolate Cake (page 375) or Chocolate Sweetness (page 373).

Chicken with Basil and Tarragon

PREPARATION TIME:
20 to 30 minutes

COOKING TIME:
35 minutes

SERVES:
4

1   *4-pound chicken, cut into 8 pieces*
4   *tablespoons butter*
½   *cup heavy cream*
¼   *cup* glace de volaille
¼   *cup fresh basil leaves, roughly chopped*
2   *tablespoons fresh tarragon leaves, or ½ tablespoon dried*
    Watercress leaves for garnish
    Salt
    Freshly ground pepper

1. Wash the chicken pieces and pat them dry with paper towels. Lightly salt and pepper.

2. Melt the butter over medium heat in a 12- to 14-inch skillet and sauté the chicken thighs and legs first, for 10 minutes, turning them once. Add the breast and wing pieces and continue to sauté these together with the legs and thighs, turning them over every 5 minutes so that they don't burn. Continue to sauté until they cook through, and a crusty exterior forms. This should take a total of 30 to 35 minutes, or until the juices of the leg run clear yellow. (*Note:* If the butter begins to burn, cover the skillet, lower the heat, and steam the chicken through although by doing this, the crisp exterior will not form.)

3. Remove the chicken pieces to a platter and keep them warm while you are finishing the sauce.

4. Over medium heat, degrease the skillet. Add ½ cup water to the skillet, scraping the browned particles into the liquid. Reduce this liquid by half.

5. Add the heavy cream, *glace de volaille*, and herbs and reduce by half again, or until the sauce lightly coats a spoon. Adjust the seasonings and strain the sauce if you wish to eliminate the browned particles. ●

PRESENTATION

Place the chicken pieces on a platter, pour sauce over them, and garnish the platter with watercress leaves.

MENU ACCOMPANIMENT

Almost any fish or shellfish recipe can precede this, as could any soup without cream. Serve the chicken with any of our vegetable purées, along with Fresh Snow Peas with Shallots and Basil (page 351) or Shredded Carrots with Orange Juice (page 332). Any dessert would be appropriate.

Chicken Breasts with Hot Tomato Vinaigrette

O**NE USUALLY** expects vinaigrette to be cold. In this case it is warm and combines beautifully with the chicken. If you serve this with a garnish of sautéed zucchini and warm, steamed avocado slices, the color combination is most appetizing.

PREPARATION TIME:
2 hours and 10 minutes

COOKING TIME:
10 minutes

SERVES
4

2   *whole chicken breasts, boned and skinned*
      Juice of 2 lemons
4   *tablespoons butter*
1   *recipe Tomato Vinaigrette Sauce (see page 366)*
      Salt
      Freshly ground pepper

    1. Flatten the chicken breasts out by placing them between two pieces of wax paper and pounding them down with a mallet.
    2. Marinate the breasts in the lemon juice in a glass or porcelain bowl for 2 hours. Just before sautéing, remove and pat them dry on paper towels.
    3. Heat the butter in a 12-inch skillet. When hot, sauté the chicken breasts over medium-high heat for 3 to 4 minutes on each side. Season with ½ teaspoon salt and ¼ teaspoon pepper.

4. While you are sautéing the chicken, heat the tomato vinaigrette over low heat. It should never get so hot that the oil in the vinaigrette starts to give off a cooked oil taste. It should just be warm to the touch. If it gets too hot, turn off the heat.

PRESENTATION

In the center of each warmed dinner plate spoon out a portion of the hot vinaigrette. Place the chicken on top of the sauce in the middle of it. If you are serving Sautéed Shredded Squash and Steamed Avocado, place a portion of zucchini in the middle on top of the chicken, and pieces of steamed avocado surrounding the outside of the chicken, each piece half on the chicken, half on the sauce.

MENU ACCOMPANIMENT

Begin the meal with the Black Bean Soup (page 78). Garnish with Sautéed Shredded Squash (page 362) and Steamed Avocado (page 328). For dessert, serve Chocolate Chip Tartlets (page 400) or Fresh Cherries in Puff Pastry (page 392).

Chicken Wings with Tamarind and Garlic

THIS IS an easy dish to prepare and it makes an excellent appetizer. The longer the chicken wings marinate in the tamarind mixture, the more flavorful and pungent the taste. You may chill the wings overnight after they have been cooked and serve them cold.

PREPARATION TIME:
20 minutes
(plus 6 hours marinating time)

COOKING TIME:
35 minutes

SERVES:
8

2   *pounds chicken wings*
½   *cup olive oil*
4   *cloves garlic, minced*
3   *tablespoons tamarind paste*
¼   *cup red wine vinegar*
     Salt
     Freshly ground pepper

1. Wash the chicken wings and pat them dry with paper towels. Separate the wings at the second joint and reserve the wing tips for use in making stock. In a large mixing bowl, season the chicken with ½ teaspoon salt and ¼ teaspoon pepper.

2. Pour the oil into a skillet and sauté the garlic over medium heat for approximately 2 minutes, or until it becomes translucent.

3. Add the tamarind and vinegar to the skillet and blend all the ingredients together.

4. Pour this mixture over the chicken, and using a large spoon, coat the chicken with the tamarind marinade. Allow the chicken to marinate in the mixture for at least 6 hours, or overnight.

5. Preheat the oven to 400 degrees.

6. Transfer the chicken to a large baking dish and bake for 35 minutes, or until the skins of the chicken begin to crisp. Baste and turn the chicken occasionally during the cooking process. Remove from the oven, taste, and adjust the seasoning.

PRESENTATION

The chicken wings may be served hot, cold, or at room temperature.

MENU ACCOMPANIMENT

Follow with a vegetable dish such as Sautéed Summer Salad (page 90) or a dish of mixed vegetable purées of your own choice. Follow this with a small portion of a fish dish such as Stuffed Sea Bass Steamed in Lettuce (page 121) or Salmon with Fresh Vegetables (page 112). Keep the dessert light—serve either a fruit ice or Chocolate-Dipped Strawberries (page 435).

Cornish Game Hens with Plantains and Pine Nuts

I F GREEN BANANAS or plantains are unavailable, you may easily substitute ripe yellow bananas.

PREPARATION TIME:
1 hour

COOKING TIME:
1 hour and 45 minutes

SERVES:
4

14 *tablespoons butter*
2   *medium onions, thinly sliced*
1   *carrot, thinly sliced*
2   *cloves garlic, minced*
1   *plaintain, or 1 banana*
4   *fresh rock cornish game hens, each one weighing about 1 ½*
       pounds
2   *tablespoons pine nuts*
½   *teaspoon thyme*
    Coarse salt
½   *cup glace de volaille*
    Salt
    Freshly ground pepper

    1. Preheat the oven to 425 degrees.
    2. In 6 tablespoons butter, sauté the onions, carrot, and garlic for 20 minutes over medium heat.
    3. Peel the plantain or banana and cut it into ½-inch slices. Sauté it along with the onions for 5 minutes more, if

you are using a plantain, or 1 minute for a banana.

4. While the onions are sautéing, wash and dry the cornish hens. Season the inside cavities with salt and pepper.

5. Add the pine nuts to the onions and bananas and stuff equal amounts of stuffing into the cavity of each bird. Truss the hens. (See illustration, page 238.) If done in advance, refrigerate now and remove 30 minutes before roasting. ●

6. Arrange the hens in a baking pan without a rack, and just large enough to accommodate them without crowding.

7. In a small saucepan, melt 4 tablespoons butter over low heat and add the thyme, 1 teaspoon coarse salt, and ¼ teaspoon pepper.

8. Place the baking pan with the hens on the lowest shelf of the oven and roast them for about 50 minutes or until the juices run clear yellow when you prick the thigh with a fork. Baste the birds every 15 minutes with the melted butter, thyme, salt, and pepper.

9. Remove the hens from the oven and keep them warm while you are making the sauce.

10. Discard the grease from the roasting pan. Add ¾ cup water to the pan and bring this to a boil over medium heat, scraping the browned particles into the liquid. Add the *glace de viande* and reduce so that the sauce lightly coats a spoon.

11. Whisk in 4 tablespoons butter and season with salt and pepper, if necessary.

PRESENTATION

Remove the trussing string. Split each bird in half. Place the opened rock cornish game hens on warmed dinner plates. Spoon the sauce over the stuffing, down the middle. Serve any vegetable garnishes on separate plates.

Purées of turnips (page 365) and leeks (page 341), and wild rice as garnishes would be fine for contrast in flavors and textures. Because of the richness of this dish, follow with a plain green salad. End the meal with Cranberry Soufflé (page 413).

Cornish Game Hens in Cumin and Vinegar

R OCK CORNISH game hens are, on their own, rather bland in taste, so to liven them up in this recipe, they are marinated for 6 to 8 hours in a simple mixture of vinegar and cumin. They are then stuffed with a mixture of green beans sautéed with shallots, and roasted using the marinade for basting.

PREPARATION TIME:
20 minutes
(plus 10 hours marinating time)

COOKING TIME:
50 minutes

SERVES:
4

4   fresh rock cornish game hens, each weighing about 1 ½
        pounds
¾   cup white wine vinegar
2   tablespoons ground cumin, plus ¼ teaspoon
¾   pound trimmed green beans
9   tablespoons butter
2   tablespoons minced shallots
     Salt
     Freshly ground pepper

1. Wash the hens inside and out, and dry them with paper towels. With a fork, prick the skin and flesh of the hens so that the marinade will penetrate into the flesh.

2. Combine the vinegar with 2 tablespoons cumin and marinate the birds in a glass, porcelain, or stainless steel bowl for 8 to 10 hours, in the refrigerator. Turn them frequently, as the marinade will be in the bottom of the bowl and there is not enough to cover the entire body of the hens.

3. Parboil the green beans in salted water for about 5 minutes or until cooked but crunchy. Drain the beans, cut them in half, and set aside.

4. Melt 3 tablespoons butter in a skillet and sauté the shallots over medium heat until soft. Add the green beans to the shallots with ½ teaspoon salt, ¼ teaspoon pepper, and ¼ teaspoon cumin. Toss the beans with this mixture. Remove from the heat after 2 minutes.

5. Preheat the oven to 400 degrees for 20 minutes.

6. Remove the cornish game hens from the refrigerator. Stuff each bird with one-quarter of the green beans and shallots. Truss the bird. (See illustrations, page 238.) Rub them with the remaining 6 tablespoons butter, and salt and pepper them.

7. Place the marinade on the bottom of a roasting pan just big enough to hold the birds in one layer with not too much room around them. Roast them on one side for 10 minutes; on the other side for 10 minutes; and finally place them breast side up and roast for the last 30 minutes. Baste them every 10 minutes using the marinade and butter from the bottom of the pan.

8. Remove the rock cornish game hens to a platter and keep them warm. Remove trussing strings.

9. Degrease the juices in the pan and season them with salt and pepper.

PRESENTATION

Place one whole bird in the middle of each warmed dinner plate and pour the juice over the bird.

MENU ACCOMPANIMENT

To start, serve the Mussels in Puff Pastry (page 140). Accompany the hens with Souffléed Acorn Squash (page 356) as a side dish. Any dessert but those calling for puff pastry or pastry dough if you serve the mussels as a first course, would be appropriate.

Cornish Game Hen Stew

THIS IS NOT a traditional stew since the meat and vegetables do not simmer together for very long. They are first cooked separately, then together for a brief time, merely to blend the flavors. It is both hearty because of the abundance of vegetables and yet delicate in flavor because of the choice of vegetables. Steaming the cornish hens in red wine imparts flavor to these bland little birds and keeps them juicy.

PREPARATION TIME:
1 hour

COOKING TIME:
1 hour

SERVES:
6 to 8

1 *pound fresh asparagus*
1 *bulb of fennel*
1 *medium cucumber*
4 *fresh rock cornish game hens, each weighing about 1 ½*
     pounds
5 *medium carrots, sliced into 1-inch rounds*
1 *pound onions, sliced into 1-inch rounds*
10 *tablespoons butter*
2 *cups red wine*
2 *cups brown stock, or ½ cup* glace de viande *or*
     glace de volaille
½ *teaspoon thyme*
    Salt
    Freshly ground pepper

    1. Cut off 2 inches from the bottoms of the asparagus stalks. Remove the stalks from the fennel bulbs and discard. Cut the bulb in half, cut out the core and discard, then continue cutting the bulb into 2-inch pieces.

    2. Peel the cucumber, cut it in half, scoop out the seeds, and chop into 1-inch pieces. Toss them with ½ teaspoon salt and put the pieces in a sieve placed over a bowl to drain them of their excess water.

    3. Wash the cornish hens inside and out and pat them dry with paper towels. With poultry shears, cut each one into 4 pieces and lightly salt and pepper each piece.

4. In a 12- to 14-inch skillet, sauté the onions and carrots in 4 tablespoons butter for 10 minutes, over low heat. Add the fennel to the skillet and sauté for another 10 minutes.

5. Meanwhile, pour the red wine into a 6- to 9-quart casserole and place the cornish game hen pieces, skin side down, in the wine. Bring to a boil, reduce the heat and simmer, covered, for 15 minutes.

6. After the hen pieces have simmered for 15 minutes, remove them to a bowl, and pour the wine and juices through a strainer into the skillet with the vegetables.

7. Add the *glace de viande* or *glace de volaille* to the skillet and simmer for another 5 minutes. Remove from the heat.

8. In 2 batches, using 3 tablespoons butter for each batch, sauté the pieces of cornish hen in the same casserole you steamed them in. Sauté them over medium heat, until golden brown on each side.

9. When all the pieces are brown, add the vegetables and their juices from the skillet to the casserole. Add 1 teaspoon salt, ½ teaspoon pepper, and the thyme. ●

10. Lay the asparagus stalks in a row across the top of the meat and vegetables. Cover the casserole and cook until the asparagus are soft but still have some crunch, about 10 minutes.

11. Add the cucumbers and cook them, covered, for another 3 minutes. Taste, and adjust the seasonings.

PRESENTATION

Transfer the contents of the casserole to a soup tureen or very deep serving dish. Serve this dish in deep soup plates. Spoon out the vegetables first, the meat on top of them, followed by a few stalks of asparagus, crisscrossed on top of the meat, and finally the juices over everything.

See menu accompaniments for Chicken in Spinach Broth with Fresh Vegetables (page 240), omitting Asparagus with Japanese Dressing as a first course.

Roast Duck

AMERICAN ducks are very fatty so this recipe combines both steaming and roasting to cook the fat out. By steaming it first, you keep the flesh juicy and render out much of the fat. You finish the duck by roasting it for an hour to make the skin crisp and golden.

PREPARATION TIME:
1 hour

COOKING TIME:
1 hour and 15 minutes

1   *4-to 5-pound duck*
Coarse salt
Freshly ground pepper

    1. Remove extraneous fat underneath the skin and at the neck of the duck. Wash it inside and out and pat dry with paper towels.
    2. Slip your fingers between the flesh and the skin around the back and sides to loosen. This is done so that the fat will run out of, rather than into the flesh.
    3. Cut away the neck skin. Work the backside flaps of skin into the duck cavity.

4. Truss the duck with butcher's twine. Starting at the duck's ankle, twist the string around one foot, then the other, then around both in a figure 8 pattern. Continue in this fashion two more times.

5. Wrap the string in between the joined ankles vertically alongside the back of the duck and around the belly. Continue this two more times, then change directions and work horizontally around the sides of the duck, leaving the wings outside the string as you work. In other words, you are wrapping the duck as you would an ordinary package. Tie the string tightly in the middle.

6. Liberally sprinkle the duck with coarse salt and pat it into the flesh.

7. Tie 1 long piece of string around each wing and let the strings hang so that you can fasten them to the handles of a stockpot.

8. Tie each string securely and tightly to each handle of the stock pot, making sure the duck is suspended 2 to 3 inches from the bottom of the stockpot. Cut off any extraneous string hanging from the stockpot.

9. Put 1½ inches of water in the stockpot. Bring the water to a boil, reduce it to a simmer. Cover the pot with foil and a cover and steam the duck this way for 45 minutes.

10. Turn off the heat, uncover the pot, and let the duck cool, still suspended over the water, for another half an hour.

11. Preheat the oven to 500 degrees.

12. Detach the duck from the stockpot. Salt and pepper the duck and place it on its side on a rack in a shallow roasting pan. Roast it on its side for 10 minutes on the lowest rack in the oven.

13. Turn it over to its other side and roast it for another 10 minutes. Finish the roasting by turning it on its back, breast side up, and roasting for another 20 minutes, or until the skin is crispy.

14. Remove it from the oven and let it rest 10 minutes before carving.

Roast Duck Stuffed with Fruit

PREPARATION TIME:
1 hour

COOKING TIME:
2 hours

SERVES:
4

1   *4- to 5-pound duck*
½   *pound chestnuts in the shell*
1½   *cups (½ pound) dried, pitted prunes, cut into quarters*
½   *cup (2 ounces) dried apricots, cut into quarters*
2   *pounds McIntosh apples*
1   *large onion*
9   *tablespoons butter*
3   *tablespoons tarragon, champagne, or white wine vinegar*
½   *cup* glace de canard *or* glace de volaille
2   *tablespoons minced parsley*
       Salt
       Freshly ground pepper

1. Follow through step 10 of the Roast Duck recipe, page 273, to steam the duck. While it is cooling, prepare the stuffing, if you did not make it in advance.

2. With a sharp knife, cut the chestnuts in half vertically. Peel off the tough outer skin. There is an inner light brown skin that will come off later.

3. Bring 2 cups water to a boil. Parboil the chestnuts for 3 minutes (they should not begin to turn soft). Drain them and quickly peel off the light brown inner skin while they are still hot, otherwise it will not come off. Cut the halved chestnuts in half again and put them in a mixing bowl. (*Note:* If you have difficulty removing the inner skin, scrape away at it, even if you take away some of the chestnut in the process.)

4. Add the prunes and the apricots. Season with 1 teaspoon salt and ¼ teaspoon pepper. Peel, core, and roughly dice the apples. Add them to the mixing bowl. ●

5. Preheat the oven to 500 degrees.

6. Remove the trussing from the steamed duck. Pat it dry. Season the inside cavity with salt and pepper and stuff the inner cavity with as much stuffing as possible. Then stuff the cavity at the neck. Sew up the neck and rear with thread. Season the outer skin with salt and pepper and prick the skin all over, especially around the fatty rear parts, to give the fat an opportunity to run out.

7. Place the duck on a rack in a roasting pan on its side and roast it for 10 minutes. Prick the skin again and turn the duck onto its other side; roast for another 10 minutes. Prick the skin again and roast the duck, breast side up, for another 25 minutes.

8. Purée the onions in a food processor or mince them by hand and finish puréeing in a blender.

9. Melt 3 tablespoons butter over low heat in a medium saucepan and sauté the puréed onions for 20 to 30 minutes, stirring occasionally, until the mixture begins to turn a light brown.

10. Add the vinegar to the purée and simmer for an additional 2 to 3 minutes. Add the *glace de canard* or *glace de volaille* and bring the mixture back to a simmer. Turn off the heat.

11. Remove the duck and let it rest for 10 minutes.

12. Gently reheat the sauce while you carve the duck. Place the duck on a carving board with rims to catch any juices. Remove the twine. With the tip of a chef's knife, starting at the top of the breast, cut through the duck vertically. With poultry shears, cut through the back bone. You now have 2 equal halves.

13. Carefully, so as not to disturb too much of the

stuffing, turn one duck half over. Cut the duck in half again, along the thigh, through the joint. Repeat with the other half. Now you have 4 pieces. Cover loosely with foil to keep warm.

14. Add the juices the duck has given off to the sauce and beat in the remaining butter, tablespoon by tablespoon. Turn off the heat and adjust seasonings.

PRESENTATION

Spoon any stuffing that is loose onto the center of each warmed dinner plate. Place a duck piece on top and spoon simmering sauce over that. Sprinkle parsley on the sauce that has dribbled down onto the plate. Repeat for the other servings.

MENU ACCOMPANIMENT

Start with Steamed Vegetable Salad (page 92) or Cold Bay Scallops with Cumin Vinaigrette (page 147) or Mussel and Saffron Soup (page 85). Serve steamed green beans, broccoli, or cauliflower as a vegetable garnish to this dish. A Souffléed Chocolate Cake (page 375) or a Chocolate Almond Cake (page 370) would be fitting desserts to this grand meal.

Boning a Duck

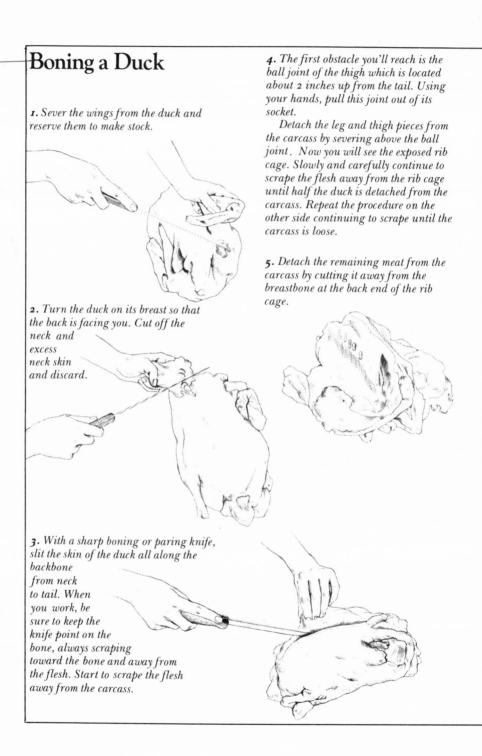

1. Sever the wings from the duck and reserve them to make stock.

2. Turn the duck on its breast so that the back is facing you. Cut off the neck and excess neck skin and discard.

3. With a sharp boning or paring knife, slit the skin of the duck all along the backbone from neck to tail. When you work, be sure to keep the knife point on the bone, always scraping toward the bone and away from the flesh. Start to scrape the flesh away from the carcass.

4. The first obstacle you'll reach is the ball joint of the thigh which is located about 2 inches up from the tail. Using your hands, pull this joint out of its socket.

Detach the leg and thigh pieces from the carcass by severing above the ball joint. Now you will see the exposed rib cage. Slowly and carefully continue to scrape the flesh away from the rib cage until half the duck is detached from the carcass. Repeat the procedure on the other side continuing to scrape until the carcass is loose.

5. Detach the remaining meat from the carcass by cutting it away from the breastbone at the back end of the rib cage.

6. At this point you will have two large flaps of skin containing both the meat and the surrounding breast fat. With your knife, outline the contours of these pieces close to the meat. Shown is duck with extraneous skin cut away.

7. If your recipe calls for skinless breast and thigh meat, proceed as follows: Remove the skin from the flesh with the tip of your knife; the skin detaches easily. It is best to work with your fingers at this point.

Shown below is, left to right, skinless breast meat, detached skin, and contoured skin with breast meat attached.

8. To bone thigh and leg meat: With the tip of the knife, make an incision all along the thigh and leg bone. Push the meat away from the bone with the knife so that you see exposed bone, joints, cartilage, and ligaments. Slip the tip of the knife underneath the bone to free the underneath flesh.

9. Hold the bone in one hand and scrape away cutting through ligaments when necessary to free the flesh from the bone. Sever the tendon at the end of the bone and pull the bones out. Repeat this with the leg.

Duck with Cranberries

FRUIT AND DUCK have traditionally been good companions. The tart cranberries contrast well with the rich duck and lend a deep red color to the sauce. The meat cooks in its own fat and skin which is removed before serving.

PREPARATION TIME:
1 hour and 20 minutes

COOKING TIME:
20 minutes

SERVES:
4

¼ *cup sugar*
2 *cups fresh cranberries*
   Filleted breast and thigh meat from a 4- to 5-pound duck
      (see page 278)
4 *tablespoons butter*
1 *tablespoon minced shallots*
½ *cup* glace de canard
   Salt
   Freshly ground pepper

1. Bring 2 cups water and the sugar to a boil in a heavy saucepan. Reduce to a simmer, add the cranberries, and simmer, covered, for 5 minutes, or until the skins pop. Remove from the heat, and drain the cranberries, reserving the juice for some other use. ●
2. Meanwhile, begin to sauté the meat, skin side down, in a 10-inch skillet over medium heat. Cook the meat

for about 8 to 10 minutes in all, turning frequently to brown both sides.

3. When brown, remove the meat to a carving board and keep warm, covered loosely with foil. The meat will still be somewhat pink inside.

4. Degrease the skillet, add 2 tablespoons butter, and melt them over medium heat. Add the shallots and sauté for 1 minute.

5. Add the *glace de canard* and the reserved cranberries to the pan. Over medium heat, scrape all the browned particles into the sauce. Reduce the sauce for 2 minutes.

6. Remove the sauce from the heat. Strain out the cranberry skins. Return the strained sauce to the skillet; season with ½ teaspoon salt and ¼ teaspoon pepper, and keep warm over low heat while you carve the duck.

7. Remove the skin and fat from the duck pieces and discard. Slice the duck across the grain, into ¼-inch thick slices.

8. Whisk the remaining butter into the simmering sauce. Taste, and adjust the seasonings.

PRESENTATION

Place some thigh and breast slices in the center of each warmed dinner plate. Surround the meat with spoonfuls of sauce.

MENU ACCOMPANIMENT

Duck is rich, so start with a light appetizer, such as Broiled Oysters with Vegetable Julienne (page 143) or the Seven Vegetable Broth (page 76). Serve the duck with Oven-Baked Sliced Potatoes (page 347) and Floating Broccoli (page 329) or Leek Pureé (page 341) for color and contrast in texture. Upside-Down Pecan Pie (page 403) would be good for dessert.

Duck with Oranges and Grapes

HERE IS AN untraditional way of using a traditional combination of flavors. The flavor and freshness of the oranges comes through and is underscored by the sweet grapes.

PREPARATION TIME:
1 hour and 30 minutes

COOKING TIME:
20 minutes

SERVES:
4

2   *navel oranges*
     Filleted breast and thigh meat from a 4-to 5-pound duck
¼   *cup* glace de viande
     Grated peel of half an orange
1   *cup seedless grapes*
2   *tablespoons butter*
     Salt
     Freshly ground pepper

1. With a sharp knife, remove all skin and white part from the oranges and discard. Cut each orange into 4 pieces; there should be no pits. Blend the oranges in a food processor or blender, pass the pulp through a sieve and discard. Reserve the juices.

2. Sauté the duck, skin side down in a 10-inch skillet over medium heat. Cook the meat for about 12 to 15 minutes in all, turning frequently to brown both sides. When brown, remove the meat to a carving board and keep warm, covered loosely with foil. The meat will still be pink inside.

3. Degrease the skillet. Add the orange juice and *glace de viande* and deglaze the pan by scraping all the browned particles into the sauce.

4. Add the orange peel, ½ teaspoon salt, and ¼ teaspoon pepper and reduce for 2 to 3 minutes over medium heat. Taste for seasoning and keep sauce warm over very low heat.

5. Remove the skin and fat from the duck pieces and discard. Slice the meat, across the grain, into ¼-inch thick slices.

6. Whisk the grapes and butter into the sauce and continue whisking until blended. Serve immediately.

PRESENTATION

Place some thigh and breast slices in the center of each warmed dinner plate. Surround the meat with the spoonfuls of sauce and grapes.

MENU ACCOMPANIMENT

See Duck with Cranberries (page 280).

Duck Fillets with Green Peppercorn Sauce

O NCE YOU have mastered boning a duck this becomes a fast and delicious recipe. The fillets of duck
are cooked like steak. Then they are sliced and arranged on top of the peppercorn sauce.

PREPARATION TIME:
45 minutes

COOKING TIME:
20 minutes

SERVES:
4

1   *4- to 5-pound duck*
½   *cup* glace de canard *or* glace de volaille
1   *cup heavy cream or* crème fraîche
4   *teaspoons water-packed green peppercorns*
2   *tablespoons butter*
     Salt
     Freshly ground pepper

1. Bone and fillet the duck, following the instructions on page 278.
2. Sauté the duck pieces over high heat, skin side
down (no additional oil is necessary), in a preheated heavy
skillet for approximately 3 to 4 minutes, or until the fat
becomes crisp and the meat immediately adjacent to the fat
starts to lose its reddish color. Turn the duck pieces over
and cook for about 2 minutes on the other side. At this
point the outside of the duck should be crisp and the inside

rare, tender, and juicy. If you prefer your duck well done, leave the duck pieces in the skillet for a few minutes more. Transfer the duck to a warm platter and cover loosely with tin foil.

3. Place the *glace de canard* in a 9-inch skillet and bring it to a simmer over medium-low heat. Add the cream and bring the mixture slowly to a boil. Add the green peppercorns and whisk all the ingredients together. Reduce the sauce for about 5 minutes, or until the mixture lightly coats a spoon.

4. Turn down the heat until the sauce is barely simmering and whisk in the butter. Season with ½ teaspoon salt and ¼ teaspoon pepper.

PRESENTATION

Carve each piece of duck across the grain, slicing the pieces as thin as possible. Spoon portions of the sauce onto warmed dinner plates. Arrange the slices of duck on top of the sauce in an overlapping pattern. Make sure that each plate has equal amounts of breast and thigh meat.

MENU ACCOMPANIMENT

Avoid cream based dishes as a first course. For color contrast, serve a Sweet Potato Sauté (page 363) as one vegetable garnish and steamed snow peas, green beans, or broccoli as a second one. Fruit ice or sherbet along with Butter Cookies (page 407) would make a good dessert.

Duck with Olives and Scallions

DUCK IS strong enough to stand up to the taste of olives, so be sure that you use olives that have flavor. Use your discretion as to how many you use—this depends on how much you appreciate their taste.

PREPARATION TIME:
1 hours and 15 minutes

COOKING TIME:
20 to 30 minutes

SERVES
4

½   cup pitted olives
9   tablespoons butter
    Filleted breast and thigh meat from a 5- to 6-pound duck
½   cup glace de canard, glace de volaille, or
       glace de viande
½   bunch scallions, sliced into ⅛-inch pieces (use up to 2 inches
       of the green as well)
1   cup heavy cream
    Salt
    Freshly ground pepper

1. Melt 4 tablespoons butter over medium heat. When hot, add the 4 duck pieces (2 breasts and 2 thighs) and sauté over high heat for 5 minutes. Turn the duck and sauté for another 5 minutes or a little longer. Do not overcook—the meat should be pink inside, not gray.
2. When the duck is finished, remove the pieces to a carving board, and cover them loosely with foil to keep them warm.

3. Degrease the skillet, then deglaze it with which-ever *glace* you are using.

4. Add the olives and heavy cream. Reduce this in the skillet for about 5 minutes, or until the sauce coats a spoon.

5. While you are reducing the sauce, in a separate small skillet, sauté the sliced scallions over medium heat in 1 tablespoon butter for 2 minutes only—just to cook them a little bit.

6. Add the sautéed scallions and any juices the duck has given off to the sauce.

7. Whisk in the remaining 4 tablespoons butter, tablespoon by tablespoon. Season the sauce with ½ teaspoon salt and ¼ teaspoon pepper.

PRESENTATION

Slice the duck meat, on a diagonal, into ¼-inch slices. Serve each person some thigh meat and breast meat, with the breast slices covering the thigh meat. Spoon the sauce around the duck and serve any garnishes on a separate plate.

MENU ACCOMPANIMENT

See the menu accompaniments for Duck Fillets with Green Peppercorn Sauce (page 284).

Squabs on a Bed of Chestnut Purée

I N THIS dish, the squabs are surrounded on all sides by chestnuts. Inside there is a marvelous chestnut and on-ion stuffing, outside a bed of chestnut purée, and over the top, a sauce containing some of the purée as a tasty thickener.

PREPARATION TIME:
45 minutes

COOKING TIME:
1 hour for squabs
10 minutes for sauce

SERVES:
4

1   *pound fresh chestnuts*
2   *medium onions, thinly sliced*
11   *tablespoons butter*
4   *fresh squabs*
⅔   *cup heavy cream*
½   *cup* glace de canard *or* glace de volaille
     Salt
     Freshly ground pepper

1. Preheat the oven to 425 degrees.
2. With a sharp paring knife, cut the chestnuts in half and parboil them in boiling water for 15 minutes.
3. Drain the chestnuts and place them in a bowl of hot water. Remove the·tough outer skins and beige inner skins, working on a few at a time while leaving the others in

the water (otherwise they are hard to peel). Set aside.

4. Sauté the onions over medium heat in 3 tablespoons butter for about 7 to 8 minutes or until soft and tender. Add half the peeled chestnuts and sauté these along with the onions for another 5 minutes. Remove from the heat and set aside.

5. Wash the squabs very well, inside and out. Pull out any follicles of hair remaining on the birds. Pat them dry with paper towels. Season well with 1 teaspoon salt and ¼ teaspoon pepper. Spoon one-fourth of the onion and chestnut stuffing into each bird.

6. Melt 8 tablespoons butter over low heat in a casserole big enough to hold the 4 birds comfortably without leaving too much room around each one. When the butter has just melted, remove the casserole from the heat and allow it to cool. Once cool, roll the birds around in the melted butter, coating each one completely.

7. Place the squabs, breast side up, in the same casserole. Place the casserole on the bottom rack of the oven. Bake the birds, basting occasionally, for 1 hour.

8. While the birds are baking, purée the remaining chestnuts with the heavy cream in a blender or food processor. Season well with ¾ teaspoon salt and ½ teaspoon pepper. Keep this warm in the top of a double boiler, over low heat.

9. When the squabs are done, remove them and keep them warm on a platter covered loosely with foil.

10. Transfer the casserole drippings to a 9-inch skillet. Remove as much fat as possible from the drippings, and discard. Add the *glace de canard* to the drippings and bring to a simmer.

11. Whisk in 6 tablespoons of the chestnut purée. Season with salt and pepper to taste. The sauce should have a thick consistency but be quite dark in color. It should not taste heavily of the chestnut purée.

PRESENTATION

To serve, place a spoonful of the warm chestnut purée in the center of each warmed dinner plate. Place the squab on top of the purée and spoon some of the sauce over each bird. Serve immediately.

MENU ACCOMPANIMENT

You could start with Broccoli and Apple Soup (page 72) or Cold Oyster and Tamarind Soup (page 83). Serve a Green Salad with Walnut Oil (page 98) afterwards. Finish with the Cranberry Soufflé (page 413), Pumpkin Pie (page 405), or Lemon Almond Cake (page 380).

Boning a Turkey Breast

1. Before proceeding, remove the package of giblets from inside the turkey, wash the turkey inside and out and pat dry with paper towels.

With a sharp knife, cut the wings off at the first joint (see Boning a Duck, page 278, step 1). Keep these for your stockpot. Take care not to remove much breast meat with the wing.

2. Cut along the rib cage on either side of the breastbone, freeing the breast. Pull the whole breast toward you until you hear a cracking sound. Cut around the neck to free the breast from the carcass; remove the wishbone.

3. Turn the breast fleshside down. Holding the knife with the blade pointing toward the carcass, cut the breast from the bones pulling the bones up as you cut. Remove the flesh from both sides of the breastbone without splitting the breast in two. Remove any extraneous cartilage from the meat.

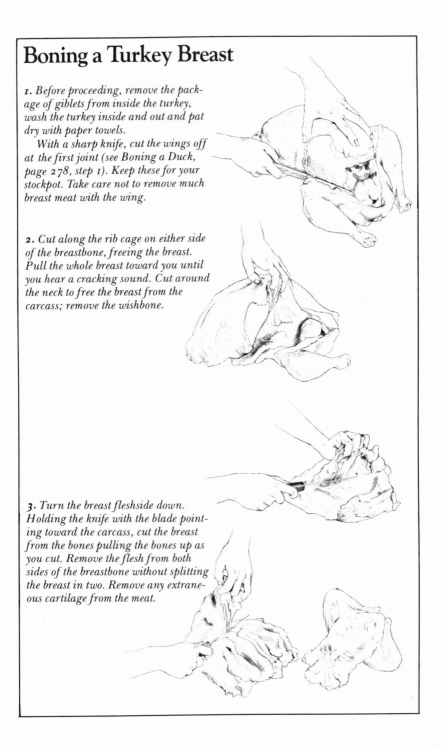

Stuffed Turkey Breast

THIS IS A lovely way to use turkey because the meat remains so moist. If you use flavorful olives the stuffing becomes a spicy contrast to the mild taste of the turkey meat. This dish tastes excellent cold.

PREPARATION TIME:
2 hours

COOKING TIME:
1 hour and 45 minutes

SERVES:
6 to 8

1   *8-pound fresh turkey*
1   *cup dry white wine*
½   *cup olive oil*
¼   *cup tarragon vinegar*
2   *large bay leaves*
1   *teaspoon thyme*
11 *tablespoons butter, plus 4 tablespoons softened*
½   *pound ground pork*
¼   *cup heavy cream*
2   *tablespoons minced shallots*
1   *small carrot, thinly sliced*
1   *small onion, minced*
1   *clove garlic, minced*
¼   *cup currants*
10 *imported pitted black olives*
2   *tablespoons fresh lemon juice*
½   *cup* demi-glace

4   *tablespoons minced fresh mint, optional*
    Salt
    Freshly ground pepper

1. Bone out the turkey breast. (See illustration, page 290.)

2. In a deep 8-quart enameled, glass, or stainless steel pot, combine the white wine, oil, vinegar, bay leaves, thyme, 1 tablespoon salt, and 1 tablespoon pepper. Marinate the breast in this mixture for 1 hour at least, while you prepare and cook the stuffing.

3. In one skillet, melt 2 tablespoons butter and sauté the ground pork over fairly high heat until it loses its pink color. Add the cream and reduce it over medium heat for about 5 to 7 minutes, or until it has been absorbed by the meat. Remove from the heat and cool to room temperature.

4. In a separate skillet, melt 3 tablespoons butter and sauté the shallots, carrot, onion, and garlic. Then cover and cook until soft. Remove from the heat and cool to room temperature.

5. When both mixtures are cool, combine them with the currants, olives, 1 tablespoon lemon juice, ½ teaspoon salt, and ¼ teaspoon pepper.

6. Preheat the oven to 450 degrees.

7. Remove the turkey from the marinade and pat dry. Stuff the breast and sew the two sides together to make a neat package. Place the turkey in a roasting pan.

8. Melt 6 tablespoons butter. When melted, brush about half the butter onto the turkey.

9. Place the turkey in the roasting pan on the bottom shelf of the oven. Roast for 1 hour, basting every 10 minutes with a combination of the butter that is browning on the bottom of the roasting pan and with the remaining melted butter.

10. Remove the turkey from the oven and allow it to rest in the pan for 10 minutes. Remove the turkey to a platter and keep it warm while you finish the sauce.

11. Discard the burnt butter from the pan, but keep the particles that are on the bottom of the roasting pan. Add the remaining shallots and ½ cup water to the pan and return the pan to the top of the stove. Bring the water to a boil, scraping up the browned particles into the water, creating a brown liquid sauce.

12. Add the remaining lemon juice and *demi-glace* and continue to heat over moderate heat for about 1 minute.

13. Whisk in the softened butter, tablespoon by tablespoon, and season with ½ teaspoon salt and ¼ teaspoon pepper.

PRESENTATION

Cut slices from the stuffed turkey and place them in the center of each warmed dinner plate. Spoon the sauce around the meat and place the mint leaves, if you are using them, on top of the sauce.

MENU ACCOMPANIMENT

First, serve either Wilted Greens Salad (page 96) or Smoked Fish Salad (page 106). Serve Floating Broccoli (page 329) and Souffléed Acorn Squash (page 356) as vegetable garnishes, on separate plates. For dessert, serve fresh fruit along with some Chocolate Truffles (page 408).

Game and Variety Meats

Venison Steak with Caper Sauce

PREPARATION TIME:
15 minutes
(Marinating: 24 hours)

COOKING TIME:
20 minutes

SERVES:
4

2   *1-pound venison steaks*
8   *tablespoons red wine vinegar*
4   *tablespoons olive oil*
1   *cup* demi-glace
1   *teaspoon Dijon mustard*
2   *tablespoons chopped capers*
1½ *cups heavy cream*
2   *tablespoons butter*
2   *tablespoons minced parsley*
    Salt
    Freshly ground pepper

1. Remove the center bone from the venison steaks. Cut each one in half, making 4 steaks out of the 2.

2. In a covered non-aluminum dish, marinate the steaks overnight in the refrigerator, in 2 tablespoons vinegar and 2 tablespoons oil.

3. An hour before serving, in a 10- or 12-inch skillet, reduce the remaining vinegar over high heat until only 2 tablespoons remain.

4. Add the *demi-glace*, mustard, capers, and cream to the vinegar and reduce in the skillet over medium heat, for about 5 minutes, or until the sauce coats a spoon. Season with salt and pepper to taste.

5. Transfer the sauce to a bowl and cover with a buttered piece of brown paper cut from a grocery bag. Set aside.

6. Remove the steaks from the marinade and pat them dry.

7. Heat 2 tablespoons oil and 2 tablespoons butter in the 12-inch skillet. When hot, add the steaks and sauté for about 5 minutes on each side. Remove them to a carving board and keep warm.

8. Degrease the skillet, and return it to the heat. Deglaze the skillet with the reserved sauce, scraping up all the browned particles into the sauce. Season with salt and pepper to taste.

PRESENTATION

Slice each steak across the grain into ¼-inch slices. Place some sauce in the center of warmed dinner plates. Pose sliced pieces of venison on top and sprinkle the sauce with minced parsley.

MENU ACCOMPANIMENT

Venison is an elegant fall or winter dish. Therefore, the rich Mussels in Puff Pastry (page 140) would be a fitting starter. You could serve the Souffléed Acorn Squash (page 356) on the side. Sautéed Grapes (page 336) or Sweet Potato Sauté (page 363) would also provide the right touch of color and sweetness for the venison. Cranberry Soufflé (page 408) and Chocolate Truffles (page 413) would be a glorious end to such a meal.

Rabbit with Raisin, Currant, and Red Wine Sauce

T HE SWEETNESS of the sauce in this recipe complements the gaminess of the rabbit. For this recipe you may buy frozen rabbit if your butcher does not have a source for fresh.

PREPARATION TIME:
30 minutes

COOKING TIME:
50 minutes

SERVES:
4

1   *whole rabbit, cut into 9 pieces*
½   *cup flour, mixed with ½ teaspoon freshly ground pepper and*
      1 teaspoon salt
13 *tablespoons butter*
½   *cup raisins*
¼   *cup dried currants*
1   *cup* glace de viande *or* demi-glace
1   *cup red wine*
¼   *cup minced chives*
      Salt
      Freshly ground pepper

   1. Preheat the oven to 400 degrees.
   2. Dredge 5 pieces of rabbit in the seasoned flour. Shake off any excess flour.

A rabbit cut in 9 pieces.

3. In a 12- to 14-inch skillet melt 3 tablespoons butter. Sauté these pieces over medium heat, for 5 minutes on each side, then transfer them to a rack placed on a large baking sheet.

4. Dredge the remaining rabbit pieces in the flour. Shake off any excess flour. Add an additional 3 tablespoons butter to the skillet and cook the final four pieces of rabbit in the same way.

5. Place all the rabbit on the rack and bake in the middle of the oven for 40 minutes.

6. While the rabbit is baking, combine the raisins, currants, 1 tablespoon butter, and ½ cup *glace de viande* in a saucepan. Cook for 1 minute and transfer the ingredients to a food processor. Purée in the processor until the mixture is smooth.

7. Five minutes before removing the rabbit from the oven, reduce the red wine by two-thirds in the skillet used to cook the raisins. Add the additional ½ cup *glace de viande* and the raisin and currant mixture. Whisk together until smooth.

8. Whisk 6 tablespoons softened butter and the minced chives into the sauce. Season with ¾ teaspoon salt and ½ teaspoon pepper.

PRESENTATION

Arrange the pieces of rabbit on a serving platter or on a warmed plate. Spoon the sauce over the meat.

MENU ACCOMPANIMENT

This rich and zesty dish should be ushered in by the Sweet Potato Soup (page 80). Serve it with a Leek Purée (page 341) and a Julienne of Winter Root Vegetables (page 345). Follow this with salad and end with Mocha Cream (page 415) or a Chocolate Sweetness (page 373).

Calves Liver with Leek Purée

WHEN BUYING liver, remember that it should be pale beige in color. A butcher who sells you deeply purpled liver as calves liver is selling you a tall story as well.

PREPARATION TIME:
35 minutes

COOKING TIME:
10 minutes

SERVES:
4

1   *medium-sized leek, white part only*
4½ *tablespoons butter*

2   *tablespoons heavy cream*
1   *pound calves liver*
½   *cup* glace de viande *or* demi-glace
    Salt
    Freshly ground pepper

How to cut a leek.

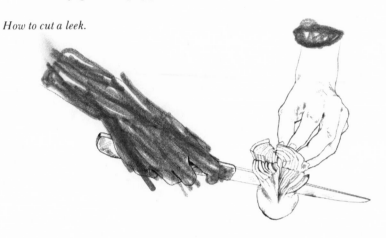

1. Cut the root end off the leek. With a sharp knife cut slashes in a cross pattern into the leek, starting at the stem end to within ½ inch above the root end. Wash the leek thoroughly, making sure it is entirely free of sand. Cut the leek into ¾-inch pieces.

2. In a small saucepan, combine the leek with ½ cup water and ½ tablespoon butter. Bring to a boil, cover, turn down the heat, and simmer gently for 30 minutes or until very soft. Add more water if it evaporates before the leek is tender. When it is cooked, the leek should have absorbed all the liquids; if not, drain off any excess.

3. Purée the leek in a blender or food processor with the heavy cream, ¼ teaspoon salt, and ⅛ teaspoon pepper. Set aside.●

4. Slice the liver into ⅛-inch thick slices. The slices should be cut on a slight diagonal, parallel to the longer side. (You should get about 14 slices out of 1 pound of liver.)

5. In a 12-inch skillet, melt 4 tablespoons butter over medium heat. When hot (and the bubbles have subsided) turn down the heat to a bare simmer. Add half the liver. Simmer on the gentle heat for 1 minute on the first side and 1½ minutes on the other. Remove to a plate and cover loosely with foil to keep warm and repeat the procedure with the second batch of liver.

6. Degrease the skillet. Add the *glace de viande* or *demi-glace* and any juices the liver may exude while resting. Simmer for 1 minute. Whisk in the leek purée and simmer for 1 minute.

PRESENTATION

Spoon some sauce on each of 4 warmed dinner plates and place slices of liver on top of the sauce.

MENU ACCOMPANIMENT

Precede this dish with a plate of assorted vegetables, such as Pumpkin Purée (page 349), Cauliflower Purée with Celery (page 331), and Sautéed Spinach (page 352). Serve the liver as a separate course and follow it with a simple salad.

Calves Liver with Currant Glaze

T HE TRICK to cooking liver well is to cut it into paper thin slices and literally float them in hot butter until they are cooked. Don't cook the liver at a high heat or it will toughen.

PREPARATION TIME:
40 minutes

COOKING TIME:
8 minutes

SERVES:
4

½   *cup dried currants*
2   *tablespoons red wine or sherry vinegar*
2   *tablespoons Cognac or brandy*
1   *pound calves liver*
6   *tablespoons butter*
1   *tablespoon minced shallots*
    Salt
    Freshly ground pepper

    1. In a small bowl, marinate the currants in the vinegar and Cognac for 30 minutes.●
    2. Meanwhile, using a razor-sharp knife, slice the liver into ⅛-inch thick slices. The slices should be cut on a slight diagonal, parallel to the longer side. (You should get about 14 slices out of 1 pound of liver.)
    3. In a 12-inch skillet, melt 4 tablespoons butter over medium heat. When hot (and the bubbles have subsided), turn down the heat to a bare simmer. Add half the liver. Simmer on this gentle heat for 1 minute on the first side and 1½ minutes on the other. Remove to a plate and cover loosely with foil to keep warm and repeat the procedure with the second batch of liver.
    4. Discard all but 1 tablespoon butter from the skillet. Add the shallots and sauté for 30 seconds.
    5. Add the currants with the vinegar and Cognac, as well as any juices the liver may have exuded while resting.

Raise the heat and cook over high heat for 30 seconds to burn off the alcohol. Turn the heat down and simmer for 1 minute, or until the currants are syrupy.

6. Whisk in the remaining 2 tablespoons butter, and remove from the heat immediately.

PRESENTATION

Place the liver on 4 warmed dinner plates. Season it with salt and pepper to taste. Spoon some currant glaze on each portion and serve immediately.

MENU ACCOMPANIMENT

See suggestions for Calves Liver with Leek Purée (page 300).

Sweetbreads with Cassis and Whole Shallots

ALL THE liquids in this sauce should be reduced almost to a syrup, which will coat each slice of sweetbread. We find it is best to slice sweetbreads after they are braised and reheat them in the sauce to ensure that each mouthful is enveloped in the luscious sauce. There is a classic tradition of weighting down sweetbreads, after they have been blanched. This is done in order to extract some of the moisture and firm up the flesh to make slicing them easier.

PREPARATION TIME:
2 hours and 45 minutes

COOKING TIME:
1 hour and 15 minutes

SERVES:
6 as a first course
4 as a main course

2 *pounds fresh veal sweetbreads*
1 *small onion*
1 *stalk celery*
1 *carrot*
4 *tablespoons butter*
2 *cups beef or chicken stock*
½ *cup Zinfandel red wine*
5 *tablespoons cassis*
32 *shallots*
¼ *cup* demi-glace
1 *tablespoon red wine or sherry vinegar*
3 *tablespoons minced parsley*
   Salt
   Freshly ground pepper

   1. Place the sweetbreads in a bowl. Cover them with cold water and soak them for 1 hour, changing the water three times.
   2. Drain the sweetbreads. Place them in a sauté pan, 3 inches high and about 9 inches wide. Cover them with water and, over low heat, very slowly bring the water to a boil. As the water comes to a boil, turn the sweetbreads over with tongs, and simmer them gently for 1 minute. Drain and refresh them under cold water. Discard the poaching water.
   3. Remove the white fatty particles and the grayish rubbery gristle from the sweetbreads. If you pull some membrane away as you remove the fat and gristle, it is all right. Wrap the cleaned sweetbreads in a cloth. Place them between two boards and weight them down under a 5-pound weight (a bag of sugar or flour) for 1 hour.

4. While you are weighting down the sweetbreads, mince the onion, celery, and carrot.

5. In the same sauté pan you used to parboil the sweetbreads, melt 2 tablespoons butter over medium heat. When the butter is just melted, add the minced vegetables and ½ teaspoon salt. Cover and stew the vegetables over low heat for 15 to 20 minutes, or until tender.

6. When the vegetables are tender and the sweetbreads have been weighted down, place the sweetbreads on top of the vegetables. Add the stock, wine, 4 tablespoons cassis, the whole shallots, 1 teaspoon salt, and ¼ teaspoon pepper. Raise the heat and bring to a boil, then lower the heat to simmer. Cover the pan, and cook for 40 minutes.

7. After the sweetbreads are cooked, remove them to a cutting board. Strain out the solids from the liquid and reserve only the liquid and the whole cooked shallots while discarding the rest.

8. Put the strained liquids in a 10-inch skillet. Add the *demi-glace*, the remaining cassis, and the vinegar. Bring to a boil over high heat, skim off the fat, and reduce the liquids to 1 cup. Season with ½ teaspoon salt and ¼ teaspoon pepper. (The sauce may seem salty at this point, but when the sweetbreads are added, the seasoning will correct itself.)

9. Slice the sweetbreads into ¼-inch thick slices across the grain.

10. Reheat the cup of liquid in a 10-inch skillet. Add the sweetbreads and whole shallots and heat through, uncovered, over high heat for about 5 minutes, reducing the liquid until it coats the sweetbreads and is syrupy. Remove from the heat.

11. Whisk in the remaining 2 tablespoons butter and stir until it is melted into the sauce. Taste, and adjust the seasoning. Add the parsley to the skillet and toss the sweetbreads around to coat them with the parsley.

PRESENTATION

Serve each portion in the center of a warmed dinner plate.

MENU ACCOMPANIMENT

If you serve this as an appetizer, follow it with Veal Loin Laced with Peppercorns (page 220) or Pork with Cracked Peppercorns (page 188), or plain roast chicken or roast lamb. If served as a main course, precede with a plate of 5 assorted vegetable purées and sautés. End the meal with a sherbet or ice.

Cold Sweetbreads with Oranges

I N THIS recipe, the sweetbreads are completely separated into fine nodules. The resulting texture is quite smooth. The unusual combination of oranges with sweetbreads works well, if you make sure to remove all the white bitter pith when peeling the oranges.

PREPARATION TIME:
3 hours and 45 minutes

COOKING TIME:
45 minutes

SERVES:
6 as first course
4 as main course

2 *pounds veal sweetbreads*
4 *navel oranges*
   Juice of 1 lemon
½ *cup white wine*
½ *cup sliced onions*
5 *tablespoons olive oil*
2½ *tablespoons tarragon vinegar*
1 *tablespoon minced shallots*
1 *egg yolk*
   Salt
   Freshly ground pepper

1. Place the sweetbreads in a deep bowl. Cover them with cold water and soak for 1 hour, changing the water three times.

2. Drain the sweetbreads. Place them in a sauté pan, 3 inches high and about 9 inches wide. Cover them with water and very slowly bring the water to a boil over low heat. As the water comes to a boil turn the sweetbreads over, with tongs, and simmer them gently for 1 minute. Drain and refresh them under cold water. Discard the poaching water.

3. Remove the white fatty particles and rubbery grayish gristle from the sweetbreads. Wrap the cleaned sweetbreads in a cloth. Place them between two boards and weight them down under a 5-pound weight (a bag of sugar or flour) for 1 hour.

4. While you are weighting the sweetbreads down, peel 3 of the oranges over a bowl. Use a sharp paring knife and peel the oranges so that both the outer skin and inner white membrane are removed. Then section out triangular pieces of orange from within the inner membrane. Place these in the bowl and set aside.

5. After the sweetbreads have been weighted down, combine the lemon juice, white wine, 1 cup water, and sliced onions in the same pan you used to parboil the sweetbreads. Add the sweetbreads, cover, and bring to a boil over medium heat. Turn the heat down and simmer gently for 35 minutes. Turn off the heat and leave sweetbreads in the pan for 10 minutes longer.

6. Cut the remaining orange in half and squeeze out its juice. Grate the peel of one of the halves and combine it in a food processor or blender with the juice from the orange, the oil, vinegar, shallots, and any juice the sectioned oranges have given off in the bowl. Blend all these together for 1 minute in the processor or blender. Season with salt and pepper to taste and set aside. This is now an orange vinaigrette.

7. When the sweetbreads are cooked, remove them from the cooking liquids and pat dry with paper towels.

8. With your fingers, separate the sweetbreads from their fine, enveloping white membrane. Sweetbreads will separate naturally into nodules ranging from ¼-to¾-inch in size. Place these in a deep bowl and cover with one-half of the orange vinaigrette. Season with salt and pepper to taste and marinate in the refrigerator for 1 hour.

9. After an hour, remove the sweetbreads from the marinade. Reserve the marinade if there is any left.

10. Blend the egg yolk for 30 seconds in food processor. Very slowly, in a steady stream, blend the reserved orange vinaigrette and any reserved marinade into the egg yolk. Season with salt and pepper to taste.

PRESENTATION

Spoon some sauce on 4 chilled dinner plates. Place the sweetbreads on top and place peeled orange sections on top of the sweetbreads, in a cartwheel pattern.

If this is a main course, then serve it along with a spinach or mixed green salad. Precede it with a soup. If you serve this as a first course, follow it with a simple roast dish such as plain Roast Duck (page 273) garnished with two vegetable purées, perhaps Turnip (page 365) and Butternut Squash (page 360). For dessert, serve Upside-Down Pecan Pie (page 403).

Frogs' Legs with Fresh Herb and Butter Sauce

T HE STEAMING process in this recipe keeps the frogs' legs moist and tender. They are then quickly sautéed to a golden brown. The contrasting texture of the flesh and the crisp skin is quite delicious.

PREPARATION TIME:
20 minutes

COOKING TIME:
15 minutes

SERVES:
4

6   pairs cleaned frogs' legs
13 tablespoons butter
½   cup flour for dredging, mixed with ½ teaspoon freshly
      ground pepper and 1 teaspoon salt
¼   cup minced shallots
4   cloves garlic, minced
1   cup white wine
1   tablespoon lemon juice
½   cup loosely packed chopped basil
     Salt
     Freshly ground pepper

1. Bring to a boil 2 inches of water in a 4-quart saucepan. Put 3 pairs of frogs' legs in a vegetable steamer and place the steamer in the saucepan. Steam the legs, covered, for 3 minutes over medium heat. Set aside. Repeat for the remaining 3 pairs of legs.

2. Melt 8 tablespoons butter over medium heat in a 9-inch skillet. When the butter is melted, turn off the heat and let it cool for 5 minutes.

3. Preheat the oven to 250 degrees.

4. Dip 3 pairs of legs in the butter and then immediately dredge with the seasoned flour, shaking off any excess flour.

5. In another 9-inch skillet, heat the remaining melted butter until it begins to bubble. Place the legs in the hot butter and sauté over high heat for 6 minutes. Turn frequently so the legs don't stick to the bottom of the pan.

6. Transfer the legs when they are sautéed to a rack on top of a cookie sheet and place them in the oven to keep them warm and crisp. Repeat dredging and sautéing for the remaining 3 pairs of legs.

7. Clean the skillet and in it melt 4 tablespoons butter. Add the shallots and garlic and sauté then for 1 minute over medium heat.

8. Add the white wine and the lemon juice and reduce this by one-half.

9. Add the basil, and continue cooking for 30 seconds. Whisk in 1 tablespoon butter and season to taste with salt and pepper.

PRESENTATION

Place 2 to 4 legs on each plate and spoon a small amount of sauce over each pair.

MENU ACCOMPANIMENT

If you start with a soup, serve the Kohlrabi (page 74) or Jerusalem Artichoke (page 81). You might also begin with a salad, such as the Smoked Fish (page 106), Piquant Chicken Liver (page 100) or Steamed Vegetable (page 92). Whether the frogs' legs are served as a first or second course, follow them with a simple dish like the Veal Laced with Peppercorns (page 220) or the Beef Fillet with Pan Juices (page 168) and a medley of vegetables. For dessert, serve Fresh Cherries in Puff Pastry (page 392).

Ices

Grapefruit Sherbet

A SHERBET differs from an ice in that it has milk as one of its ingredients. Most American sherbets call for a high ratio of milk to fruit juice and pulp; the French sorbets call for a higher ration of fruit pulp. We have developed a recipe which is somewhere in between. If the syrup looks a bit curdled when you add the milk, don't worry, this all smooths out in the freezing process.

PREPARATION TIME:
25 minutes

COOLING TIME:
5 hours or overnight

FREEZING TIME:
2 hours

SPECIAL EQUIPMENT:
Ice cream freezer

SERVES:
10 (makes about 1½ quarts)

1   *cup sugar*
3   *to 4 grapefruits*
1   *cup milk*

1. Combine the sugar and 1 cup water in a 2-quart, heavy-bottomed saucepan. Bring to a boil over low heat, stirring the bottom once in a while so that the sugar crystals dissolve. Boil the mixture for 2 minutes then remove it from the heat and cool while you proceed with the grapefruit.

2. Remove all the outer skins and white pith from the grapefruit. Remove triangular sections of the fruit from within the inner white membranes. Remove all the pits. Place all the fruit in a food processor and blend for 1 minute, or until the pulp and juice are puréed together.

3. Measure out 2 cups puréed fruit and add them to the sugar syrup. When the sugar syrup and fruit are completely cool, refrigerate until cold.

4. Right before freezing, add the milk to the cold mixture and proceed with the directions that come with your ice cream maker. Freeze until hard.

Lime Ice

P ARTICULARLY REFRESHING in the summertime, you can garnish this ice with fresh strawberries and a dash of white rum.

PREPARATION TIME:
30 minutes

COOKING TIME:
10 minutes

FREEZING TIME:
5 hours or overnight

SERVES:
4 to 6

1   *cup freshly squeezed lime juice (from approximately 8 to 10 limes)*
1   *cup sugar*
    Grated peels of 2 limes
½   *pint washed and hulled strawberries, optional*
2   *tablespoons white rum, optional*

1. Combine 2 cups water and the lime juice in a 2-quart saucepan. Dissolve the sugar in this mixture.

2. Place the saucepan on a low heat and slowly bring the mixture to a boil. Using a pastry brush, clean the sides of the pan down with cold water to eliminate any sugar crystals.

3. Once the mixture has come to a boil, let it simmer for exactly 5 minutes. Any more cooking time will evaporate too much water and leave you with an ice that is too sweet. Remove it from the heat and cool to room temperature.

4. Add the grated rind. Then transfer the ice to empty ice trays or a shallow bowl, and freeze for at least 5 hours, scraping down the sides of the pan into the mixture every hour.

5. Just before serving, place the ice in a food processor with a tablespoon of the white rum. (This step can be omitted if you are not adding in the rum.)

PRESENTATION

Serve the lime ice in wine glasses, garnish with the strawberries, and/or a splash of white rum.

Mango Ice

USE VERY RIPE mangoes to make this ice terrific. If a mango is soft to the touch and smells fragrant it is ripe. This is best eaten the same day it is made.

PREPARATION TIME:
30 minutes

FREEZING TIME:
2 hours

SPECIAL EQUIPMENT:
Ice cream maker or food processor

SERVES:
6

½   *cup sugar*
2   *to 2 ½ pounds ripe mangoes, peeled and cubed*
Juice of ½ lemon
Pinch of salt

1. Slowly bring 1½ cups water and the sugar to a boil in a 2-quart saucepan. Using a pastry brush dipped in cold water, wipe down the sides of the pan in order to eliminate any sugar crystals. Boil for 5 minutes exactly. Remove it from the heat and cool to room temperature.
2. While the syrup is cooling, purée the fruit in either a blender or food processor. You should have about 2 cups of purée. Stir in the lemon juice and a pinch of salt.
3. Stir the cooled syrup into the mango purée and freeze according to the directions of your ice cream maker. (You can make this by simply freezing it in an ice tray and

stirring it once or twice during the freezing process. You would, however, have to purée the ice in a food processor just before serving in order to achieve a good eating consistency.)

PRESENTATION

Serve this in tall chilled wine or champagne glasses.

Tomato and Basil Ice

MOST OF US are used to sweet fruit ices and sherbets, so this savory tomato ice will come as a surprise to your guests. It is really like a frozen gazpacho—slightly piquant, simple to make, and exceedingly refreshing on a hot summer day. Because it contains no sugar syrup, there is nothing to prevent the mixture from freezing into a solid block of ice if it sits in the freezer too long. Therefore, it is necessary to eat the ice immediately after it has frozen but is still somewhat mushy. If you miss the timing on this, you can break down the ice by giving it a whirl in a food processor until you again have a mushy consistency.

PREPARATION TIME:
25 minutes

FREEZING TIME:
2 hours

SERVES:
6 to 8

1½ pounds tomatoes, peeled, seeded, and roughly chopped
½ tablespoon minced shallots
2 tablespoons minced fresh basil or parsley
 Minced parsley for garnish
 Salt
 Freshly ground pepper

1. In a blender or food processor, blend the tomatoes, shallots, and basil or parsley, ¾ teaspoon salt, and ¼ teaspoon pepper until it is all liquefied.

2. Pour the mixture into refrigerator ice trays and freeze for about 2 hours, stirring every 30 minutes.

PRESENTATION

Serve in tall wine or champagne glasses the way you would any other sherbet or ice. Sprinkle minced parsley on the top of each portion.

MENU ACCOMPANIMENT

Serve this sherbet as an "intermezzo" or as a starter in the summertime. Avoid dishes with tomato in them in courses to follow.

Vegetables

Artichoke and Walnut Sauté

T HE CRUNCHY walnuts in this dish are a perfect foil for the artichokes — their flavor really comes through, unobscured by the addition of a pungent sauce.

PREPARATION TIME:
30 minutes

COOKING TIME:
1 hour and 15 minutes

SERVES:
4

3   *large (10-ounce) artichokes*
1   *lemon*
⅓   *cup walnuts, roughly chopped*
4   *tablespoons softened butter*
3   *tablespoons minced parsley*
     Salt
     Freshly ground pepper

1. Wash the artichokes well and put them in an 8-quart heavy-bottomed stainless steel or enamel pot. Cover with water. Squeeze the juice from a half lemon into the water, then add the squeezed lemon half to the pot. Cover, bring to a boil over high heat, then lower the heat and simmer for 45 minutes, or until the artichokes are tender. Drain the artichokes, upside down in a colander, and cool for 15 to 25 minutes.

2. Using a tablespoon, scrape off the soft part of each artichoke leaf into a bowl. Don't scrape off the upper part of the leaf, or the vegetable will be bitter. From each heart, remove the inner choke and discard. Cut each heart

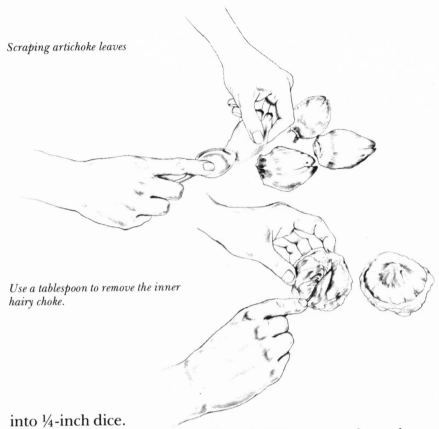

Scraping artichoke leaves

Use a tablespoon to remove the inner hairy choke.

into ¼-inch dice.

3. Squeeze the remaining half lemon and set the juice aside.●

4. Just before serving, melt 2 tablespoons butter over medium heat in a 9-inch skillet. When hot, add the artichoke pieces, walnuts, ¾ teaspoon salt, and ¼ teaspoon pepper. Sauté for 1 to 2 minutes, or until hot throughout. Remove from the heat.

5. Add the reserved lemon juice, remaining 2 tablespoons butter, and the minced parsley. Mix it all together and serve immediately.

MENU ACCOMPANIMENT

In the summertime, this is a novel garnish for meat, poultry, or fish. Avoid serving with powerful recipes, as the delicate flavor of the artichokes might be overwhelmed.

Sautéed Asparagus

I F YOU prepare this dish for an elegant occasion, perhaps you should consider using only the asparagus tips.
But, if you are conscientious about peeling the stalks,
they, too, are delicious when steamed and sautéed correctly.

PREPARATION TIME:
30 minutes

COOKING TIME:
15 minutes

SERVES:
6

4   *pounds medium-sized asparagus*
4   *tablespoons butter*
3   *tablespoons minced shallots*
1   *tablespoon wine vinegar*
    Salt
    Freshly ground pepper

1. Cut the ends off the asparagus about 2 to 3 inches
from the bottom of the stalk, and discard. With a vegetable
peeler, peel the asparagus down from the tip.

2. Bring to a boil 2 inches of water in a 4-quart
saucepan. Place a vegetable steamer in the saucepan, lay
the asparagus pieces in the steamer, cover, and steam the
asparagus pieces for 5 minutes. Make sure the asparagus
are above the water level.

3. Melt the butter in a skillet. Add the shallots and
cook gently over low heat for 1 to 2 minutes. Mix in the

steamed asparagus and stir until the shallot and butter mixture completely coats the vegetables. Sauté for 3 to 5 minutes more, or until the asparagus are tender.

4. Add the vinegar and turn up the heat for 30 seconds while you rapidly stir the contents of the pan. Season with salt and pepper to taste, and serve immediately.●

MENU ACCOMPANIMENT

As long as asparagus are in season, serve this with meats, poultry, and fish.

Asparagus Spears and Hollandaise Sauce in Puff Pastry

THIS ELEGANT DISH makes an excellent appetizer or first course. Take special care with the hollandaise sauce—it is better to serve it tepid, than risk curdling the eggs by overheating.

PREPARATION TIME:
30 minutes

COOKING TIME:
1 hour

SERVES:
6 to 8

6   *to 8 triangles puff pastry (see page 388)*
16 *to 32 asparagus spears, depending on size*
4   *egg yolks*
1   *tablespoon lemon juice*
6   *tablespoons heavy cream*
½   *pound butter, cut into 16 tablespoon-sized pieces*
    Salt
    Freshly ground pepper

1. Preheat the oven to 450 degrees.

2. Remove the pastry rectangles from the freezer and place them on a baking sheet which has a lip around all its edges. This will catch any butter leaking out of the pastry. With a sharp paring knife, make decorative cross-hatch lines on top of each rectangle. Bake for 10 minutes.

3. Lower the temperature to 375 degrees and bake for another 15 to 20 minutes or until the pastry has turned golden brown and the inner layers are baked. To check this, remove one of the baked rectangles from the oven and pull it apart. If the inside looks very pasty and wet, bake for 10 minutes more.

4. Remove the pastry from the oven and set aside to cool on a cake rack. When cool enough to handle, separate each rectangle in half horizontally as you would 2 halves of a sandwich.

5. While the puff pastry squares are baking, trim 2 to 3 inches of stalk from the bottom of the asparagus and discard. Using a standard vegetable peeler, gently hold the tip of the asparagus in the palm of your hand and peel the stalk from just below the tip of the asparagus towards the bottom.●

6. About 15 to 20 minutes before serving, bring 2 inches of water in a 6-quart saucepan to a boil. Place a vegetable steamer in the bottom of the pot and lay the asparagus in neat rows in the steamer. The asparagus should be above, not in the boiling water and may be stacked on top of each other. Gently steam the asparagus, covered, for 5 to 10 minutes, depending on their size. They should be tender but still retain their crunch.

7. Remove the asparagus from the heat and set aside. Pat them dry with paper towels.

8. While the asparagus are steaming, make the sauce. In a non-aluminum saucepan, over very low heat, beat the egg yolks, lemon juice, and cream together with a wire whisk for approximately 2 minutes, or until the mixture forms ribbons.

9. When the eggs feel lukewarm to the touch, begin whisking in the butter, piece by piece. (If the butter gets too hot it will begin to separate. If this does happen, remove the pan from the heat and stir in a few additional tablespoons of cream. The mixture should smooth itself out. If the mixture gets very hot, the eggs will curdle and you will have to start over again.)

10. Continue adding the butter until all of it has been whisked into the sauce. Season the sauce with ½ teaspoon salt and ¼ teaspoon pepper. Remove from the heat.

11. Keep the sauce in a warm place (not in the oven!) while you begin to assemble the dish. Stir the sauce every minute or so to prevent a crust from forming.

PRESENTATION

Place one puff pastry half on a plate. Arrange a layer of asparagus spears on the pastry then spoon sauce on top. Top off with the second half of the pastry. The sauce should flow over the asparagus and the bottom half of the pastry onto the plate.

MENU ACCOMPANIMENT

This should be served as an appetizer to an elegant dinner party. Follow it with Boned Saddle of Lamb (page 206), for example. Avoid rich cream sauces in the second course because the hollandaise sauce is very rich.

Steamed Avocado

THIS GARNISH IS unusual and goes well with chicken or fish. Be sure to pick ripe avocados as they have more flavor. To choose a ripe avocado, check to see if the narrower tip (blossom end) is soft.

PREPARATION TIME:
5 minutes

COOKING TIME:
5 minutes

SERVES:
4

2   *large ripe avocados*
1   *lemon, cut in half*
    Salt
    White pepper

1. Bring ½- to 1-inch of water in the bottom of a 4-quart saucepan to a boil. Place a vegetable steamer in the saucepan.

2. While the water is coming to a boil, peel the avocados and cut them into vertical slices about ¼-inch thick. Sprinkle the slices with lemon juice so that they don't discolor.

3. Place the avocado pieces in the steamer in a neat layer. Make sure they are above the water level. Cover the pot and steam for 3 minutes, or until the avocados are just warm. They should not cook longer or they will begin to turn gray and lose their crunch. Season with salt and pepper to taste.

This is wonderful as a garnish for Chicken Breasts with Hot Tomato Vinaigrette (page 262).

Floating Broccoli

IN THIS DISH, the broccoli stalks are cooked separately from the flowerets and puréed with butter and cream. The flowerets are steamed and half are then folded into the purée. The remaining half are placed on top of the purée as if they were floating.

PREPARATION TIME:
15 minutes

COOKING TIME:
20 minutes

SERVES:
4

1   *bunch of broccoli*
4   *tablespoons butter*
2   *tablespoons heavy cream*
    Salt
    Freshly ground pepper

1. Trim 3 inches from the bottom of the broccoli stalks and discard.

2. Separate the tiny flower heads from the remaining stalks, making sure you break them into little pieces.

3. Bring to a boil 2 quarts of water with 1 tablespoon salt. Drop the broccoli stalks into the boiling water and cook them for 15 minutes, or until tender. Drain well.

4. In a food processor, or with a food mill, purée the cooked stalks with the butter, cream, ¾ teaspoon salt, and ¼ teaspoon pepper until very smooth.

5. Reheat the purée in the top of a double boiler.

6. While the purée is reheating, steam the flowerets over water for 5 minutes, or until tender but still bright green. Remove them from the heat, drain, and pat them dry with paper towels.

PRESENTATION

Fold half the flowerets into the purée and spoon the purée into a serving bowl. Place the remaining flowerets on top, flower side up, covering the surface of the purée.

MENU ACCOMPANIMENT

Served by itself, this is a wonderful appetizer. As a vegetable garnish it would overpower a delicate fish dish, but would be excellent with beef, pork, lamb, poultry, and venison.

Cauliflower Purée with Celery

PREPARATION TIME:
20 minutes

COOKING TIME:
35 minutes

SERVES:
4

1 head (14 to 16 ounces) cauliflower, trimmed and cut into
     flowerets
½ cup heavy cream
3 tablespoons long grain rice
3 tablespoons butter
2 stalks celery, cut into ¼-inch dice
3 small or 2 medium shallots, minced
     Salt
     Freshly ground white pepper

1. Put cauliflower flowerets, cream, 1 cup water, rice, and ½ teaspoon salt in a 4-quart saucepan. Cover and bring to a boil over medium heat. Lower the heat to a simmer, and cook, covered, for 10 to 12 minutes, or until the rice has absorbed the liquid and is tender. Remove from the heat and set aside.

2. Melt the butter in a 1-quart saucepan. Add the celery, shallots, ½ teaspoon salt, and ½ teaspoon white pepper. Cover and simmer for 15 minutes, or until the celery is tender but still has a crunch. Be sure to cook this over low heat so that celery and shallots do not brown.

3. In a food processor, purée the cauliflower and rice with salt and white pepper to taste. Fold the cooked celery into purée and reheat in the top of a double boiler.

Shredded Carrots with Orange Juice

T HIS SIMPLE way of preparing carrots is bound to convert many of the people who normally cannot abide this vegetable cooked.

PREPARATION TIME:
30 minutes

COOKING TIME:
10 minutes

SERVES:
4 to 6

1 *pound peeled carrots*
8 *tablespoons butter*
Grated rind and juice of 1 large navel orange
Salt
Freshly ground pepper

1. Shred the carrots on the large holes of a hand grater or in a food processor.

2. In a 9- or 10-inch skillet, melt the butter. When hot, add the shredded carrots and the grated orange rind. Sauté together over high heat for 2 minutes, turning them frequently with a slotted spoon.

3. Add the orange juice and reduce over high heat for 1 or 2 minutes longer. Season with salt and pepper to taste. (If you make this in advance, remove the carrots to a bowl with a slotted spoon. Reduce the liquids in the skillet to 1 tablespoon and reserve. To reheat, sauté the carrots in

1 tablespoon butter over high heat for 1 minute or until hot. Add the tablespoon of reduced liquid and serve.)

Shredded Cucumber with Dill

M OST PEOPLE use cucumbers in a summer salad or as a garnish for a sandwich. When served hot, they make a lovely light vegetable dish. The marriage of cucumber and dill is traditional, but take care to sauté the cucumbers rapidly or they will lose their crunch.

PREPARATION TIME:
2 hours and 20 minutes

COOKING TIME:
3 minutes

SERVES:
4

4   *pounds (6 medium) cucumbers*
6   *tablespoons butter*
1½ *tablespoons freshly snipped dill*
     Salt
     Freshly ground pepper

1. Two hours before sautéing, peel the cucumbers and slice each one lengthwise. With a small spoon, scrape out and discard the seeds. Grate them on the large holes of a hand grater, Mouli grater, or in a food processor. Place them with 1 teaspoon salt in a sieve, over a bowl. After 2 hours, press down on the cucumbers with your hands to extract as much moisture as possible.●

2. Just before serving, melt the butter in a skillet over medium high heat. When the butter is just about to turn brown, sauté the cucumbers for 1 minute. Sprinkle on the dill, season with ½ teaspoon salt and ¼ teaspoon pepper.

PRESENTATION

If this is to be used as the sole vegetable garnish to a dish, place the cucumbers in a ring around the entrée.

MENU ACCOMPANIMENT

Because this has a delicate flavor and texture, serve it with milder flavored recipes, such as veal, chicken, sweetbreads, or fish.

Eggplant Flan

THIS FLAN is made of ingredients ordinarily used in a ratatouille, which are then set in a custard of egg and cream. Be sure to cook the vegetables long enough so that they mellow and taste sweet.

PREPARATION TIME:
1 hour

COOKING TIME:
1¼ hours to 1½ hours

SERVES:
6

1   *eggplant*
12   *tablespoons butter*
2   *small (¼-pound) onions, minced*
1   *red pepper, cut into ¼-inch julienne pieces*
1   *pound tomatoes, peeled, seeded, and chopped*
1   *egg*
½   *cup heavy cream*
     Salt
     Freshly ground pepper

    1. Cut the eggplant into ½-inch thick slices and then cut each slice into quarters. Sprinkle the eggplant with 1 teaspoon salt. Lay the eggplant between paper towels and place a weight on top. Leave for 45 minutes to extract the juices.
    2. Meanwhile, melt 4 tablespoons butter in a 12-inch skillet. When hot, add the onions and sauté over medium heat for about 3 minutes. Add the peppers and con-

tinue to sauté for about 15 minutes, stirring frequently so the vegetables don't burn. Add the tomatoes and simmer over very low heat for another 10 minutes, or until the liquid has evaporated. The tomatoes should be melted into a near purée. Season with ½ teaspoon salt and ¼ teaspoon pepper. Remove from the heat and set aside.

3. When the eggplant slices have been weighted for 45 minutes, melt the remainder of the butter in a large skillet. When the butter is about to turn brown, add the eggplant and sauté over medium high heat for a few minutes, or until the eggplant has absorbed the butter and has turned golden brown. Cover the skillet, reduce the heat, and simmer for about 20 minutes, or until the eggplant is very soft. Remove the cover and sauté for a few minutes more to evaporate any water. Season with salt and pepper to taste.●

4. Preheat the oven to 350 degrees.

5. Combine the eggplant with the cooked peppers, onions, and tomatoes. Taste, and adjust the seasonings. Spoon the mixture into a 9-inch round glass or ceramic oven-proof dish.

6. Combine the egg with the cream. Season with ¼ teaspoon salt and ¼ teaspoon pepper. Spoon the liquid over the vegetables. With a fork lift the vegetables here and there so that cream can seep to the bottom of the dish. Bake for 20 minutes or until the custard has firmed but is still creamy.

PRESENTATION

Cut into wedges and serve immediately.

MENU ACCOMPANIMENT

A rich and robustly flavored garnish, serve this with roasted meats, such as Herbed Leg of Lamb with Anchovy Butter (page 200) or Boneless Rib Roast with Roasted

Garlic (page 170). The flan works very well as a first course, provided you do not follow it with a course in which cream dominates or one which will not stand up to this hearty flavor.

Fennel Purée

ALTHOUGH THIS vegetable is puréed, there remains quite a bit of texture in it because of the slight crunch of the rice and of the fennel. One could, after it is puréed, pass it through a sieve to eliminate that coarse texture, but we find it is not as interesting.

PREPARATION TIME:
20 minutes

COOKING TIME:
35 minutes

SERVES:
4

2   *medium-sized fennel bulbs*
6   *tablespoons butter*
2   *tablespoons long grain rice*
¼   *cup heavy cream*
     Salt
     Freshly ground pepper

1. Cut the fennel bulbs from the stalks at the junction where the stalks sprout out from the bulb; discard the stalks. Cut the root end off the bulb. Cut each bulb in two.

You will see a white, triangular-shaped core. Cut that out and discard it. Wash the fennel in cold water and roughly chop it into large pieces.

2. Melt 4 tablespoons butter in a 10-inch skillet over medium heat. When hot and bubbly, add the fennel and ½ teaspoon of salt. Lower the heat, cover, and simmer gently for 30 minutes, or until the fennel is tender. If you find while you are simmering the fennel that it is sticking to the bottom of the skillet, add some water.

3. While the fennel is cooking, bring ½ cup water to a boil in a small saucepan. When boiling, slowly add the rice, lower the heat, cover the saucepan, and simmer for 12 to 15 minutes, or until the rice is tender. Remove from the heat and set aside.

4. Put the rice, cooked fennel, and any liquid in the skillet in the container of a food processor, along with 2 tablespoons butter, the cream, ¼ teaspoon salt, and ¼ teaspoon pepper. Purée, and adjust the seasonings. Serve immediately so that the mixture does not get too cold. (*Note:* If you do not own a food processor, you may pass the fennel and rice through a food mill, then beat in the additional butter, cream, and seasonings.) If you are not going to eat the purée right away, you may reheat it in a double boiler until hot. Don't overheat or the butter will weep out of the purée.

MENU ACCOMPANIMENT

This rich purée should not be served with another purée in which cream dominates. Serve with Shrimp in Bordelaise Sauce (page 157), Steak with Bordelaise Sauce (page 182), Pork with Cracked Peppercorns (page 188) or Sautéed Rib Lamb Chops with Rosemary and Thyme (page 215).

Sautéed Grapes

WHEN LIGHTLY dusted with flour and sautéed, grapes make a fine accompaniment to duck, rock cornish game hens, or lamb.

PREPARATION TIME:
10 minutes

COOKING TIME:
5 minutes

SERVES:
4

¾   *pound seedless green grapes*
⅓   *cup flour*
2   *tablespoons butter*
     Salt

1. Remove the tiny stems from the grapes. You should end up with about 2 cups of the fruit.

2. Roll the grapes around in a shallow dish filled with the flour. Transfer them to a sieve and shake off any excess flour.

3. Melt the butter in a 9-inch skillet. When hot, add the grapes and sauté them over medium heat, rolling them around and shaking the pan so that all sides cook.

4. After 2 minutes remove from the heat. Season with ¼ teaspoon salt or to taste. (The grapes may be quickly reheated just before serving by sautéing over a high heat for 30 seconds to 1 minute until the grapes are hot.)

Kale Simmered in Cream

KALE IS a lovely vegetable, too often overlooked. Its slight bitter edge is softened here by the addition of cream. This dish goes particularly well with pork.

PREPARATION TIME:
20 minutes

COOKING TIME:
20 minutes

SERVES:
4

¾ *pound fresh kale*
1 *cup heavy cream*
¼ *teaspoon grated lime rind*
Salt
Freshly ground pepper

1. Trim the kale of its tough outer stalk and wash it well because, like spinach, it is usually very sandy.

2. In a 9-inch skillet, reduce the cream over medium heat until only ½ cup remains.

3. In a 4-quart saucepan, bring 1 inch of water to a boil. Drop the kale into the pan and cook, uncovered, over medium heat for 10 to 15 minutes, or until the leaves are tender but still have some bite to them.

4. Drain and rinse the kale under cold running water. Squeeze out the excess moisture from the leaves and chop them roughly. Set aside.●

5. Just before serving, bring the reduced cream to a simmer in the skillet. Add the chopped kale leaves, lime rind, salt, and pepper. Heat, and serve immediately.

Leek Purée

U NFORTUNATELY, leeks are overpriced in this country so this has become an extravagant dish. The secret to this purée and most other purées, is to add butter rather than cream to smooth it out. It may seem like a lot of work for the amount of purée that remains, but each mouthful is heavenly. When you take the trouble to pass the purée through a sieve to remove any stray vegetable fibers, this purée will literally melt in your mouth.

PREPARATION TIME:
30 minutes

COOKING TIME:
45 minutes

SPECIAL EQUIPMENT:
China cap, drum sieve or fine meshed sieve

SERVES:
4

4   *pounds leeks, white bulb with 1 inch of the green stalk left on*
½   *cup chicken stock, or ¼ cup* glace de volaille *combined with*
      ¼ cup water
8   *tablespoons butter*
     Salt
     Freshly ground pepper

    1. Cut the root ends off the leeks. Slice them in half and wash each piece thoroughly, making sure they are entirely free of sand. Cut them crosswise into ¾-inch pieces.
    2. Put the stock and 4 tablespoons butter in a 9-inch skillet and bring this to a boil over medium heat. Add

the leeks, cover the pan, lower the heat, and simmer for 45 minutes, or until the leeks are very tender. If all the liquid evaporates before the leeks are soft, add some water and continue to simmer.

3. When all the liquid is absorbed and the leeks are meltingly tender, purée them in a blender, food mill, or food processor with the remaining butter, ¾ teaspoon salt, and ¼ teaspoon pepper.

4. If you wish, pass the purée through a China cap, drum sieve or fine meshed sieve to make it silky smooth.

5. Reheat in a double boiler until hot.●

MENU ACCOMPANIMENT

This is perfect with most roasted meats and fowl. Avoid serving this with fish dishes, as the flavors might compete.

Caramelized Onions

THIS IS our version of one of the more unusual vegetable garnishes served in a three-star restaurant. Raising and lowering the heat as you cook the onions helps to release their natural sugars and therefore caramelizes them.

PREPARATION TIME:
30 minutes

COOKING TIME:
1 hour and 45 minutes

SERVES:
4

3½ pounds Bermuda onions
8   tablespoons butter
3   tablespoons red wine vinegar
     Salt
     Freshly ground pepper

1. Cut the onions in half lengthwise. Remove the hard root end as it will not soften completely no matter how long you cook the onions. Slice the onions into ⅛-inch thick slices.

2. Melt the butter in a heavy 14-inch skillet. Add the onions, cover, and stew them, over gentle heat, until tender, for about 30 minutes.

3. Remove the lid, and stew uncovered, stirring every now and then, to keep the onions from sticking to the skillet. Raise the heat to begin to caramelize the onions. As soon as the onions begin to brown (in about 10 minutes), lower the heat. Cover and repeat these steps a few more times. (Caramelizing the onions will take an hour more.)

4. Add the vinegar, 1 teaspoon salt, and ½ teaspoon pepper. Stir the onions over high heat with a wooden spoon until the vinegar has evaporated, about 5 minutes. Serve immediately. (If you make this dish in advance, re-heat, covered, over low heat for 10 minutes or until hot.)

MENU ACCOMPANIMENT

This goes well with any poultry or meat course. Avoid dishes in which garlic or shallot is the dominant flavor.

Baked Wild Rice with Onions, Carrots and Mushrooms

THERE IS nothing new about this way of making wild rice. The recipe is included, however, because it is a lovely accompaniment to poultry recipes, such as the Chicken with Garlic Sauce.

PREPARATION TIME:
1 hour

COOKING TIME:
1 hour

SERVES:
4 to 6

1   *cup wild rice*
    Coarse salt
4   *tablespoons butter*
½   *cup minced carrot*
¾   *cup minced onion*
½   *pound mushrooms, rinsed and chopped*
2   *tablespoons minced shallots*
2   *teaspoons fresh thyme, or ½ teaspoon dried*
1   *large bay leaf*
1½ *cups beef stock*
    Salt
    Freshly ground pepper

1. Soak the wild rice in water to cover for 1 hour. Drain, and discard the water.

2. Bring 1½ quarts of water to a boil with 1 tablespoon coarse salt. Plunge the rice in the water and parboil for 5 minutes after water has returned to a boil. Drain the rice and set aside.

3. Preheat the oven to 375 degrees.

4. Melt the butter in a 9- or 10-inch skillet. Add all the vegetables at once and stew, covered, over low heat for about 10 minutes, or until soft.

5. Mix the rice with the vegetables and continue to cook for another 2 minutes. Add 1 teaspoon salt, ½ teaspoon pepper, the thyme, bay leaf, and stock and stir them into the rice.

6. Transfer the mixture to a 2-quart oven-proof baking pan. Cover the pan with a piece of aluminum foil and bake for 35 to 40 minutes or until the rice has absorbed the liquid. (This may be reheated in a 350-degree oven for 20 minutes, if the rice has been refrigerated. Reheat for 10 minutes only, if the rice has been kept at room temperature.)

MENU ACCOMPANIMENT

As a side dish, this goes well with everything, including fish.

Julienne of Winter Root Vegetables

ALTHOUGH WE suggest you cut the vegetables to the same size, if they are cut in slightly uneven thicknesses, don't despair. This adds an interesting touch to the dish because the vegetables will cook at different rates, and thus have different textures.

PREPARATION TIME:
30 to 40 minutes

COOKING TIME:
8 to 10 minutes

SERVES:
4

4   *tablespoons butter*
½   *medium onion, thinly sliced*
2   *medium parsnips, peeled and cut into 2- by ¼-inch
      julienne pieces*
2   *medium carrots, cut into 2- by ¼-inch
      julienne pieces*
1   *large (8-ounce) white turnip, cut into 2- by ¼-inch
      julienne pieces*
1   *teaspoon sugar*
    Juice of 1 lime
    Salt
    Freshly ground pepper

1. In a 9-inch skillet, melt the butter over high heat until very hot. Add the onion slices, reduce the heat to medium, and sauté for 2 minutes, or until wilted.

2. Add the rest of the vegetables, 1 teaspoon salt, ¼ teaspoon pepper, and 1 teaspoon sugar. Sauté for 1 minute then cover the skillet, lower the heat, and simmer for 5 minutes.●

3. Uncover the skillet, raise the heat, add the lime juice, and evaporate all the liquid until the vegetables are slightly syrupy and glazed. Adjust the seasoning if necessary.

This goes well with pork and lamb dishes, such as the Sautéed Rib Lamb Chops with Rosemary and Thyme (page 215), or Pork with Cracked Peppercorns (page 188).

Oven-Baked Sliced Potatoes

THIS IS A classic recipe with a delicious flavor and texture. It is a simple way to make potatoes and is a fine accompaniment to any main course. This cannot be made in advance and reheated because the potatoes will toughen and dry out.

PREPARATION TIME:
20 minutes

COOKING TIME:
35 to 45 minutes

SERVES:
4

1   *pound boiling potatoes*
6   *tablespoons melted butter*
    Coarse salt
    Freshly ground pepper

   1. Preheat the oven to 400 degrees.
   2. Peel and slice the potatoes in even ⅜-inch thick slices. Lay them in a single layer on paper towels and pat them dry.
   3. Spread half of the melted butter on a large cookie sheet with sides or on a jelly roll pan, making sure the bottom is entirely coated so that the potatoes won't stick. Lay

the potato slices on the pan in a single layer, just overlapping slightly. Pour the rest of the butter over them. Season the potatoes with 2 teaspoons coarse salt and ¼ teaspoon pepper. Bake for 35 to 45 minutes, or until the potatoes are cooked through and crispy. (They should have absorbed the butter.)

MENU ACCOMPANIMENT

These are perfect with roasted, sautéed, or sauced meats and poultry.

Pea Purée

THIS VEGETABLE IS a perfect accompaniment for a variety of meat and chicken dishes. The color alone brightens up any entrée.

PREPARATION TIME:
40 minutes

COOKING TIME:
10 minutes

SERVES:
4

1	*small carrot, roughly chopped*
1	*small onion, roughly chopped*
8	*tablespoons butter*
2½	*pounds fresh peas in the shell*
	Salt
	Freshly ground pepper

1. In a 7-inch skillet, sauté the chopped carrot and onion in 4 tablespoons butter over a low heat. The vegetables should become tender but should not burn. Allow the remaining butter to soften to room temperature.

2. Steam the peas in a vegetable steamer for 4 minutes. Add the peas to the carrot and onion mixture and sauté for an additional 3 minutes.

3. Scrape the contents of the pan into a food processor. Add the remaining 4 tablespoons butter, which have been softened, to the mixture and purée. Season the purée with ¾ teaspoon salt and ¼ teaspoon pepper.

4. Remove the purée to a saucepan and simmer over very low heat until hot. Stir occasionally so the bottom does not scorch. (This purée may be made in advance and reheated in a double boiler. Before reheating, brush the top of the purée with one tablespoon melted butter to prevent a crust from forming.)

Pumpkin Purée

ONE HAS TO make this dish in a large quantity because it is difficult to find very small pumpkins. The very smooth texture and orange color make the purée lovely company for beef and poultry.

PREPARATION TIME:
45 minutes

COOKING TIME:
30 minutes

SERVES:
8

1	*5-pound pumpkin*
½	*cup chopped onion*
6	*tablespoons butter*
¼	*cup long grain rice*
½	*cup chicken stock*
⅛	*teaspoon allspice*
⅛	*teaspoon mace*
2	*teaspoons brown sugar*
2	*tablespoons heavy cream*
	Salt
	Freshly ground pepper

1. Halve the pumpkin. Scoop out the seeds and discard them.

2. Cut the pumpkin into large pieces with a sharp knife. Cut the tough outer skin away and discard it. Chop the pulp into 1-inch pieces and set aside.

3. Sauté the onion in a 12-inch skillet in 4 tablespoons melted butter over medium heat. When the onion is soft, add the rice, chicken stock, pumpkin, 1 teaspoon salt, and ¼ teaspoon pepper. Lower the heat and simmer these together, covered, for 30 minutes, or until the rice and pumpkin are soft. Remove from the heat.

4. If there is a lot of liquid left, strain it out. Blend the pulp and rice in a blender or food processor, a bit at a time, so that the hot purée does not "explode" in the blender.

5. Strain the mixture through a sieve to remove any large rice pieces.

6. Return the purée to a pan to heat it through. Add the spices, sugar, 2 tablespoons butter, the cream, and adjust the seasonings. As the purée heats, it will bubble and splatter madly so be sure to stand back.

PRESENTATION

Spoon the hot purée under slices of roast or on the side of the entrée.

Fresh Snow Peas with Shallots and Basil

T HE USE OF *glace de viande* with snow peas is unusual, and it gives the crisp snow peas an interesting flavor.

PREPARATION TIME:
20 minutes

COOKING TIME:
10 minutes

SERVES:
4

1 *pound fresh snow peas*
4 *tablespoons butter*
2 *tablespoons minced shallots*
¼ *cup* glace de viande
2 *tablespoons chopped fresh basil*
   Salt
   Freshly ground pepper

1. Clean the snow peas by removing the string-like fibers on both edges.

2. In a vegetable steamer, steam the snow peas for 2 to 3 minutes, or until they are barely tender. Make sure the water level comes below the steamer. Drain and set aside.

3. Melt the butter in a 10- to 12-inch skillet. When the foam begins to subside, add the *glace de viande* and simmer over medium heat for 1 to 2 minutes or until the shallots are soft.

4. Add the snow peas to the skillet. Raise the heat and stir constantly with a wooden spoon for approximately 1 minute. Make sure the shallots and butter evenly coat the snow peas. Season with salt and pepper to taste. (These may be reheated just before serving by quickly sautéing over a high heat for 30 seconds to 1 minute until the snow peas are hot.)

PRESENTATION

Spoon out the snow peas and sprinkle each portion with fresh basil.

MENU ACCOMPANIMENT

This is especially good with Capon Stuffed with Wild Rice (page 234), Pork Medallions in Fig Coulis (page 194), Herbed Leg of Lamb with Anchovy Butter (page 200), and Veal Loin with Capers (page 223).

Sautéed Spinach

YOU MUST FINISH this recipe after the rest of the main course has already been cooked. The spinach can not be in the skillet for more than 10 seconds and should look like hot spinach salad rather than wilted spinach. You may vary this basic recipe by first sautéing pine nuts and/or dried currants soaked in Madeira before you add the spinach.

PREPARATION TIME:
30 minutes

COOKING TIME:
1 to 2 minutes

SERVES:
4

¾ *pound fresh spinach*
4 *tablespoons butter*
1 *tablespoon minced shallots*
  Salt
  Freshly ground pepper

1. Stem and wash the spinach thoroughly. Drain well and set aside.

2. After you have finished all the steps for the other parts of the meal, heat the butter in a 14-inch skillet. When the butter is hot, toss in the shallots and, over high heat, cook them for 30 seconds.

3. Add the spinach and, with tongs, constantly move the spinach around so that all surfaces get heated with some of the butter. You are essentially stir-frying the spinach leaves or just coating them with the butter. Remove from the heat as soon as you see the leaves begin to wilt. Season with salt and pepper to taste.

Spinach Soufflés

THESE ARE NOT traditional soufflés. There is no white sauce to bind the vegetable. This is a purée of spinach and shallots bound by egg yolk and lightened with egg white. They puff up just a little bit, and therefore can be easily unmolded. The rich and creamy, slightly sweet sauce which accompanies these little soufflés is an interesting flavor contrast to the slightly acidic taste of the spinach.

PREPARATION TIME:
45 minutes

COOKING TIME:
30 minutes

SPECIAL EQUIPMENT:
Four ⅓-cup oven-proof ramekins

SERVES:
4

4½ tablespoons butter
2   tablespoons minced shallots
1½ pounds fresh spinach
¾   cup heavy cream
2   eggs, separated
⅓   cup onions, thinly sliced
2   carrots, sliced into ¼-inch rounds
¼   cup chicken stock or water
      Salt
      Freshly ground pepper

1. Preheat the oven to 400 degrees.

2. Stem, wash, and drain the spinach thoroughly. Butter the ramekins with about ½ tablespoon butter in all. Set aside.

3. Melt 2 tablespoons butter in a 3-quart saucepan. Add the shallots and cook for 1 minute over medium heat, stirring with a wooden spoon. Add the spinach and continue to stir over medium heat until the spinach is just wilted. This should take only about another minute or so.

4. Remove from the heat and drain the spinach in a sieve. When cool enough to handle with your hands, squeeze out any excess moisture.

5. In a blender or food processor, blend the spinach and shallots with 2 tablespoons heavy cream, ½ teaspoon salt, ¼ teaspoon pepper, and the egg yolks. Blend until smooth. Taste for seasoning. Again, drain out excess moisture from the spinach, if there is any. Transfer the spinach to a mixing bowl.●

6. Whip the egg whites with a pinch of salt until stiff, but not dry. Gently fold the egg whites into the spinach purée and spoon this into the prepared ramekins. The spinach mixture should reach to almost the top of each ramekin.

7. Set the ramekins in a baking pan with 2-inch-high sides. Fill the baking pan with hot water which should reach three-quarters of the way up the sides of the ramekins. Place the baking dish in the oven and bake for 25 minutes.

8. While the soufflés are baking, melt 2 tablespoons butter in a 10-inch skillet. Sauté the sliced onions and carrots over medium heat for about 1 minute. Turn the heat down and add ¾ teaspoon salt and ¼ teaspoon pepper. Cover the skillet and simmer gently for 20 minutes, or until the carrots are tender.

9. Add the remaining heavy cream and stock or water. Bring to a boil and reduce the mixture over high heat for 1 minute.

10. Transfer the contents of the skillet to the container of a blender or food processor, and purée until smooth. Pass the sauce through a drum sieve to further refine it. Taste for seasoning and return the sauce to a clean skillet.

11. Remove the soufflés from the oven and off the baking pan. Let them settle for half a minute. Run the tip of a knife around the inside edges of the ramekins to loosen the soufflé. Gently reheat the sauce.

PRESENTATION

Turn the soufflés upside down on warmed dinner plates using pot holders so you do not burn yourself. Spoon some sauce around each soufflé and serve.

Souffléed Acorn Squash

THIS IS A wonderful way of turning an ordinary, inexpensive vegetable into an elegant dish. What is unique about these soufflés is that there is no white sauce base. The acorn squash shells make perfect containers for the individual soufflés.

PREPARATION TIME:
30 minutes

COOKING TIME:
1 hours and 40 minutes

SERVES:
4

2   *small (¾-pound) acorn squash*
4   *tablespoons butter*
4   *teaspoons brown sugar*
    Scant ¼ teaspoon ground cinnamon
    Grating of fresh nutmeg
1   *large egg, separated*
    Salt
    Freshly ground pepper

1. Preheat the oven to 400 degrees.

2. Wash the outside of the squash well to rid it of any grit.

3. Using a sharp knife, cut a very thin slice off at both ends of the squash so that, when presented on a plate, each half stays stable on the dish and doesn't wobble. Cut the squash in half and with a spoon, scoop out the seeds and discard them.

4. Place the halved squash, skin side up, in ½ inch of water in a baking dish so that the flesh steams and remains moist while it bakes. Bake for 30 minutes.

5. Remove the baking dish from the oven. With a large spoon and tongs, turn the squash cut side up and place 1 tablespoon butter in each half. Return the squash to the oven and continue baking for another 30 minutes, or until the flesh is tender.

6. Using tongs, very carefully remove each squash half from the baking pan. As you remove them, pour the melted butter from the center of each into a mixing bowl.

7. Carefully so as not to pierce the soft shell, spoon out the cooked squash from each and place it in the bowl. Make sure to leave some flesh all around the inside cavity of each half. Do not pierce the skin or the soufflé mixture will run out.

8. In a blender or food processor, purée the squash (in two batches if necessary to prevent the mixture from "exploding" from the heat as you purée it) and reserved melted butter with the sugar, spices, ½ teaspoon salt, ¼ teaspoon pepper, and the egg yolk. Pour this into a mixing bowl.●

9. In another bowl, whip the egg white with a pinch of salt until stiff. Fold it into the puréed squash.

10. Pour equal amounts of the soufflé mixture into each hollowed-out cavity and bake on a baking sheet for 25 minutes or until the tops are nice and brown and begin to crack.

PRESENTATION

Serve in the squash shells as an appetizer or side dish.

MENU ACCOMPANIMENTS

The presentation of this dish is elegant enough to make it a fine beginning course to fall and winter meals. It is also perfect as a side dish to beef, lamb, poultry, and especially pork.

Squash Cakes

THE ALTERNATING colors of the different squash make for a pretty vegetable accompaniment or appetizer.

PREPARATION TIME:
1 hour

COOKING TIME:
40 minutes

SPECIAL EQUIPMENT:
Four ⅓-cup oven-proof ramekins

1   *pound young yellow summer squash*
½   *pound young zucchini*
6   *tablespoons butter*
2   *cloves garlic*
1   *egg yolk*
⅓   *cup heavy cream*
     Salt
     Freshly ground pepper

1. Slice off the tops and bottoms of the squash and discard. Wash the squash well.

2. Shred the squash on the large holes of a hand grater or with the shredding disk of a food processor, taking care to keep the yellow squash entirely separate from the zucchini.

3. Place the yellow squash in one sieve and the zucchini in another. Place each sieve over a bowl. Toss each squash with ½ teaspoon salt and let stand in the sieves for 30 minutes. Then press down hard on the squash with your hands to expel excess water.

4. Melt 4 tablespoons butter in 1 skillet and 2 tablespoons butter in another, smaller one. When hot, add 1 garlic clove to each skillet, and then the yellow squash to the larger skillet and the zucchini to the smaller one. Sauté both over medium heat for about 5 minutes or until hot.

5. Remove the skillets from the heat, discard the garlic cloves, and let the squash and zucchini cool for 10 minutes.

6. In a small mixing bowl, combine the egg yolk with the heavy cream and combine ⅓ of this mixture with the cooled zucchini and the rest with the cooled yellow squash.

7. Butter the ramekins and in each one spoon a ½-inch layer of yellow squash followed by a ½-inch layer of zucchini, topped by a ½-inch layer of yellow squash.●

8. Put the ramekins in a baking pan with 2-inch sides. Pour hot water three-quarters of the way up the sides of the ramekins. Bake for 30 minutes.

9. To unmold, let the little custards settle for about 3 minutes. Then run a sharp knife around the inside edges of the ramekins and unmold them onto a plate. Take care to protect your hands with a cloth when you do the unmolding because the ramekins are very hot.

MENU ACCOMPANIMENT

Serve this as a first course before fish, meat, or poultry. If used as a garnish, avoid serving with entrées rich in cream or butter sauces. You could also serve this as a second course between a fish appetizer and meat or poultry entrée.

Butternut Squash Purée

BECAUSE SQUASH tends to be watery, one needs to include an egg to bind the purée. Mashed potatoes or rice could be used instead, but the purée would not be as light. This dish shoud be eaten right away, in order to avoid reheating.

PREPARATION TIME:
30 minutes

COOKING TIME:
1 hour and 30 minutes

SERVES:
4

3   *pounds butternut squash*
6   *tablespoons softened butter*
1   *egg*
1   *tablespoon sliced scallions*
    Salt
    Freshly ground pepper.

1. Preheat the oven to 350 degrees.

2. Trim a thin slice from each end of the squash and discard. Wash the squash well and cut it into quarters.

3. In a baking pan large enough to accommodate the squash in a single layer, place the pieces, flesh side down, in ½ inch of water. Bake until soft for about 1¼ to 1½ hours.

4. Remove the squash from the pan and let it cool for 20 minutes, until you can handle it without burning your hands. As you would squeeze juice out of an orange half, with your hands gently squeeze out the excess moisture from each squash quarter. Then, with paper towels, sponge off any remaining water.

5. Scoop the flesh out of the skins and into a blender or food processor. Purée the squash flesh with the softened butter, egg, ½ teaspoon salt, and ¼ teaspoon pepper. Serve right away or reheat in a double boiler, whisking all the while, to help prevent water separation. Fold in the sliced scallions at the last minute.

MENU ACCOMPANIMENT

Because this purée tastes sweet, avoid serving it with dishes in which fruit is the dominant flavor. Since its texture is fluid, the purée should be served alongside entrées which have firmer textures, such as Veal Packets Stuffed with Fresh Vegetable Julienne (page 229), Pork with Cracked Peppercorns (page 188), and Sautéed Rib Lamb Chops with Rosemary and Thyme (page 215).

Sautéed Shredded Squash

THIS IS A classic way to cook squash and makes an excellent accompaniment to almost any dish. By shredding the squash first, you create many surface areas, allowing the vegetable to cook quickly and so retain a crunch. Be sure to choose small tender squash since they are sweeter.

PREPARATION TIME:
45 minutes

COOKING TIME:
5 minutes

SERVES:
4 to 6

2½   *to 3 pounds young yellow summer squash or zucchini*
6   *tablespoons butter*
2   *cloves garlic*
     Salt
     Freshly ground pepper

    1. Slice off the tops and bottoms of whichever squash you choose and discard. Wash the squash well.

    2. On the large holes of a hand grater, Mouli, or food processor, shred the squash. Toss the shredded vegetables with 1 tablespoon salt and place in a sieve over a bowl for 30 minutes. Then press down hard on the squash with your hands to expel as much moisture from it as possible.●

3. Melt the butter in a 10-inch skillet and, when hot, add the whole garlic cloves, and then the squash. Sauté over medium heat for 5 minutes. Discard the garlic cloves. Add ¼ teaspoon salt and ¼ teaspoon pepper or to taste. Serve while piping hot. (Do not add too much salt at once because there is quite a bit of salt remaining in the vegetable from the salting process in Step 2.)

MENU ACCOMPANIMENT

This goes as well with meat and poultry as it does with fish and other vegetables.

Sweet Potato Sauté

THIS IS A bit like hash-brown sweet potatoes. Simple but delicious.

PREPARATION TIME:
20 minutes

COOKING TIME:
45 minutes

SERVES:
4.

8 *tablespoons butter*
1½ *pounds sweet potatoes, peeled and cut into ¼-inch slices*
    Salt
    Freshly ground pepper

1. In 14-inch skillet, melt the butter and add the sliced sweet potatoes. With a wide spatula, turn them, making sure the potatoes are all coated with some butter. Cover, and cook over medium heat for 10 to 15 minutes, or until the potatoes are semi-soft throughout.

2. Remove the cover, raise the heat slightly and, with the spatula, turn the potatoes every 3 minutes or so as they continue to cook. At this point, the moisture given off by the softening potatoes will evaporate and they will continue to sauté in the melted butter. You must turn the potatoes frequently or they will stick to the pan as the natural sugar in them begins to caramelize. Don't, however, turn so frequently that they get no chance to brown. It is the combination of the browned bits and the softened potato that makes the flavor interesting and different. The potatoes will break up as you turn them.

3. After 20 to 25 minutes the potatoes should have absorbed nearly all the butter. Season with 1 teaspoon salt and ¼ teaspoon pepper or to taste. Serve while hot. (This may be reheated just before serving by sautéing the potatoes over a medium heat for 1 to 2 minutes or until the potatoes are hot.)

MENU ACCOMPANIMENT

This is a fine accompaniment to any hearty main meat or poultry course. This is too sweet a dish to serve with fruity tastes such as Roasted Duck Stuffed with Fruit or Veal with Lemon Comfit.

Puréed Turnips with Garlic

PREPARATION TIME:
10 to 15minutes

COOKING TIME:
15 minutes

SERVES:
4

2   *pounds white turnips, peeled and cut into ½-inch pieces*
     Coarse salt
12   *tablespoons butter*
12   *cloves garlic*
     Salt
     Freshly ground pepper

1. Bring 4 quarts of water to a boil with 1 tablespoon coarse salt. Parboil the turnips for 7 minutes, then drain.

2. In a 10-inch skillet, melt 8 tablespoons butter and cook the turnips and garlic, partially covered, over low heat for 5 minutes.

3. Transfer the contents of the skillet to a food processor and purée until smooth. Add 4 tablespoons butter to the mixture with the machine turned on.

4. Season heavily with salt and freshly ground pepper. The purée may be reheated in a double boiler.

MENU ACCOMPANIMENT

This is good with any kind of poultry or meat, and is particularly satisflying with pork. It would, however, overpower delicate veal or fish dishes.

Tomato Vinaigrette Sauce

THE BASIS for this sauce is a fresh tomato reduction which is easily made and is far superior to canned tomato paste. We have included this recipe in this section because it is our only sauce recipe and is used in several different dishes.

PREPARATION TIME:
1 hour and 15 minutes

COOKING TIME:
45 minutes

MAKES:
1½ cups

3 *pounds ripe fresh tomatoes*
4 *tablespoons olive oil*
2 *tablespoons champagne vinegar*
2 *tablespoons chopped Italian parsley*
1 *tablespoon chopped tarragon, optional*
   Salt
   Freshly ground pepper

1. In a 4- to 5-quart saucepan, bring 3 quarts of water to a boil. Plunge some of the tomatoes in for 10 to 20 seconds. Remove them and immediately place in cold water to stop the cooking process. Repeat the procedure with all of the tomatoes. This process makes the skins easy to remove.

2. Peel the tomatoes. Then, with a sharp knife, dig in at one end and remove the core.

3. Cut each tomato in half horizontally. With a teaspoon, scoop out and discard the seeds and excess juice from each half. Chop up the remaining pulp and put them in a sieve placed over a bowl.

4. Using a wooden spoon, push the pulp and juice through the sieve. Discard any remaining seeds and bits of skin that remain in the sieve.

5. In a non-aluminum saucepan or skillet, reduce the tomato pulp and juice over high heat stirring occasionally with a wooden spoon, until only 1 cup of purée remains. This should take approximately 10 minutes. Let it cool to room temperature. At this point it is a tomato purée.

6. Mix in the remaining ingredients and chill until serving time.●

PRESENTATION

Spoon a portion of the sauce on the plate first, then place the entrée with which you are serving the sauce *on top*.

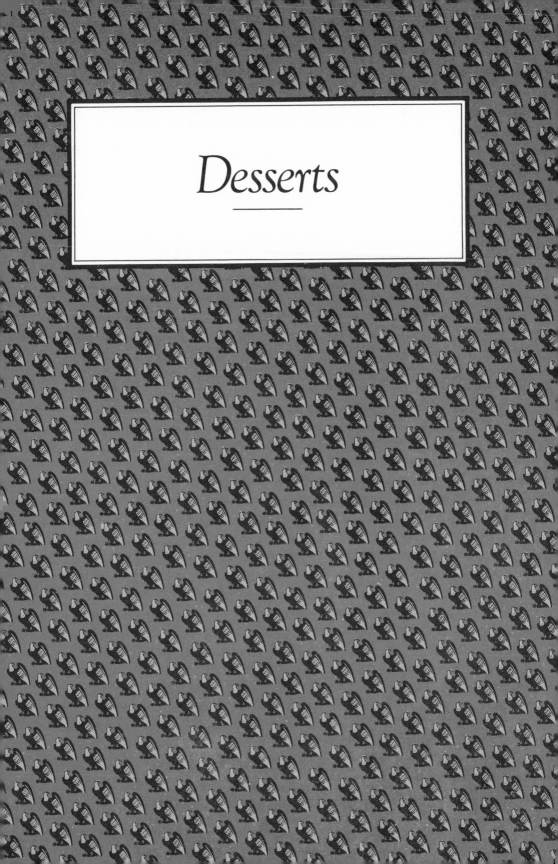

Desserts

Chocolate Almond Cake

OR THIS CAKE it is essential that you use an excellent brand of chocolate such as Lindt or Tobler. These brands carry an "extra-bittersweet" variety which would be the best to use, but the bittersweet would do.

PREPARATION TIME:
1 hour and 30 minutes

COOKING TIME:
40 minutes

SPECIAL EQUIPMENT:
Candy thermometer

SERVES:
10 to 12

Cake

6   ounces extra-bittersweet chocolate
8   tablespoons butter, plus 1 tablespoon softened
¼   cup flour, plus 1 tablespoon
¾   cup sugar
6   large eggs, separated
1   tablespoon instant (not freezed-dried) coffee
8   ounces almonds in skins, finely ground
     Salt

Mocha Buttercream

2   ounces bittersweet or extra-bittersweet chocolate
6   tablespoons sugar
2   egg whites
1   tablespoon instant (not freeze-dried) coffee
6   tablepoons butter

½   *cup heavy cream*
2   *teaspoons confectioners' sugar*
    Salt

1. Melt the chocolate in the top of a double boiler over hot, not boiling water. Let the chocolate cool.

2. Generously grease two 8- by 8- by 1½-inch cake pans with ½ tablespoon softened butter each. Add ½ tablespoon flour to each cake pan and roll it around the bottom and sides of each pan. Shake out any excess flour. Set aside.

3. In your food processor or mixer, cream 8 tablespoons butter with ¼ cup sugar until ivory colored. Add the egg yolks, one at a time, and beat until fluffy. Add the instant coffee, half the almonds and the melted and cooled chocolate. Set aside.

4. Preheat the oven to 350 degrees.

5. Using an electric mixer, beat the egg whites with a pinch of salt until stiff. Add the remaining sugar, a tablespoon at a time, beating well after each addition, until all the sugar is dissolved, and the egg whites are stiff and shiny.

6. Fold one-quarter of the beaten egg whites into the nut batter to lighten it. Pour this lightened batter back into the egg whites. Add the remaining nuts and sift the ¼ cup flour on top. Rapidly fold all the ingredients together so that no more white shows. Work rapidly so you do not deflate the egg whites.

7. Pour half of the batter in each pan. Rap the pans gently on a table to eliminate air pockets and to level off the tops. Bake for 10 minutes. Lower the oven temperature to 325 degrees and bake for another 20 to 25 minutes or until a cake tester or knife, plunged in the center of the cake, comes out dry.

8. While layers are baking make the mocha buttercream. Melt the chocolate in the top of a double boiler over hot, not boiling water. Let the chocolate cool.

9. In a small saucepan, combine the sugar and ¼ cup water. (You must use a small saucepan. The sugar syrup will evaporate too quickly on a wider surface.) Place the mixture over medium heat to dissolve the sugar. Stir occasionally with a spoon. Dip a pastry brush in cold water and run it around the inside of the pan to dissolve any sugar crystals that may have formed there. When all the sugar is dissolved, turn the heat to very low.

10. Begin to beat the egg whites with a pinch of salt until frothy. It is best to do this in a stationary mixer so that you can let the egg whites whip while you attend to the sugar syrup.

11. When the egg whites are frothy, raise the heat under the sugar syrup and boil it rapidly until the syrup registers 238 degrees on a candy thermometer.

12. Return to the egg whites and rapidly beat them with an electric mixer until they are stiff. Pour the sugar syrup, in a steady stream, into the beaten egg whites and continue to beat until the mixture is cool. When cool, beat in the coffee and butter. As you beat in the butter, the mixture will deflate. Add the cooled melted chocolate and mix well. Refrigerate while you make the whipped cream.

13. In a chilled bowl, beat the cream until semi-stiff. Add the confectioners' sugar, beat until stiff, then refrigerate.

14. When both the butter cream and the whipped cream are chilled, fold them together. Don't wait too long or the butter cream will harden too much. When combined, chill until harder but still of spreading consistency.

15. Remove the layers from the oven and let them settle in the pans for 10 minutes. Run a knife around the inside edges of the layers to loosen them from the pans; turn them upside down on a cake rack to cool. Let them cool completely before filling with buttercream.

16. To assemble the cake, first trim the layers so that both are equal and the tops are horizontal. Smooth the sides so they are straight. Brush off excess crumbs. Place one layer, bottom facing up, on a serving platter. Place 4 narrow strips of wax paper around and underneath the layer in a square pattern to catch any excess buttercream. Spread the layer with one-third of the buttercream. Place the second layer, also bottom side facing up on top of the butter cream. Spread the remaining buttercream around the sides and on top of the cake. Carefully remove the wax paper from the cake and cover it with a large bowl turned upside down so that the cake does not absorb refrigerator odors. The bowl should not touch the cake. Refrigerate until serving time.

Chocolate Sweetness

THE GROUND HAZELNUTS and praline paste give this cake an elegantly smooth texture. Keep the portions small as this is a very dense and rich dessert.

PREPARATION TIME:
30 minutes

COOKING TIME:
25 minutes

SERVES:
12 to 16

1   *pound bittersweet chocolate*
10 *tablespoons butter, plus 1 tablespoon softened*
1   *tablespoon flour*
⅓   *cup praline paste*
¼   *cup heavy cream*
5   *eggs, separated*
½   *cup sugar*
½   *cup hazelnuts, toasted and finely ground (see David's Cake, page 377, step 1)*
     Confectioners' sugar

1. Preheat the oven to 350 degrees.

2. Melt 10 tablespoons butter in the top of a double boiler over hot, not boiling water. Pour the butter in a bowl and set aside.

3. Melt the chocolate with the praline paste in the top of a double boiler over hot, not boiling, water. When the chocolate mixture has just melted, stir in the heavy cream. Take it off the heat and set aside.

4. While the chocolate and praline paste are melting, prepare a 9- by 9½- by 1½-inch false-bottomed cake pan. Grease the pan with the remaining softened butter, then sprinkle with flour. Roll the flour around the inside of the pan so that it is well coated. Shake out any excess and set the pan aside.

5. With a electric mixer, beat the egg whites. When they are frothy, continue beating and gradually add the sugar, tablespoon by tablespoon, until soft peaks form. Set this aside.

6. In a second bowl, lightly beat the yolks with a whisk, then add them to the egg whites, beating all the while. Beat for an additional 3 minutes.

7. Sprinkle half the hazelnuts, half the melted butter, and half the melted chocolate mixture on top of the beaten eggs then, with a rubber spatula, fold them together.

8. Add the remainder of these ingredients to the batter and fold them in. Make sure the ingredients are completely blended.

9. Turn the batter into the prepared cake pan. Place in the middle of the oven and bake for 25 minutes.

10. Cool the cake in the pan for 45 minutes. If you make this cake in advance and then refrigerate, be sure to bring it back to room temperature before serving.

PRESENTATION

Center the cake on a platter, and right before serving, lightly dust the top with confectioners' sugar.

Souffléed Chocolate Cake

TYPICALLY French, this delicious dessert has an underbaked middle which is the secret to its lightness and richness.

PREPARATION TIME:
40 minutes

COOKING TIME:
30 minutes

SERVES:
8

9 *ounces extra-bittersweet chocolate*
9 *tablespoons butter, plus 1 tablespoon softened*
1 *tablespoon flour*
6 *eggs, separated*
½ *cup sugar*
6 *tablespoons cornstarch*
   Confectioners' sugar

1. Preheat the oven to 350 degrees.

2. In the top of a double boiler, melt the chocolate over hot, not boiling, water. When the chocolate has melted, remove it from the heat and set aside to cool a bit.

3. In a small saucepan, melt 9 tablespoons butter over medium heat; cool it and when it is lukewarm, whisk it into the melted chocolate.

4. While you are melting the chocolate and butter, prepare a 9- by 9½- by 1½-inch false-bottomed cake pan by greasing it with 1 tablespoon softened butter. Dust it with 1 tablespoon flour, shaking out the excess. Set aside.

5. With an electric mixer, beat the egg whites until soft peaks form. Add the sugar, tablespoon by tablespoon, until all the sugar is incorporated.

6. With a fork, lightly beat the egg yolks and add them to the beaten egg whites. Continue to beat with the electric mixer. After the yolks have been completely incorporated, continue to beat for 3 minutes more.

7. Through a strainer, sift one-half of the cornstarch onto the beaten egg mixture, and add one-half of the melted chocolate and butter mixture on top of this. Fold everything together.

8. Add the remaining half of the ingredients in the same way and fold them in. Be careful to reach all the way to the bottom of the mixing bowl—otherwise you will miss some of the chocolate, which tends to sink to the bottom.

9. Turn the batter into the prepared cake pan and bake for 30 minutes. The insides should remain moist.

10. Cool the cake for 10 minutes in the pan. Then, with a spatula, loosen the edges and remove the cake from the cake pan. When completely cool, turn the cake upside down on a plate so that the slightly crusty top will be hidden on the bottom. If you bake this cake in advance, be sure to bring it back to room temperature before serving, so that the texture will be correct.

Right before serving, dust the top through a doily, with some confectioners' sugar. Remove the doily.

David's Cake

THIS DESSERT, made of crunchy nut meringue cakes and rich cream fillings, is exquisite and great for large parties. Making it is a lengthy affair but worth the effort. You can prepare the cake in advance; as a matter of fact, it improves with age. It should be made at least two days before you plan to serve it and will keep for up to a week in the refrigerator.

PREPARATION TIME:
2 hours

COOKING TIME:
1 hour and 15 minutes

SPECIAL EQUIPMENT:
Either a non-stick jelly roll or cookie sheet with ½-inch rim around it, or a regular jelly roll pan or cookie sheet lined with silicone-treated baking paper

SERVES:
20 to 24 portions

Cake:

7   *ounces blanched almonds*
5   *ounces hazelnuts*
1¼ *cups sugar*
4   *tablespoons flour*
1   *tablespoon butter*
8   *egg whites*

Fillings:

1   *pound bittersweet chocolate*
3   *cups heavy cream*
¼   *cup superfine sugar*
1   *teaspoon vanilla*
4   *tablespoons butter*
4   *ounces praline paste*

1. Preheat the oven to 400 degrees.

2. Using separate shallow pans, roast the almonds and hazelnuts separately until you can begin to smell the aroma of roasted nuts or until they turn golden brown. This should take 10 to 15 minutes.

3. Remove them from the oven and right away, while the hazelnuts are still hot, rub their skins off between two kitchen towels. Lower the oven temperature to 325 degrees.

4. In a food processor, or with a hand nut grater, grind the nuts together until nearly as fine as flour, without letting them turn oily. In a bowl, fold the sugar and 2 tablespoons flour into the ground nuts and set aside.

5. With softened butter generously grease a large (13- by 17-inch or 12- by 15½-inch) non-stick jelly roll pan. If the corners of the pan do not meet, fill them in by wrapping them with foil and creating your own corners. This will also help you remove the cake from the pan after baking. Dust the pan with a little flour and shake off any excess. (If you do not have a non-stick pan, use a regular jelly roll pan but line it with silicone-treated paper.)

6. Using an electric mixer, beat the egg whites with

a pinch of salt until stiff. Using a rubber spatula, fold the beaten egg whites into the ground nut and sugar mixture.

7. Spread this mixture on the prepared baking pan and bake in the oven for 35 to 45 minutes, or until the cake is golden brown, crisp on top but still pliable.

8. While the cake is baking, make the fillings. For the chocolate cream filling, melt the chocolate over simmering water in the top of a double boiler. Let the chocolate cool so that it is cool enough to touch but is still soft and pliable. Mix it with 1 cup heavy cream. Cool the mixture in the refrigerator until it is of spreading consistency, but don't leave it too long or it will be too hard to spread.

9. For the plain buttercream filling, combine the superfine sugar and 4 tablespoons butter in a small saucepan or skillet. Cook them, over low heat, for about 2 minutes, or until the sugar begins to melt into the melting butter. Cool and add the vanilla. Whip 2 cups heavy cream until stiff. Fold the vanilla and sugar mixture into half of the whipped cream. Refrigerate until ready to use.

10. For the praline cream, use a wooden spoon to work the praline paste until it is smooth and any oil that has separated has been rehomogenized. Take ¼ cup of the remaining whipped cream and work it into the praline paste to loosen the texture. This can be done in a food processor. Gently fold the rest of the cream into the praline paste. Refrigerate until of spreading consistency.

11. Remove the cake from the oven and, using pot holders to protect your hands, immediately turn the pan upside down onto a clean kitchen towel. Use two spatulas if necessary. If you have lined the pan, remove the paper. It is not unusual for the cake to break so don't despair; it more or less gets "glued" back together in the icing process. When slightly cool, cut the cake into 4 long vertical strips, each one measuring about 17 by 3 inches (or slightly smaller if you have used the smaller cake pan).

12. Assemble the cake. Start with a strip of cake on which you spread one-third of the chocolate cream. Top this with a second layer of cake and spread this layer with the plain buttercream. Place the third strip of cake on top of the plain buttercream and spread it with the praline cream. Finish with the fourth strip of cake.

13. At this point, refrigerate the dessert to firm it up before the final icing. This should take approximately 30 minutes.

14. When firmed, frost the top and sides of the cake, except for the short ends, with the remaining chocolate cream. Decorate the top by making either vertical lines or cross-hatch marks on top of the cake with a knife or the tines of a fork. Cut off a thin slice from each end of the cake to even up the ends. To keep the cake from drying out protect the ends with plastic wrap. Store in the refrigerator until serving time. This is hard to cut so use a serrated knife.

Lemon Almond Cake

THIS CAKE IS made, as is a *génoise*, with melted butter incorporated into the batter. The only leavening in the cake is the beaten eggs. The contrast of the tart lemon to the sweet almond paste is a real palate pleaser and makes for a wonderful ending to a special meal.

PREPARATION TIME:
30 minutes

BAKING TIME:
30 to 40 minutes

SERVES:
8

8   tablespoons melted butter, plus 1 tablespoon softened
1   tablespoon flour
½   cup (4 ounces) almond paste
2   egg yolks
¼   cup lemon juice
1½ teaspoons lemon rind
4   eggs
¾   cup sugar
½   cup finely ground blanched almonds
¼   cup cornstrarch
2   tablespoons apricot preserves
¼   cup almonds, sliced and toasted
    Salt

1. Preheat the oven to 350 degrees.

2. Prepare a 9½- by 1½-inch round cake pan by greasing it with 1 tablespoon softened butter and sprinkling 1 tablespoon flour around the inside. Roll the flour around the bottom and inside edges of the cake pan. Shake out any excess flour and set aside.

3. In a large bowl, combine the almond paste with 1 egg yolk. You might have to do this with your hands as the almond paste is hard to work with a fork or whisk.

4. Add the lemon juice and rind to the almond paste. Then whisk in the melted butter with a pinch of salt. Set aside.

5. Whisk the 4 eggs and the remaining yolk with the sugar in the top part of a double boiler set over simmering, not boiling, water. Beat the eggs with a hand mixer until they have doubled in volume, and turned an ivory color.

6. Remove from the heat. Fold one-quarter of the beaten eggs into the almond paste batter to lighten it, then fold in the rest.

7. Sprinkle the nuts over the batter and, using a sieve, sift the cornstarch in as well. Very quickly fold all these ingredients together until no cornstarch shows. Work fast so that you do not deflate the eggs.

8. Pour the batter into the prepared cake pan and

bake for 30 to 40 minutes, or until a cake tester, when inserted into the center of the cake, comes out dry. If the cake browns too quickly, cover it loosely with a piece of foil.

9. While the cake is baking, strain the apricot preserves through a fine strainer to remove any large pieces of fruit.

10. Once baked allow the cake to cool in the pan for 15 minutes. Then unmold it and spread the strained apricot preserves around the sides of the cake. Pat the sliced almonds onto the apricot preserves which should hold them in place.

PRESENTATION

Bring the cake to the table on a doily-covered round platter. Cut portions at the table.

Fine Orange Cake

THIS CAKE is named for the color of the various raw ingredients that combine to make this a glorious dessert. Serve thin slices of this dessert—it is very rich and filling.

PREPARATION TIME:
2 hours

COOKING TIME:
1 hour and 15 minutes

SERVES:
12 to 16

Cake:
7   ounces pecans
5   ounces hazelnuts
1½   cups sugar
3   tablespoons flour
2   tablespoons softened butter
8   egg whites
     Salt

Fillings:
1   cup (4 ounces) dried apricots or peaches
2   tablespoons Grand Marnier
¼   cup superfine sugar
8   ounces bittersweet chocolate
2½   cups heavy cream
⅓   cup (4 ounces) apricot preserves

1. Preheat the oven to 400 degrees.

2. Using separate shallow pans, roast the pecans and hazelnuts separately for 10 to 15 minutes, or until you can begin to smell the aroma of the roasted nuts as they turn golden brown.

3. Remove the nuts from the oven and while the hazelnuts are still hot, rub their skins off between two kitchen towels. Lower the oven temperature to 325 degrees.

4. In a food processor, or with a hand nut grater, grind the nuts until fine. Do not overprocess these or they will turn oily. Fold the sugar and 2 tablespoons flour into the ground nuts and set aside.

5. Generously grease with butter 3 round 9- by 1½-inch cake pans. Dust the pans with 1 tablespoon flour and shake out any excess. You may cut out rounds of silicone-treated baking paper and lay them on the bottom of the cake pans.

6. With an electric mixer, beat the egg whites with a pinch of salt until they are stiff. Fold the beaten egg whites into the ground nut mixture.

7. Divide the batter into three equal portions and spread on the bottoms of each of the prepared cake pans. Bake for 35 to 40 minutes, or until the layers are golden brown, crisp on top, but still pliable. If you are baking this cake on a humid day, you might have to bake the layers a little longer for them to be crisp. They will shrink from the pan sides when done.

8. Make the fillings while the layers are baking. Soak the dried apricots for 30 minutes in ¼ cup water mixed with the superfine sugar and Grand Marnier. While they are soaking, proceed to the next step.

9. Melt the chocolate in the top of a double boiler over hot, not boiling water. Let the chocolate cool so that it is cool to the touch but still soft and pliable. Mix it with ½ cup heavy cream and place it, covered, in the refrigerator until it is of spreading consistency. Don't allow it to get too hard or it will not be spreadable.

10. Combine the apricot preserves with ½ cup heavy cream in a food processor. Mix until the two are completely blended and set aside.

11. Place the soaking apricots and the soaking liquid in a food processor with ½ cup heavy cream. Process until they are completely blended and set aside.

12. Whip the remaining heavy cream with an electric mixer until stiff. Fold one-half of the whipped cream into the dried apricot cream and the other half into the apricot preserves mixture.

13. Remove the layers from the oven and immediately turn them onto a clean kitchen towel. Should they break, which they might well do, don't despair. They more or less get "glued" back together in the icing process. When slightly cool, place the first layer on a plate or platter and assemble the cake.

14. Spread the chocolate mixture as evenly as possible on the bottom cake layer. Place another layer of cake on top of the chocolate and press down until the upper layer is level. Spread the dried apricot mixture on this second layer. Again, try to spread the cream evenly. Place the last piece of cake on top of the dried apricot cream and level this surface. Ice the cake on the top and sides with the apricot preserve cream. If the creams begin to melt, place the cake in the refrigerator for 10 to 15 minutes until they chill and harden so you can begin icing the cake again.

Once the cake is iced, return it to the refrigerator. To prevent the cake from absorbing refrigerator odors, cover it with a large bowl turned upside down. The bowl should not touch the cake. Let it set for at least 8 hours.

PRESENTATION

Remove the cake from the refrigerator. Dip a sharp knife in hot water before cutting each slice.

Penuche and Raisin Layer Cake

I N THIS delicious layer cake the texture of the brown sugar, bourbon, and raisin frosting is lightened by the addition of whipped cream. It is best to make this cake a day in advance.

PREPARATION TIME:
40 minutes

COOKING TIME:
30 minutes

½ cup white raisins
3 tablespoons bourbon or rum
9 tablespoons butter, plus 1 tablespoon softened
2 cups sifted flour, plus 1 tablespoon
1 cup sugar
3 eggs
⅔ cup milk
1 teaspoon vanilla
1 teaspoon baking powder
2 cups brown sugar
2 cups heavy cream
   Salt

1. Preheat the oven to 400 degrees.

2. Soak the raisins in the bourbon and set aside.

3. Grease two 9- by 1½-inch cake pans with ½ tablespoon softened butter each. Sprinkle ½ tablespoon flour in each pan. Roll the flour around the inside of the pans to coat the bottom and sides. Shake out any excess.

4. By hand, with a wooden spoon, or in a mixer or food processor, cream 5 tablespoons butter and the sugar together for a minute or so, or until pale and frothy.

5. Add the eggs, one at a time, and beat until ivory-colored. In a separate bowl, combine the milk with the vanilla and set aside.

6. Sift the baking powder and ¼ teaspoon salt into 2 cups sifted flour and set aside.

7. Sift the flour mixture into the egg mixture and add one-third of the milk mixture. Fold quickly together. Repeat this procedure in two more batches. Do not overmix. Just mix and fold until no more flour shows.

8. Divide the batter between the two prepared cake pans, making sure you even out the tops of the batter with a spatula so that the layers rise evenly. Bake for 25 to 30 minutes, or until a cake tester, when plunged into the center of the layers, comes out dry.

9. While the layers are baking, prepare the frosting. In a heavy duty 4-quart saucepan combine the brown sugar and 1 cup heavy cream. Bring this to a boil and brush down sides of pan with a brush dipped in cold water to dissolve any sugar crystals. Once this comes to a boil, lower the heat and let the syrup cook for about 15 minutes, or until it reaches 238 degrees on a candy thermometer.

10. Remove from the heat and add 4 tablespoons butter. Let the pan of syrup cool in a bowl filled with cold water and ice until the syrup temperature reaches 160 degrees.

11. Add the raisins and bourbon and stir it all together until the mixture is well blended. When it reaches room temperature place it in the refrigerator for about 15 minutes.

12. Once the layers are out of the oven, let them settle for 5 minutes in the cake pans. Run a knife around the inside edges of the layers and turn them upside down onto cake racks to cool. When cool, split each layer in half, horizontally, producing 4 thin layers each about ⅓-inch thick.

13. Whip the remaining cup heavy cream and fold this into the chilled frosting, and chill for another 15 minutes.

14. Spread the filling evenly between the layers so that the cake stands level. Frost the top and sides with the remainder and refrigerate the cake overnight. To prevent the cake from absorbing refrigerator odors, cover it with a large bowl turned upside down. The bowl should not touch the cake.

Puff Pastry

PUFF PASTRY is much easier to make than is generally realized. There are only a few rules you must follow to make it light and delicious. One is to handle the pastry as little as possible. Another is to always work the pastry when it is very cold. You will find that the colder the pastry is when you roll it out, the lighter and flakier it bakes.

YIELD:
Sixteen 2½- by 8½-inch rectangles

PREPARATION TIME:
5 hours

COOKING TIME:
Depends on how the pastry is used

2¾ *cups unbleached flour*
¾   *cup cake flour*
1   *pound chilled butter*
1   *cup ice water*
    Salt

　　1. Mix the flours and 2 teaspoons salt together in a food processor with the blade already in place. Reserve ½ cup flour from the mixture and set aside.
　　2. Cut 8 tablespoons butter (¼ pound) into at least 16 small pieces. Put the butter into the food processor and process for 15 seconds to incorporate the butter into the flour.
　　3. Turn the machine back on and quickly pour 1 cup iced water through the tube into the bowl. Turn off the machine as soon as the dough gathers into a ball around

the blade, which should take less than 15 seconds.

4. Lightly dust an 18-inch piece of wax paper. Scrape the dough out of the food processor bowl onto the wax paper. Gather the dough into a rough ball and dust this ball with flour. Wrap the dough in the wax paper, place it on a plate, and let it rest in the refrigerator for at least 1 hour.

5. While the dough is resting, take the remaining butter out of the refrigerator and place it on your work surface. Pound it with a rolling pin to make it pliable. When it begins to soften, sprinkle on one-half of the reserved flour and work it into the butter. Once this flour has been absorbed, sprinkle on the remaining flour. The best way to work the butter and flour together is by quickly kneading the mixture with your fingers, not with the hot palms of your hands. Remember the less you touch the butter, the better, so work fast. When the flour has been worked in, form the butter into a rough 2- by 6-inch oval. Place it on a plate and refrigerate.

6. After the dough has rested in the refrigerator for at least an hour you are ready to combine it with the butter.

7. Lightly dust your pastry area with flour and place the ball of dough in the middle. Dust your hand with flour and run it up and down the rolling pin. This will facilitate the rolling process. Roll the dough into approximately a 16-inch circle. (It doesn't have to be exact.) Place the bundle of butter into the center of the dough and pinch the edges of the dough up over the butter so that you are sealing the butter in the dough.

8. Dust the pastry board and the rolling pin again with flour and turn the dough and butter packet seal side down. On the pastry board, gently roll out the dough so that you have a rectangle of pastry that is approximately 8 by 18 inches. It is important to try to roll the butter evenly throughout the dough. At this point you are ready to make what is referred to as the first turn. Turn one third of the strip up toward the center of the dough and then fold the top third of the pastry over the first fold so that you have three layers. In essence you fold the pastry as if you were folding a business letter. The folded open edge is positioned on your right. When you roll out the dough, lift it up and dust the work surface with flour to prevent sticking. Roll out the folded pastry into another 8- by 18-inch strip and repeat the folding process. You have now completed 2 turns. Wrap the pastry in wax paper and let it rest in the refrigerator for at least an hour. If a patch of butter should emerge through the dough while you are rolling it out, dust it with flour and continue.

9. When the pastry has rested, turn the pastry a third and fourth time, following the same folding procedure as mentioned above. Remember, speed is essential. The faster you get at rolling out the puff pastry, the lighter and more tender it will be when eaten. Rest the dough for another hour (or overnight).

10. After the pastry has rested, turn it a fifth and sixth time. Rest it in the refrigerator for at least another hour. The pastry is now ready to be rolled and formed into its final baking shape.

11. Remove the pastry from the refrigerator. Lightly flour and roll the dough into a shape approximately 11 by 14 inches. Use a ruler if you want to be exact. Use a bench scraper to trim the edges of the pastry. (*Note:* The edges may be used to make *palmiers* .) The sheet of pastry should be ⅜-inch thick. Using a ruler and a bench scraper or a chef's knife, divide the pastry into 16 small rectangles. They should each be about 2¾ by 3¼ inches.

12. Layer the rectangles of pastry between wax paper and wrap the whole package in foil. Place the package in the freezer and use the pastry as the recipes dictate. Puff pastry should always be baked straight from the freezer. It tends to bake more evenly.

Almond Puff Pastry Squares

THIS IS A lighter variation of the classic Napoleon. The filling consists of whipped cream blended with almond paste instead of the more traditional *crème patissière*.

PREPARATION TIME:
1 hour

COOKING TIME:
45 minutes

SERVES:
4

8   *unbaked puff pastry rectangles (see page 388)*
3   *tablespoons sugar*
1½ *cups heavy cream*
2   *tablespoons confectioners' sugar*
¼   *teaspoon vanilla*
8   *ounces almond paste*

1. Preheat the oven to 450 degrees.
2. Remove the puff pastry rectangles from the freezer and place them on a lightly buttered baking sheet. Prick the pastry with a fork at 1-inch intervals and sprinkle them with sugar.
3. Bake for 15 minutes, then lower the temperature to 375 degrees and bake for 20 minutes more or until the pastry has turned golden brown. Remove from the oven and let cool.
4. While the pastry is baking, make the filling. In a chilled bowl, whip 1 cup heavy cream until semi-stiff. Beat in the confectioners' sugar and vanilla. Reserve the

whipped cream, covered, in the refrigerator.

5. With either a whisk or in a food processor, soften the almond paste by combining it with the remaining ½ cup heavy cream. Fold the softened almond paste into the whipped cream and reserve, covered, in the refrigerator until you are ready to fill the pastries.

PRESENTATION

Assemble the squares just before serving or the pastry will become soggy. Split each pastry rectangle in half, horizontally, so you have 16 layers. Place 2 tablespoons or so of the almond cream on a layer. Top with a second layer of pastry, then almond cream, with a third layer of pastry, a third layer of almond cream, and then with a final layer of pastry, which should be one which has a light sugar coating on top. Repeat the procedure for the three other portions. Each portion should have 4 layers of pastry and 3 of cream.

Fresh Cherries in Puff Pastry

T HE BEAUTY of this recipe is that all of the components may be prepared in advance and then the dish assembled at the last minute. The color contrast of the two different creams with the burgundy of the cherries makes this delicious dessert a visual delight.

PREPARATION TIME:
1 hour

COOKING TIME:
30 minutes

8   unbaked puff pastry rectangles (see page 388)
2   tablespoons egg white
1   tablespoon brown sugar
1½   cups heavy cream
2   tablespoons confectioners' sugar
2   egg yolks
¾   cup sugar
¼   cup kirsch
½   cup milk
1   vanilla bean
1½   pounds Bing cherries

1. Preheat the oven to 450 degrees.

2. Remove the puff pastry rectangles from the freezer and place them on a lightly buttered baking sheet. Score the top of the pastry rectangles with a knife in a decorative pattern. Mix the egg white with brown sugar and brush each piece with this glaze.

3. Bake the pastry for 15 minutes at 450 degrees; then lower the temperature to 375 degrees and continue baking for 20 minutes, or until the pastry has turned nut brown. When the pastry is baked, remove it from the oven and set aside.

4. While the pastry is baking you can begin to prepare the whipped cream and the custard sauce. In a chilled mixing bowl whip 1 cup heavy cream until it forms soft peaks. Add the confectioners' sugar and whip until stiff. Reserve the finished whipped cream, covered, in the refrigerator.

5. Combine the two egg yolks and the sugar in a mixing bowl and beat with an electric mixer for 3 minutes at high speed. Add the kirsch and continue beating for an additional minute at low speed.

6. In a 4-quart non-aluminum saucepan bring the milk, ½ cup heavy cream, and the vanilla bean to a boil over medium heat. Pour the hot liquid directly into the egg yolk mixture. Keep the vanilla bean in the bottom of the saucepan.

7. With a whisk, beat the custard sauce for 1 minute, making sure the liquid doesn't splash over the side of the mixing bowl. Pour the sauce back into the saucepan and return it to a medium heat whisking all the while. Don't stop stirring or the bottom will scorch. When steam begins to rise from the saucepan, or the temperature of the custard reaches 175 degrees on a candy thermometer, turn off the heat and put the custard sauce on a back burner.

8. Pit the cherries with a cherry pitter or with a paring knife. Roughly chop three-quarters of the cherries into ¼- by ½-inch pieces. Leave the rest of the cherries whole (or halved if you haven't used the pitter).

9. Just before you assemble the dish, reheat the custard sauce over very low heat or until tepid.

PRESENTATION

Gently split the puff pastry in half with your fingers so you have a top layer and a bottom layer. Place the bottom half on a large dinner plate. Spread a ½-inch layer of cream on top of the pastry. Divide the chopped cherries into 8 portions. Spoon one-eighth of the cherries on top of the whipped cream. Place the other half of the puff pastry on top of the cherries to create a cherry sandwich effect. Spoon the warm custard sauce around the entire assembled pastry. About 4 to 6 tablespoons of custard sauce should be enough for each plate. Take a few whole cherries and place them around the outside of the pastry on top of the custard sauce. (*Note:* It is easier to assemble all the cherry sandwiches at one time, line them up, and then spoon the hot custard sauce around them one after another.)

While developing the cherries and puff pastry dish we discovered another dessert which is very easy to make. Follow the directions for making the kirsch custard. Pit one pound of fresh cherries. Pour the finished custard sauce into a large stainless, glass, or porcelain container and add the cherries to the sauce. Cool this mixture in the refrigerator. When the sauce is cool, cover the jar. Refrigerate overnight and serve the next day. The combination of the cherries totally covered and marinated with the kirsch custard is quite delicious.

Hot Peach and Almond Tart

THIS RECIPE makes up into a lovely large tart. The pastry is thin and the filling consists only of sliced peaches and butter, so your guests will manage to consume rather healthy portions. The nuts in the dough make for a cookie-like crust and the tartness of the fruit contrasts well with the sweetness of the pastry. You can, if you wish, cut the recipe in half and make a 7-inch tart which will serve 4 to 6 people.

PREPARATION TIME:
1 hour (plus 2 hours resting time)

COOKING TIME:
35 minutes

SPECIAL EQUIPMENT:
Large 17- by 14-inch baking sheet

1 cup unsifted flour
¼ cup sugar
16 tablespoons chilled butter, plus 2 tablespoons softened
½ cup finely ground hazelnuts
½ cup finely ground almonds
½ teaspoon vanilla
   Grated rind of 1 lemon
1 egg yolk, beaten
1½ pounds ripe peaches
3 tablespoons brown sugar
2 to 3 tablespoons confectioners' sugar, optional
   Salt

1. Make this pastry at least two hours before rolling it out or, better still, prepare it the night before and refrigerate. Place the flour, sugar, and a pinch of salt in a large mixing bowl. Cut the butter into 16 tablespoon-sized pieces and, with your fingertips, quickly rub it into the flour and sugar until the mixture is the consistency of coarse meal. This step can be done by blending the ingredients in a food processor for 15 seconds.

2. Stir the ground nuts thoroughly into the flour.

3. In a separate small bowl, mix the vanilla and lemon rind into the beaten egg yolk.

4. Make a well in the flour and nut mixture and pour the egg mixture into the center of the well. Using your fingertips, quickly gather the flour into the egg until the dough just sticks together. It will be softer and stickier than an ordinary pie dough because of the high proportion of nuts.

5. Wrap the dough in wax paper and refrigerate for at least 2 hours or overnight.

6. Preheat the oven to 375 degrees.

7. Roll out the pastry between 2 pieces of wax paper (otherwise the dough will stick mercilessly to your rolling pin) until you have formed a circle about 13 inches in diameter. Lift the top piece of the wax paper off. Holding the edges of the bottom piece of wax paper, transfer the pastry to a buttered baking sheet. Place the dough-side down on the sheet and peel off the wax paper.

8. Using your thumb and forefinger, pinch the edges of the circle up in order to form a free standing ¼-inch high lip all around the pastry. This is easy to do as the pastry is very soft and pliable.

9. Bake the dough for 20 minutes or until the pastry is light brown. Remove it from the oven.

10. While the pastry is baking, plunge the peaches in boiling water for 20 seconds. Drain and refresh them under cold water. Now you should be able to remove the skins easily. If the peaches are not ripe enough, the skins will still not slip off and you will have to peel them away with a knife. Cut each peach in half and remove the pit. Slice the peaches as thinly as possible.

11. In a small bowl, combine the 2 tablespoons softened butter and brown sugar until it forms a paste. Spread this on the pre-baked shell.

12. Arrange the sliced peaches in a circular pattern on top of the butter and sugar paste. If the peaches are not sweet enough, sprinkle them with confectioners' sugar. Bake again for 10 to 15 minutes.

PRESENTATION

Bring the hot tart on a platter to the table and cut it into large wedges.

Strawberry Tart

T HE FRESH strawberry and strawberry jam reduction is lighter and fresher tasting than the more traditional *crème patissière* used in baking the classical tart. Be sure to cook the pastry until quite golden.

PREPARATION TIME:
45 minutes
(plus 2 hours resting time)

COOKING TIME:
1 hour

SERVES:
6 to 8

1   *cup unsifted flour*
2   *tablespoons sugar*
4   *tablespoons butter, chilled and cut into ½-inch bits, plus 1*
        tablespoon softened
2   *tablespoons shortening, chilled and cut into bits*
2   *to 3 tablespoons ice water*
3   *pints strawberries, washed and hulled*
½   *cup strawberry preserves or jam*
¼   *cup apricot preserves*
1   *teaspoon Grand Marnier, cognac, or kirsch*
      Whipped cream, optional
      Salt

1. In a large bowl, rub the flour, ¼ teaspoon salt, sugar, butter, and shortening together with the tips of your fingers, until the mixture resembles coarse meal. This step may be done in a food processor by blending the ingredients for 15 seconds.

2. Make a well in the center of the mixture, pour 2 tablespoons of ice water in the center and quickly work these together into a rough ball of pastry which just holds together. The pastry should not be damp or sticky. If, however, it is too dry and there are loose particles of flour which do not adhere to the mass, sprinkle them with the additional ice water and gather them into the ball of dough.

3. Wrap the dough in wax paper or foil and rest it in the refrigerator for at least a couple of hours or overnight.

4. Preheat the oven to 375 degrees.

5. Roll the dough into a ¼-inch thick round. (If you have rested the dough for more than 2 hours, remove the dough 10 minutes before rolling it; otherwise it will be too cold and will crack.)

6. Generously grease a 9-inch false-bottomed tart pan with the softened butter and lift the dough into the mold, pressing the dough against the sides and bottom of the tart pan. Prick the dough with a fork at 1-inch intervals. Place some foil on top of the dough and fill it with dried beans or rice to hold the dough in place while it bakes. Make sure you have used enough beans so that they press against the sides of the shell to keep the sides up. Bake the dough this way for 10 minutes.

7. Take it out of the oven, remove the beans and foil and with a fork prick the bottom again. Rebake for another 15 to 20 minutes, or until the pastry is quite golden and smells like cookie dough. Remove it from the oven and cool it on a rack.

8. While the tart is baking, purée one pint of strawberries in a blender or food processor or with a food mill. Combine the purée and strawberry preserves in a non-aluminum saucepan and cook the mixture, reducing it by half, or until a little less than ¾ cup remains. While it is cooking, stir the bottom every once in a while so that it does not burn. Cool to room temperature.

9. Split the rest of the strawberries in half.

10. A few hours before serving, remove the pastry from the false-bottomed pan, and spread the strawberry filling in the bottom. Place the split strawberries in a neat pattern on top of the filling.

11. Strain the apricot preserves through a sieve into a small saucepan or skillet with the liqueur. Heat this over medium heat, stirring all the while.

12. When hot, remove the glaze from the heat and brush it lightly over the strawberries to give them a shine. Decorate further with the optional whipped cream. Keep the tart refrigerated until you are ready to eat. The longer you keep it refrigerated, however, the soggier it tends to become. Before serving, transfer the tart to a platter.

Chocolate Chip Tartlets

AFTER APPLE PIE and vanilla ice cream, chocolate chip cookies are probably as American as you can get. The idea of a crusty tartlet containing a rich chocolate chip filling is mouthwatering. What is very important in this recipe is to create your own "chips" by cutting imported bittersweet chocolate into ½-inch chunks instead of using the packaged kind.

PREPARATION TIME:
35 minutes
(plus 2 hours resting time)

COOKING TIME:
40 minutes

SERVES:

6

¾   *cup unsifted flour, plus 1 ½ teaspoons*
¼   *cup sugar, plus 1 tablespoon*
2   *tablespoons chilled shortening*
4   *tablespoons chilled butter, plus 3 tablespoons*
2   *tablespoons ice water*
¼   *cup sugar, plus 1 tablespoon*
¼   *cup brown sugar*
2   *eggs*
½   *teaspoon vanilla*
½   *cup roughly chopped walnuts or pecans*
6   *ounces bittersweet chocolate, cut into ½-inch chunks*
     Salt

1. Combine 1 cup flour, ⅛ teaspoon salt, and 1 tablespoon sugar in a 2 quart bowl. Cut the chilled shortening and 4 tablespoons chilled butter into the flour with a knife or your fingertips until the mixture resembles coarse meal. (You may do this in food processor by processing all the ingredients for 15 seconds.) Make a well in the center of the dough. Add the ice water at once and rapidly, with cupped hands, gather the dough into a rough ball that holds together. If the dough is too dry, sprinkle on more droplets of water; if it is too wet, dust with flour and mix in. Do not overwork the dough or it will be rubbery and shrink from the molds.

2. Wrap the dough in wax paper and then in foil and let it rest in the refrigerator for at least 2 hours or overnight.

3. Preheat the oven to 400 degrees.

4. Lightly butter the fluted tartlet molds. Divide the chilled dough into 6 equal pieces. Roll each about 1 inch larger than your tartlet molds. Place a piece of rolled out dough in the mold, making sure it adheres well to the inside crevices of the fluted sides. Repeat for the other molds. Prick the bottoms in several places with a fork. Line each tartlet shell with foil and place a handful of dried beans or rice in the tartlet shells.

5. Place all 6 molds on a baking sheet and bake for 5 minutes. Remove from the oven, remove the weights and paper, prick the bottoms of the dough again, and bake for another 7 minutes. Remove from the oven and cool. Turn the oven temperature to 325 degrees.

6. Cream the remaining 3 tablespoons butter with ¼ cup granulated sugar and brown sugar until light and fluffy. Beat in the eggs one at a time. Add a pinch of salt, vanilla, 1½ teaspoons flour, nuts, and chocolate chunks and mix together.

7. Spoon an equal amount into each tartlet shell. Place all 6 on a baking sheet again and bake at 325 degrees for 25 minutes or until lightly golden on top and the dough is set and no longer runny.

8. Remove from the oven and cool on a rack for 45 minutes. Ease tartlets out of the molds by first detaching the edges from the sides of the molds. When you have eased them out, finish cooling completely on a rack.

Upside-Down Pecan Pie

THE IDEA for this pie came to us when we experimented with a variation of the classic *tarte Tatin* with pecans. One recipe led to another: the apples got lost in the shuffle, but caramelizing the mold and placing the dough on top of the filling has remained from the original. The result is our Upside-Down Pecan Pie.

PREPARATION TIME:
40 minutes
(plus 2 hours resting time)

COOKING TIME:
50 minutes

SERVES:
8

1   *cup unsifted flour*
4   *tablespoons chilled lard*
2   *tablespoons chilled butter, plus 3 tablespoons melted*
2   *tablespoons ice water*
⅔   *cup sugar, plus ½ cup*
4   *large eggs*
½   *cup light corn syrup*
1½ *teaspoon vanilla*
½   *teaspoon cinnamon*
2   *cups pecans, broken into large pieces*
1   *cup whipped cream, optional*

1. Combine the flour and ½ teaspoon salt in a bowl or in the bowl of a food processor. With your fingertips, or in a food processor, work the lard and chilled butter into the flour until the mixture resembles coarse meal. Make a well in the center of flour and fat and pour in the ice water. Rapidly cup the dough with your hands, blending well until the dough just holds together. You can do this step in the food processor, processing all ingredients for 15 seconds.

2. Wrap the dough in plastic wrap and refrigerate for at least 2 hours, or overnight if possible.

3. Have a 10-inch pie plate ready near the stove. Combine ⅔ cup sugar and ¼ cup water in a small, heavy-bottomed saucepan. Heat slowly until the sugar dissolves. When the sugar is dissolved, brush the sides of the sauce-pan with a pastry brush dipped in cold water to dissolve any sugar crystals which may have clung to the sides of the pan. Let the sugar boil, undisturbed, until it begins to turn to caramel. Turn off the heat.

4. Holding the saucepan with pot holders, pour the caramel into the pie plate. Holding the pie plate with pot holders to protect your hands, twirl it around to evenly spread the caramel over the bottom of the pie plate. Set aside.

5. Preheat the oven to 325 degrees.

6. In a separate bowl, combine the remaining ½ cup sugar, eggs, melted butter, corn syrup, vanilla, and cinnamon. Mix well. Combine with the pecans and pour into the pan.

7. Roll out the dough ⅜-inch thick and about the size of the pie plate. Place the dough on the pie plate and trim the edges to line up with the edges of the pie plate. Let the dough drop over and sink down onto the filling. It should completely cover the filling, come up the sides of the pie plate and cover about ¼-inch of the rim.

8. Place the pie plate on a baking sheet and bake for 50 to 60 minutes or until a knife, when plunged in the center comes out clean. Be sure to test the center, which is the last part to bake thoroughly.

9. Remove the pie from the oven. Run the edge of

a sharp knife around the edges of the pie to loosen it from the pan. Let it rest for 5 minutes.

PRESENTATION

Place a serving plate on top of the pie plate. With towels, to protect your hands, turn the pie plate upside down. The pie plate should come off easily. If any pecans stick to the bottom, pick them up and replace them on the pie. You should be left with a beautifully shiny pecan pie, with just a hint of dough peeking through from underneath. Let the pie cool for 1 hour and serve at room temperature with whipped cream.

Pumpkin Pie

IF THERE were such a thing as the *grand dessert* cart in America, our classic Pumpkin Pie would have to be included.

PREPARATION TIME:
40 minutes
(plus 2 hours resting time)

COOKING TIME:
1 hour and 5 minutes

SERVES:
8 to 10

⅔   cup unsifted flour
1½ tablespoons sugar
6   tablespoons chilled butter, plus 2 tablespoons softened
1½ tablespoons ice water
⅓   cup ground pecans
1   cup brown sugar
2   eggs, plus 1 egg yolk
1   cup unsweetened pumpkin purée (canned or fresh)
1   tablespoon flour
¼   teaspoon cloves
¼   teaspoon cinnamon
1   cup heavy cream
1   cup whipped cream, optional
     Salt

1. Place the flour, a pinch of salt, and the sugar in a mixing bowl and mix together.

2. Cut the chilled butter into 12 pieces and add them to the flour.

3. With your fingertips work the butter into the flour until the mixture resembles coarse meal. Work fast so that the butter does not begin to turn oily. Form a well in the center of the flour and pour the ice water into the well. With your hands gather the dough rapidly into a mass that just sticks together. If the dough is too dry, add more ice water by droplets, until the dough holds together. Do not knead the dough or else you will end up with a rubbery tart. (*Note:* This step can be done in a food processor by processing all ingredients for 15 seconds.)

4. Wrap the dough in wax paper and refrigerate it for at least 2 hours or overnight.

5. Heat the oven to 400 degrees.

6. Butter a 9-inch pie plate. Roll out the pastry and fit it into the pie plate. Place foil inside the dough. Add dry beans, or rice to weight down the dough and bake it for 10 minutes. Remove the pastry from the oven and discard the foil and weights.

7. While the pastry is baking, make the filling. Combine the pecans, ⅓ cup brown sugar, and 2 tablespoons softened butter and work them into a paste. Spread this with a rubber spatula into the partially cooked pastry shell and return it to the oven for 10 more minutes. Remove the pastry from the oven.

8. While the pastry is cooking, combine in a bowl the eggs, egg yolk, the pumpkin purée, 1 tablespoon flour, ⅔ cups brown sugar, spices, ½ teaspoon salt, and cream. When the pastry is done, pour this into the pastry shell.

9. Turn the oven down to 325 degrees and bake the pie for 45 minutes.

PRESENTATION

You may serve this hot or cold with sweetened whipped cream. Portion the pie out at the table and serve whipped cream on the side.

Butter Cookies

THESE ARE incredibly easy to make and taste wonderfully rich. This recipe makes about 3 dozen butter cookies.

PREPARATION TIME:
10 minutes
(plus 2 hours resting time)

COOKING TIME:
12 to 14 minutes

9   tablespoons butter, at room temperature
1   egg, separated
6   tablespoons superfine sugar
1   cup unsifted flour
¼   cup sliced almonds

1. Combine 8 tablespoons butter, the egg yolk, sugar, a pinch of salt, and the flour in a little bowl.

2. When the ingredients are completely blended, divide the dough in half and roll each one into a cylinder, approximately 1½ inches in diameter and 6 inches long.

3. Wrap each cylinder in wax paper and then in foil. Refrigerate until hard. This should take at least 2 hours.

4. Preheat the oven to 375 degrees.

5. Grease 2 baking sheets with the remaining butter. Remove the dough from the refrigerator and slice each cylinder crosswise into ¼-inch rounds. Place each round on a baking sheet. Don't crowd them too closely together. The cookies will spread as they bake and could run into each other. Brush the tops of the cookies with the remaining egg white and place some sliced almonds on each cookie.

6. Bake for 12 to 14 minutes or until the edges begin to brown. Cool on a cookie rack.

Chocolate Truffles

A T THE END of a three-star meal in France, even after a great many desserts, platters of cookies and petits fours are brought to the table to be eaten with coffee. If you care to be this authentic and over-indulge yourself, here is a recipe for chocolate truffles which you can serve with or after dessert and coffee.

PREPARATION TIME:
1 hour

COOKING TIME:
10 minutes

MAKES:
8 truffles

6 *ounces bittersweet chocolate, cut into 1-inch pieces*
¼ *cup milk*
1 *tablespoon sugar*
½ *tablespoon butter*
¼ *pound walnuts, roughly chopped*
¼ *cup cocoa powder*

1. Place the chocolate, milk, and sugar in a heavy saucepan and melt these together over low heat, stirring constantly with a wooden spoon.

2. When the chocolate has melted, add the butter, and continue to stir over low heat with a wooden spoon until the mixture has thickened slightly. This should take about 5 minutes.

3. Add the walnuts and cook for 2 minutes longer.

4. Spread the hot chocolate and nut mixture in an 8- to 9-inch lightly, buttered dish or cake pan and let the mixture cool for about 15 minutes, or until cool but still pliable.

5. When cool, break off pieces of chocolate and roll them in your hands into 1-inch balls. They should look rough and uneven in order to simulate real truffles. Roll in cocoa powder and refrigerate until serving time.

Palmiers

THIS RECIPE is included because not only are the cookies delicious, they are a good way to use puff pastry
trimmings. Of course you can also make *palmiers*
from the large sheet of pastry and not just from the
scraps. This recipe makes about 25 cookies.

PREPARATION TIME:
15 minutes

COOKING TIME:
20 minutes

Leftover strips of trimmed puff pastry, or regular puff pastry
Sugar

1. Line up the strips of the trimmed puff pastry.
With a pastry brush dipped in water lightly moisten the
exposed edges of the pastry.

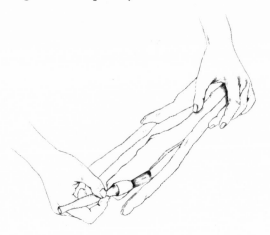

2. Push all the edges together and, lightly pack them to seal. Liberally dust the surface of the pastry with sugar and roll the pastry to approximately 4- by 10- to 12-inches. Turn the pastry over and dust the other side with sugar.

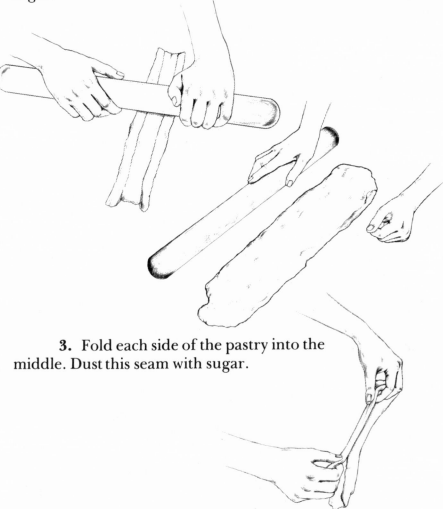

3. Fold each side of the pastry into the middle. Dust this seam with sugar.

4. Now fold the pastry in half. Gently apply pressure to the top of the folded pastry to flatten it out and even it up.

5. Take a bench scraper and cut ⅜-inch pieces from the strip of pastry. Transfer these pieces to a cookie sheet, which has been either buttered or covered with silicone-treated baking paper. Form the cookies by turning the edges out to approximate a bell shape, or by turning the edges in on themselves.

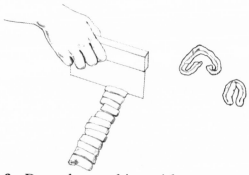

6. Dust the cookies with more sugar. Refrigerate for at least 1 hour.

7. Preheat the oven to 400 degrees.

8. Remove the cookies from the refrigerator and place them in the oven. Bake for 10 to 15 minutes, or until the sugar on top of the cookie begins to caramelize and turn golden brown. Turn them over and bake for another 5 minutes until the second side is golden brown. Watch these carefully as they bake unevenly and will burn if over-baked.

Note: The recipe explains how to make *palmiers* out of the scraps of the trimmed puff pastry. *Palmiers* can also be made by using regular puff pastry and will in fact be more tender because the dough will not have been handled as much. To make the *palmiers* out of the fresh pastry, simply cut a 2-inch strip from the large sheet of finished pastry and liberally dust with sugar. Roll the strip out until it measures 4 inches in width. At this point refer to step 2 on the *palmiers* recipe (from "turn the pastry over and dust this side with sugar"). Proceed according to instructions. A 2-by 14-inch piece of puff pastry will yield 50 *palmiers*.

Cranberry Soufflé

THIS RECIPE is sure to help elevate the "once-at-Thanksgiving" status of the cranberry. Make the soufflé whenever cranberries are in season. The amount of sauce may seem excessive but you need this much to suffuse the soufflé with a powerful cranberry flavor.

PREPARATION TIME:
1 hour

COOKING TIME:
1 hour

SERVES:
4

1	*cup sugar, plus 2 tablespoons*
3	*cups fresh cranberries*
5	*tablespoons butter, plus 2 tablespoons softened*
¼	*cup flour*
¾	*cup milk*
5	*eggs, separated*

1. In a 4-quart saucepan, bring 1½ cups water and ¾ cup sugar to a boil. When the sugar is completely dissolved, add the cranberries, cover, and simmer for 5 minutes, or until the cranberries have popped their skins.

2. Spoon this mixture into a food mill and purée the cranberries. Discard the skins and seeds. If you do not have a food mill, pass this mixture thorough a sieve into a bowl, discarding the cranberry skins and seeds which remain in the sieve.

3. Put ¾ of a cup of this strained cranberry mixture into a saucepan. Reduce this slowly until only ¼ cup remains, stirring now and then so that the bottom does not burn. The mixture will be very thick. Remove from the heat and set aside. Taste the remaining strained cranberry purée which you did not reduce. Add sugar to taste if it is not sweet enough.

4. Grease a 5- to 6- cup soufflé mold with the softened butter. Sprinkle the 2 tablespoons sugar on the bottom and all around the inside of the mold. Shake out any excess sugar. Fasten around the mold a buttered aluminum or paper collar, 2 inches higher than the upper rim of the mold. This is to support the soufflé as it rises. Set aside.

5. Preheat the oven to 400 degrees.

6. In a 2-quart saucepan, melt 3 tablespoons butter. When the bubbles have subsided, add ¼ cup flour and whisk these together. Cook, over medium heat, for a couple of minutes. Whisk in the milk and ¼ cup sugar. Bring to a boil, whisking all the while. As it reaches a boil, the soufflé base will thicken. Whisk vigorously as it thickens so that it does not get lumpy. Continue to cook for a couple of minutes after it has thickened. Remove from the heat.

7. Cool the base slightly. Whisk 4 egg yolks, one at a time, incorporating each one into the base before adding the next one. To this mixture, add the reserved ¼ cup reduced cranberry purée. If you prepare this in advance, dot the top with bits of butter so that a crust does not form on the surface of the soufflé base.

8. Beat 5 egg whites until stiff but not dry. Fold one-quarter of the beaten egg whites into the cranberry soufflé base to lighten it. Fold the rest of the egg whites into the mixture.

9. Pour the mixture into your prepared mold. Set the soufflé in the oven and bake for 5 minutes. Turn the oven temperature down to 375 degrees and bake for 40 minutes longer.

10. Five to 10 minutes before the soufflé is done, return the remaining cranberry purée to a saucepan and set it over medium heat. When hot, whisk in 2 tablespoons butter and stir until smooth. Remove from the heat and pour into a sauceboat.

PRESENTATION

Bring the soufflé to the table with the sauce in a sauceboat. Spoon some sauce on heated dessert plates and spoon one-fourth of the soufflé onto the sauce in the center of the plate. Pass the remaining sauce around.

Mocha Cream

PREPARATION TIME:
1 hour
(plus 6 hours chilling time)

COOKING TIME:
15 minutes

SPECIAL EQUIPMENT:
Candy thermometer

SERVES:
6

2   *ounces bittersweet chocolate*
½   *cup very strong coffee*
¾   *cup sugar*
4   *egg yolks*
6   *tablespoons butter*
¾   *cup chilled heavy cream*
2   *tablespoons almonds, toasted and sliced*

1. Melt the chocolate in the top part of a double boiler set over hot, not boiling, water. Set aside.

2. In a small saucepan, mix the coffee and sugar. Bring this to a boil and boil for 2 to 3 minutes, or until the coffee syrup thickens slightly. Remove from the heat.

3. With a whisk, beat the egg yolks until they are just mixed. In a very thin steady stream, pour the coffee syrup into the yolks to warm them. Whisk all the time while you are pouring so the egg yolks don't curdle.

4. Transfer this mixture to the saucepan in which you cooked the coffee and sugar syrup. With a wooden spoon, stir this constantly over medium heat until a candy thermometer registers 175 degrees. Watch this carefully, stirring all the while, to prevent the eggs from scrambling at the bottom of the pan.

5. When the mixture reaches 175 degrees, remove from the heat and stir in the butter. Continue to stir this mixture until it cools slightly. Add the melted chocolate. Refrigerate until chilled.

6. In a chilled bowl, whip up the heavy cream until stiff. Fold the whipped cream into the chilled mocha mixture. Spoon this mixture into 6 tall wine or champagne glasses. Refrigerate, covered with plastic wrap, for at least 6 hours.

PRESENTATION

Right before serving, top with the sliced almonds.

Frozen Mousse Cassis

THIS IS A variation on the classic Grand Marnier soufflé. One must make the mousse with a cooked sugar
syrup which prevents crystallization in the freezing
process.

PREPARATION TIME:
30 minutes

COOKING TIME:
15 minutes

SPECIAL EQUIPMENT:
Candy thermometer

SERVES:
6 to 8

About 40 homemade or imported ladyfingers
½   *cup imported cassis (black currant liqueur)*
⅓   *cup syrup from imported black currants packed in syrup*
⅔   *cup sugar*
4   *egg yolks*
⅓   *cup drained imported black currants packed in syrup*
1¾ *cups chilled heavy cream*

1. Soak the lady fingers in 5 tablespoons of the cassis.

2. Combine ⅓ cup black currant syrup and the
sugar in a small saucepan. Wash down the insides of the
saucepan with a pastry brush dipped in cold water in order
to ensure that there are no sugar crystals on the sides of the
pan. Bring the mixture to a boil and boil without stirring

until it reaches 238 degrees on a candy thermometer.

3. While the sugar is cooking, with an electric beater, beat the egg yolks until pale yellow.

4. Once the sugar is at the right temperature, immediately remove it from heat, and pour it in a thin steady stream into the egg yolks while you continue to beat with the electric mixer. Continue to beat for 10 minutes or until you have a thick rich cream.

5. Fold the remaining 3 tablespoons cassis and the drained black currants into the cream. Refrigerate until chilled.

6. In a chilled bowl, whip the cream until semi-stiff peaks form. Fold this into the cassis cream.

7. Line the insides of 6 to 8 wine glasses with the lady fingers. Stand them up vertically. They should adhere to the glasses because of the moisture in the cassis. Pour the cassis cream in the middle of the glass. Place the glasses on a tray so that they don't wobble in the freezer. Cover the glasses with plastic wrap and freeze overnight.

PRESENTATION

Transfer the glasses to the refrigerator 15 to 30 minutes before serving time in order to soften the mixture.

Lime Soufflé

PREPARATION TIME:
1 hour

COOKING TIME:
10 minutes

SPECIAL EQUIPMENT:
Six 8½-cup oven-proof ramekins

SERVES:
6

1 *cup sugar, plus 6 tablespoons*
4 *tablespoons superfine sugar*
2 *eggs, separated, plus 2 extra egg whites*
½ *cup freshly squeezed lime juice (5 to 6 limes)*
2 *tablespoons flour*
2 *tablespoons dark rum*
   Grated rind of 2 limes
1 *tablespoon butter*
1 *tablespoon confectioners' sugar*
   Salt

1. In a small saucepan, dissolve 1 cup sugar in ½ cup cold water. Slowly bring this mixture to a boil, brushing down the sides of the pan with a pastry brush dipped in cold water to dissolve any sugar crystals.

2. Once the sugar has dissolved into a syrup, raise the heat and let the sugar syrup cook without stirring until it begins to turn a dark golden color and smells of caramel. While sugar is turning to caramel, bring ¾ cup water to a boil in a separate saucepan.

3. Once the sugar has caramelized, turn off the heat. Measure ½ cup boiling water into a pyrex measuring cup and, drop by drop, pour the water into the caramel. At first, the water and caramel will splatter dangerously, so move away as you pour, so that you do not burn yourself. Once you have introduced some water into the caramel, you can go a little faster with the rest. Bring the caramel back to a boil, stirring all the while with a wooden spoon. Boil, stirring constantly, for about 1 minute. Remove from the heat and set aside.

4. Gradually whisk the superfine sugar into the egg yolks. Beat these together until they turn an ivory color. Meanwhile bring the lime juice to a boil. Beat the flour into the sugar and yolks and then gradually beat in the boiling lime juice.

5. Return this mixture to the heat. Bring it to a boil, whisking all the while. As it comes to a boil, the mixture will thicken. Continue to whisk for about 1 minute, reaching into the corners of the pan so that the bottom does not scorch. Remove from the heat and immediately pour in the rum and half the grated lime rind. Cool to room temperature and transfer the mixture to a larger mixing bowl. This is your soufflé base.

6. Preheat the oven to 400 degrees.

7. Butter the oven-proof ramekins. Sprinkle each one with 1 tablespoon sugar and roll the sugar around to coat all sides of the molds. Set aside.

8. With an electric mixer, beat the egg whites with a pinch of salt until they form stiff, but not dry, peaks.

9. Ladle about 1½ tablespoons of the caramel in the bottom of each of the oven-proof ramekins. Fold the rest of the caramel into the egg yolk-lime juice base. Fold one-fourth of the egg whites into the base and when this is folded together, fold in the rest of egg whites. Fold them together rapidly until no more egg whites show.

10. Gently spoon one-sixth of the soufflé mixture into each of the ramekins. Place them on a baking sheet and sift some confectioners' sugar on top of each one. Bake immediately for 10 minutes. Serve at once.

Plum and Nectarine Flan

BAKING THIS DISH in a *bain marie* insures a creamy, very tender custard. If some of the fruit juices seep below the custard while baking, just spoon them over the dessert as you serve. The ripeness of the fruit will affect the amount of liquid given off in the pan while the flan bakes.

PREPARATION TIME:
1 hour and 20 minutes

COOKING TIME:
45 minutes

SERVES:
4 to 6

2   *ripe plums, about 8 ounces each*
2   *ripe nectarines, about 8 ounces each*
¼   *cup sugar*
1   *tablespoon kirsch*
¼   *cup heavy cream*
     Pinch of salt
2   *egg yolks*

1. Wash the fruit and dry well on paper towels. Cut the fruit in half and remove the pits. Cut each half into ¼-inch slices. Keep the plums separate from the nectarines.

2. Place the plums in one bowl and the nectarines in another. To each bowl, add 2 tablespoons sugar and ½ tablespoon kirsch. Cover with plastic wrap and let marinate for 1 hour at room temperature.

3. Preheat the oven to 325 degrees.

4. Remove the fruit from the liquid and pat it dry on a paper towel. Place the fruit in a 9-inch oven-proof, ceramic, or glass pie plate that is pretty enough to serve from. Arrange the fruit in alternate slices of plums and nectarines, skin side up, in a circle around the outside edge of the pie plate. Place the fruit so that it is nearly standing upright on its inside edge. Any left over fruit should be placed in the center.

5. Transfer any remaining liquid from the fruit bowls to a measuring cup. Add enough cream to this liquid to make ½ cup in all. Add a pinch of salt. In a separate small bowl place the egg yolks and whisk in the cream mixture. Blend well and pour over the fruit in the pie plate.

6. Place the pie plate in a large baking pan. Pour hot water into the pan until the water comes three-quarters of the way up the sides of pie plate. Bake for 45 minutes. Remove the pie plate from the oven and cool for 10 minutes.

Peach Ice Cream

WAIT UNTIL you can get deliciously ripe, sweet, and fragrant peaches before trying this recipe.

PREPARATION TIME:
45 minutes
(plus 8 hours cooling and freezing time)

SPECIAL EQUIPMENT:
Ice cream maker

SERVES:
8

2   *quarts light cream*
2⅔ *cups sugar*
½   *vanilla bean*
4   *pounds very ripe peaches, plus 8 peaches*

1. Combine the cream with 2 cups sugar in a heavy 5-quart saucepan. Add the vanilla bean. Slowly bring this mixture to a boil over medium-low heat, stirring the sugar occasionally to ensure it dissolves. Don't heat the cream too quickly or it will scorch.

2. Remove the cream from the heat and let it cool to room temperature. When cool, refrigerate in a covered bowl for 5 hours or overnight.

3. Bring 3 quarts of water to a boil. In several batches, plunge in the 4 pounds of peaches for 1 minute. Drain and refresh them under cold water. With a sharp, stainless steel knife, peel off the skins. Pit the peaches and mash them with ⅔ cup sugar, either by hand or in the food processor. Refrigerate, covered, until the sugar is dissolved.

4. Later, or the next day, remove the cream and the peaches from the refrigerator. Remove the vanilla bean from the cream. Add the cream to your ice cream maker and proceed following the directions of your ice cream maker. Half-way through the freezing process, add the peaches and continue. When done, freeze the ice cream, packing it well, for 2 hours at least, to firm it up.

5. Make the garnish. Bring 2 quarts of water to a boil. Parboil the 8 peaches for 1 minute. Refresh them under cold running water and peel them. Cut each peach in half and remove the pit. Cut each peach half into ¼-inch slices.

PRESENTATION

Place the peaches in a wreath of overlapping slices on the outer edge of dessert plates. Place a hefty serving of ice cream in the center of the peach wreaths. Serve immediately.

Vanilla Ice Cream with Hot Blueberry Sauce

ANY AMERICAN nouvelle cuisine dessert cart would certainly include a vanilla ice cream. Here is a simple American version of vanilla ice cream, made without eggs. We serve it with a hot blueberry purée, but you could substitute a hot purée of any regional summer fruit in season. Just be sure the fruit you use is fragrant and ripe. The tartness of the fruit contrasts beautifully with the sweet taste of the ice cream.

PREPARATION TIME:
35 minutes
(plus 7 hours cooling and freezing time)

COOKING TIME:
30 minutes

SPECIAL EQUIPMENT:
Ice cream maker

SERVES:
8

2 *quarts light cream*
2 *cups sugar*
2 *vanilla beans*
1 *pint fresh blueberries*
   Salt

1. In a 5-quart saucepan, combine the cream and sugar. Split the vanilla beans down the middle and add them, whole, to the cream. Slowly bring this mixture to just a boil over medium-low heat stirring to dissolve the sugar. Don't heat the cream too quickly or the bottom will scorch.

2. Remove the mixture from the heat. Remove the vanilla beans and scrape any seeds in the vanilla beans into the cream. Return the beans to the cream and cool to room temperature. When cool, refrigerate in a covered bowl for at least 5 hours or overnight.

3. Remove the vanilla beans from the cream and proceed to make the ice cream according to the directions of your ice cream maker. Once ice cream is made be sure to leave it at least 2 hours in the freezer to ripen.

4. Purée the blueberries in a food processor.

5. Just before serving, bring the purée to a boil, and remove from the heat immediately.

PRESENTATION

Place some hot blueberry purée in deep bowls. Scoop cold ice cream on top. Serve immediately.

Green Tea Ice Cream

T HE FLAVOR of Chinese or Japanese tea works best in this type of ice cream. You could experiment with common varieties of tea, but the flavor would not be as unique.

PREPARATION TIME:
35 minutes
(plus 7 hours cooling and freezing time)

SPECIAL EQUIPMENT:
Ice cream maker

SERVES:
4

1   *quart light cream*
2   *tablespoons loose green tea leaves*
½   *teaspoon dried ground ginger*
1   *cup sugar*
    Salt

1. Combine the cream, green tea leaves, ginger, sugar, and a pinch of salt in a 2-quart heavy-bottomed saucepan. Whisk the ingredients together and slowly bring the mixture to a boil over a medium-low heat.

2. When it just comes to a boil, remove from the heat and let cool to room temperature. Refrigerate in a bowl, covered, for 5 hours, or overnight.

3. Remove the mixture from the refrigerator and strain through a fine strainer to eliminate any tea leaves which would catch on the dasher and prevent the freezing process. Proceed with the directions of your ice cream maker. Freeze for 2 hours or more to harden ice cream.

Apple Purée

THIS RECIPE was inspired by the beginning steps of a recipe for cold apple *mousseline* taught at Lydie Marshall's cooking school in New York. This is, essentially, an elegant and rich apple sauce.

PREPARATION TIME:
20 minutes

COOKING TIME:
25 minutes

SERVES:
4 to 6

1½ *pounds McIntosh apples*
3   *tablespoons Calvados or cognac*
8   *to 10 tablespoons sugar*
6   *tablespoons butter*
2   *egg yolks*

   1. Peel, core and cut the apples into eighths. Place them with 2 tablespoons water in a large 12-inch skillet. Cover and stew them over medium heat for about 10 minutes until soft.
   2. When they are soft, uncover, raise the heat, and, with a wooden spoon, mash the apples until they are reduced to a purée, and all the liquid has evaporated. This should take another 6 minutes or so.
   3. Add the Calvados and sugar (according to taste) and continue to stir over high heat for about 15 minutes more or until the apples turn dark golden and the sugar is just about to caramelize. The purée should be somewhat

dry at this point. Remove from heat and stir in the butter to melt it completely.

4. Transfer the contents of the skillet to a food processor, blender, or food mill and blend until completely smooth. If the purée still has pieces of apple in it, pass it through a sieve. Blend in the egg yolks and taste for sweetness. Add more sugar if you do not find it sweet enough. Serve immediately or make in advance and reheat in the top of a double boiler. You may also serve it cold the next day.

PRESENTATION:

Serve in tall wine or champagne glasses accompanied by Butter Cookies (page 407).

Melon with Honey and Rum Sauce

ALTHOUGH YOU can make this dessert using one kind of melon it is really most beautiful when done with a combination of three melons of different tastes and hues.

PREPARATION TIME:
1 hour

2 minutes

4

1   to 1 ¼ cups of diced melon per person, or about 5 cups in all,
      preferably ⅓ canteloupe, ⅓ watermelon, ⅓ honeydew
4   tablespoons honey
1   tablespoon dark rum
2   tablespoons butter
      Pinch of salt

   1. Cut the different melons into approximately ¾-inch dice. Keep each kind of melon in a separate bowl. Cover and refrigerate for 30 minutes.
   2. Just before serving bring the honey, rum and a pinch of salt to a boil in a small skillet. When it comes to a boil, turn off the heat and whisk in the butter.

PRESENTATION

Arrange a row of diced canteloupe to the right of each plate, then a row of honeydew in the center and a row of watermelon to the left. Spoon the sauce over the melon and serve.

Pineapple Gratin

H OT PINEAPPLE dishes are usually served too sweet destroying the lovely flavor of the fruit. In this recipe, the flavor of the tart pineapple marries with the cream, kirsch, and brown sugar into a pleasant combination highlighted by the slightly crunchy texture of the ground walnuts. Essential to the success of the dish is a sweet, ripe pineapple—one which smells fragrant and has top leaves which can be easily removed by pulling on them slightly.

PREPARATION TIME:
20 minutes

COOKING TIME:
8 minutes

SPECIAL EQUIPMENT:
Six ½-cup oven-proof ramekins

SERVES:
6

1   *ripe pineapple*
1   *cup heavy cream*
1   *tablespoon kirsch*
3   *tablespoons brown sugar*
½   *cup walnuts, toasted and finely ground (see David's Cake, page 377, step 1)*
2   *tablespoons butter*

   1. With a sharp stainless steel knife (so that you don't blacken the fruit) cut away the top and the skin from the pineapple. Make sure you cut away the black "eyes" from the flesh. Next cut away and discard the center core. Roughly chop the flesh and set it aside.

2. Preheat the oven to 400 degrees.

3. In a 9-inch skillet, reduce the heavy cream until only ⅓ cup remains. Mix in the kirsch, 1 tablespoon brown sugar, and the ground nuts. Combine with the chopped pineapple.

4. Butter the ramekins, then spoon in the mixture and dot the tops with cut-up pieces of butter. Place the ramekins on a baking sheet and bake for 5 minutes. Remove them from oven.

5. Turn on the broiler. Sprinkle the remaining brown sugar on top of the ramekins and broil for 1 to 2 minutes, or until the brown sugar melts and becomes slightly crusty without burning. Serve immediately.

Sautéed Pears with Raspberry Sauce

T HIS IS A recipe of contrasts. The cold whipped cream is a surprise against the hot fruit and jam; the crunch of the nuts is pleasant in contrast to the tender flesh of the pears. You may use any variety of pear for this recipe except comice, which are too watery and lose their shape sautéed.

PREPARATION TIME:
20 minutes

COOKING TIME:
20 minutes

⅓ cup heavy cream
6 pears (about 2 ½ pounds)
½ lemon
4 tablespoons butter
¼ cup Grand Marnier
½ cup raspberry preserves, strained to remove seeds
¼ cup almonds, toasted and slivered

1. In a chilled bowl, whip the cream until stiff and set aside, covered, in the refrigerator.

2. With a stainless steel knife, peel and core the pears and cut them into eighths. Rub them with the cut edge of the lemon so that they do not discolor. Set them aside in a covered bowl in the refrigerator until you are ready to use.

3. Have two 9-inch skillets ready. In the first, melt the butter and, when hot, toss in the pears and sauté them over high heat for 1 to 2 minutes, coating all the pears with the butter.

4. Turn down the heat, cover the skillet and cook the pears for another 3 minutes, or until cooked but not mushy.

5. With a slotted spoon, transfer the sautéed pears to the second skillet and keep them warm over very low heat until the sauce is ready.

6. Deglaze the pan in which you sautéed the pears with the Grand Marnier and strained raspberry preserves. Mix these with the pear juices in the skillet and cook over high heat until there are rather large bubbles forming all over the surface of the pan and the syrup is quite thick. Remove from the heat.

Spoon the pears onto 4 plates. Spoon the hot raspberry sauce over the fruit and strew the nuts over the sauce. Top with cold whipped cream and serve immediately to capture the contrast of the hot pears and the cold cream.

Pink Pear with Dark Chocolate

THIS DESSERT is a marvel on all counts. A red wine syrup turns the pear purée a beautiful pink. Lying on a bed of chocolate curls, the hot purée leaves an occasional bite of chocolate unmelted for the diner to find and delight in. The texture is light and the presentation superb. You can use any variety of pear in season.

PREPARATION TIME:
1 hour and 30 minutes

COOKING TIME:
55 minutes

SPECIAL EQUIPMENT:
Marble or plastic cutting board or Formica counter
Long flexible icing spatula

SERVES:
4

3   ounces bittersweet chocolate
1½   pounds pears
     Bowl of cold water mixed with juice of a lemon
1   cup dry red wine
1   cup water
5   tablespoons sugar
4   tablespoons butter, at room temperature

1. In the top of a double boiler over hot, not boiling, water, melt the chocolate. When it is soft, spread it onto a marble or plastic cutting board (or any other non-wood surface, such as a Formica counter). Using a long-bladed flexible icing spatula spread the chocolate all over the surface until it is paper thin. Then, still using the spatula, work the chocolate back and forth until it loses its glossy shine and begins to turn dull and hard. Leave the chocolate to harden for another 10 minutes.

2. Holding a sharp knife at a 45 degree angle from the surface, scrape up the chocolate. It will roll up onto itself as you lift, forming both long and short shavings. The shavings do not have to be all the same size. Some will be longer or fatter than others. Carefully scoop up the shavings into a bowl and reserve them in the refrigerator until later.

3. With a stainless steel knife, peel, core, and quarter the pears. Drop them in the bowl of water mixed with lemon juice so that they do not discolor.

4. In a non-aluminum saucepan, bring the wine, water, and 2 tablespoons sugar to a boil. When the mixture is boiling, add the pears, reduce the heat, and simmer, partially covered, for 7 to 10 minutes, or until the pears are soft but not mushy.

5. With a slotted spoon, remove the pears from the wine syrup and set them aside.

6. Reduce the wine syrup over high heat until only 2 tablespoons remain. When it has sufficiently reduced, it will quite miraculously change from its liquid state to a syrupy glaze. Remove from the heat immediately.

7. While the wine is reducing, purée the pears with the butter and the remaining sugar in a blender or food processor. The pears will be quite liquidy at this point.

8. Add the reduced wine syrup. The purée can now be kept in the refrigerator and you can serve it the next day if you wish. ●

9. When you are ready to serve the purée, arrange the chocolate curls on 4 dessert plates. They should be spread in a circle, reserving ¼ cup of the curls for topping.

10. In a saucepan, bring the purée to a simmer, and simmer until it is hot throughout.

PRESENTATION

Spoon one-quarter of the hot pear purée onto the center of each dessert plate, on top of the chocolate shavings. Leave a border of chocolate peeking from underneath the purée. Top each portion with 1 tablespoon of reserved chocolate curls and serve immediately.

Chocolate-Dipped Strawberries

THIS IS A simple yet elegant recipe. The trick to success is to get the chocolate to just the right temperature before dipping the strawberries.

PREPARATION TIME:
20 minutes

2   *to 3 pints large sweet strawberries*
½   *pound bittersweet chocolate.*
¾   *cup heavy cream or* crème fraîche
1   *teaspoon vegetable oil or silicone-treated baking paper*

1. Wash and thoroughly dry the strawberries. Do not remove the stems. Set aside.

2. In the top of a double boiler melt the chocolate, over hot, not boiling water. When the chocolate has melted, add the cream and blend together. Remove the chocolate from the heat, but continue to mix the chocolate and the cream until the mixture is completely smooth.

3. Cool the chocolate down to 98 to 102 degrees (check on a candy thermometer). You may place the chocolate in the refrigerator to speed this process. Make sure to mix the chocolate every 10 minutes.

4. When the chocolate is at the right temperature the strawberries are ready to be dipped. Get a large baking sheet and either lightly oil it or cover it with a piece of silicone-treated baking paper. Holding a strawberry by its stem, dip it into the chocolate. Turn the berry around so that the chocolate covers it completely on all sides. Leave the upper quarter of the berry uncovered (the part nearest the stem). Twist the berry to prevent dribbles and gently lay it on the baking sheet. Repeat this process until you run out of strawberries.

5. Place the tray in the refrigerator to set the chocolate. After the chocolate has set you can remove the berries to a serving platter by gently running a spatula under them. They should lift off the baking sheet and/or parchment paper rather easily. You can leave the strawberries on the serving platter in the refrigerator until you are ready to serve them.

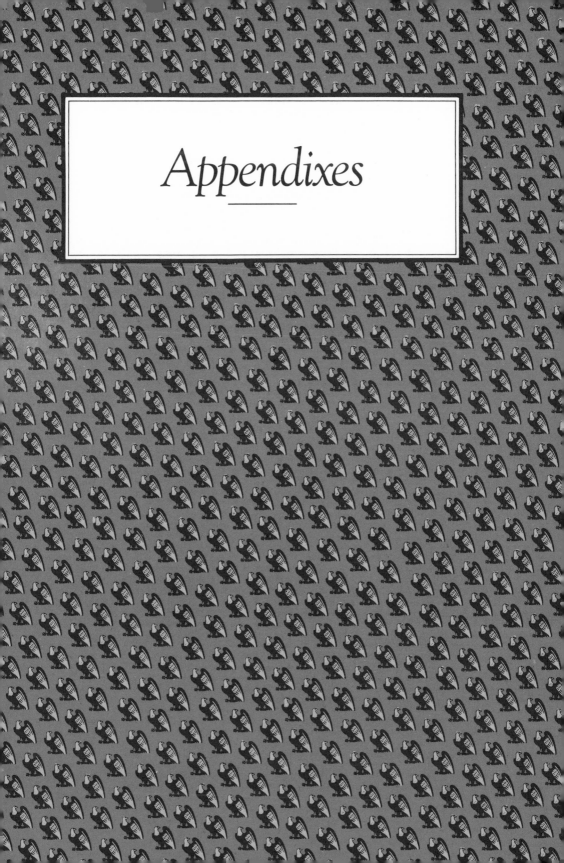

Appendixes

Glossary of Ingredients

ALMONDS *Sliced and Slivered:* These two cuts are often confused. Sliced almonds have the skin still on. Slivered almonds are skinless, elliptical in shape, and about ⅛ inch thick.

BLACK CURRANTS This berry from the currant bush is used to make the French liqueur cassis, which has become an increasingly popular ingredient in making apéritifs. You cannot get fresh currants, but you can buy them in a jar, packed in a light syrup. The best brand to buy is made in Poland, by a company called Globus, and can be found in gourmet food stores.

BLACK OLIVES When we use olives in our recipes we use the full-flavored, imported, small niçoise olives. These are the most flavorful. They can be bought, packed in jars, in gourmet food stores. The only inconvenience is that you have to pit them; the flavor, though, makes this chore worthwhile. Stay away from American olives which are virtually flavorless.

BREADCRUMBS (FRESH) This term refers to breadcrumbs made by pulverizing fresh, crustless French or Italian bread in a food processor or blender. The resulting crumbs are rather large, moist, and spongy and different from those made from dried out bread.

CELERY KNOB Also known as celeriac, this is a root vegetable available in winter months.

CHICKENS There are many grades of chicken for sale. Most brand name chickens are grown by thousands of different farmers and therefore, birds with the same brand name can still taste different. We have found that the tastiest chickens are the ones that have been allowed to scratch around in the dirt and eat real (non synthetic) food. Poultry sold in Kosher butcher shops have always been raised in this time-consuming manner. Kosher chickens will cost more, but you *can* taste the difference.

CHOCOLATE There is one very simple rule to remember when buying chocolate: "You get what you pay for." Look for chocolate which has a high cocoa ratio on the label. Good chocolate should contain at least 50 percent cocoa. The higher the cocoa ratio the more expensive the chocolate will be. The chocolate we recommend you use is bittersweet or extra-bittersweet. Usually extra-bittersweet has 10 percent more cocoa then bittersweet.

COARSE OR KOSHER SALT This is pure salt in crystal form to which no preservatives have been added. More coarsely ground than table salt, it tastes less salty when used measure for measure.

CREAM All the recipes in this book that require cream work very well with regular "heavy" or "whipping" cream. Try not to use brands that are "ultra-sterilized" or "ultra-pasteurized." Some of these brands have perservatives added to lengthen shelf life. If you are in doubt about which brand to choose, read the label carefully.

CRÈME FRAÎCHE In France, this is a naturally thick heavy cream which has a minimum of 30 percent butterfat. Because of its natural body it is often used to thicken sauces. To make a substitute in this country, stir one teaspoon of yogurt, buttermilk, or sour cream into a cup of heavy cream. Let sit in a warm place undisturbed for 8 to 10 hours or until thick. Refrigerate covered. Cream will continue to thicken and sour in the refrigerator.

DUCK Fresh duck (duck which has not been frozen) is widely available in the United States. If at all possible we suggest you use it. In mid-April many markets carry 2½- to 3-pound ducklings. The meat is very tender and roasts beautifully.

EGGS All eggs used in our book refer to U.S. Grade A Large eggs.

EGG WASH This refers to one egg mixed with about 1 teaspoon of water, usually brushed onto the surface of bread or pastry doughs to give it a golden color. An egg wash turns a lovely golden brown before the dough is baked through, so beware that your egg wash does not fool you into thinking that the dough is cooked before it really is.

FIVE SPICE POWDER This spice is used in Chinese cooking and is available in Chinese food stores. It is a combination of 5 ground spices: cinnamon, cloves, fennel, star anise, and Szechuan peppercorns.

FLOUR We recommend unbleached all-purpose flour for general use in baking. When a recipe calls for cake flour, buy a brand which does not contain baking powder. Cake flour with no preservatives or stabilizers is widely available in supermarkets.

FOIE GRAS Fresh *foie gras* is often available during the winter months in the United States. It is far superior to the *foie gras* sold in cans. If you have never tasted the fresh variety you are in for a real treat. It is incredibly rich and smooth. However, rest assured that if you can't locate the fresh product, the canned is a definite alternative.

FROGS' LEGS Many people believe that the flesh of frogs' legs tastes similar to chicken. Chinese markets in this country carry a supply of fresh legs year round and butcher shops that carry exotic game will often have a source for the frozen variety.

FRUIT OLIVE OIL This is also called green olive oil and it is derived from the first pressing of olives.

GINGER When buying fresh ginger look for plump pieces in a light tan, tight skin. If the ginger looks shrivelled up, don't buy it. To prepare ginger for use, pare away the outer skin and cut up the ginger as called for in the recipe. As our recipes don't call for much ginger you will have some leftover which you will need to store. In order to do so, pare away the outer skin, rinse it under cold water, and preserve it, covered with sherry, in a jar in the refrigerator. It will keep that way for months. Change the sherry once a month. The sherry will be flavored by the ginger and could be used in another dish.

HERB Fresh herbs are far superior to dried. If you like to cook, consider growing your own fresh herbs at home. There are several excellent books on the subject and once you have mastered the art you will have a constant supply of fresh herbs.

LEEKS This member of the onion family is particularly hard to wash. An easy way, however, is to cut off part of the stalk, or all of it, depending on the recipe. Then, with a small paring knife, start at the stalk end and make two vertical cuts at right angles to each other, thus forming a deep cross in the leek (see illustration, page 301). Do not, however, cut all the way through the root; the vegetable should remain attached at the white root end. The leaves will open up like the petals of a flower. Run the leek under cold running water and make sure you rinse each leaf to clean it of all grit. The leek is now ready to be used as indicated in the recipe.

MUSHROOMS (SPECIAL) Mushrooms called for in our book are regular, cultivated mushrooms. Look for firm white caps which are closed on the stem. The piece which joins the steam to the cap should be unbroken. "Special" mushrooms are large mushrooms which run 2 to 3 inches in diameter and which are usually used for stuffing.

MUSTARD When using mustard in our recipes use the imported French Dijon brand.

NUTS *To buy and store:* When buying fresh nuts be sure you are buying from a reputable dealer. Fresh nuts should be full-flavored—sweet without a trace of rancidity. Once you have purchased them, store, covered, in a jar in the refrigerator to prevent them from becoming rancid.
To grind: When grinding nuts you want to pulverize them into small pieces without extracting their oils and turning the mixture into a paste. The best electrical tool for this is the food processor. Follow the directions of your machine for grinding nuts. Otherwise, the best hand method is a small rotary hand grater known as a Mouli.
To roast: Preheat oven to 400 degrees. Place nuts on a baking sheet and bake them for 12 to 15 minutes, or until you can smell the aroma of the roasted nuts.

OILS We call for different kinds of oils in different recipes, depending on the flavor we are trying to achieve.
Olive oil: When we specify, we are looking for a full-bodied flavor, such as that offered in imported Spanish, French, or Italian brands. Because each flavor is so distinct, you should familiarize yourself with the different brands and settle on the ones you prefer. Stay away from cheap brands since they often have no flavor. The best supermarket brand to buy is Goya.
Sesame oil: This oil made from pressing sesame seeds has a distinctive and powerful flavor so it must be used sparingly. Obtainable in Japanese and Chinese

specialty stores.

Safflower oil: This is a light neutral oil, obtainable in health food stores.

Peanut oil: This is readily available in supermarkets.

Vegetable oil: This may be a combination of vegetable oils or just one kind. Use this when we specify a mild-flavored oil. Obtainable in supermarkets.

Walnut oil: This wonderfully fragrant oil made from pressing walnuts is delicious in salads. Because it turns rancid after it has been opened, it should be stored in the refrigerator.

PARSLEY Try to buy the flat leaf Italian parsley, which has more flavor than the curly kind. The curly kind is easier to mince and use for garnish.

To store parsley: Wash the leaves, put the stems in a cup or jar filled with about 2 inches of cold water. Cover the leaves loosely with a plastic bag. Parsley will keep this way for a week. Use this trick to store other green leafy perishables such as watercress, fresh coriander, or even asparagus.

PEPPERCORNS When using pepper always grind it fresh. You can buy *white* and *black* peppercorns in the supermarket. Keep two grinders, one for each kind. When we call for *red* peppercorns we are referring to the red *Szechuan* dried peppercorns available in Oriental food stores. *Green* peppercorns are undried peppercorns. You can buy them in fancy food stores either in cans or jars. If you have a choice, buy the ones packed in water. The ones packed in vinegar have an unpleasant aftertaste. If these are the only ones you can get, be sure to rinse them well before using.

POMEGRANATE JUICE You can make your own pomegranate juice by squeezing fresh pomegranates as you would fresh oranges. This is a tedious task because of the many seeds. You can also buy pomegranate juice in a health food store.

POTATOES There are about 9 different leading varieties of potatoes, but you should select one based on use. The moisture and starch content determine their use. The areas in which potatoes grow also affect their cooking qualities. The Idaho baking potato is grown in a type of soil which makes it very high in starch and, thus, mealy. New potatoes have a higher sugar and moisture content but are lower in starch. They will be "waxy" when cooked and hold their shape. Use boiling potatoes in dishes where they have to hold their shape, such as salads. Older potatoes are more suitable for mashing or for French fries because of their higher starch content.

PRALINE PASTE This is a mixture of roasted hazelnuts and caramelized sugar which is pulverized until it turns smooth and has a consistency similar to peanut butter. No home machine is strong enough to pulverize this mixture to that degree. This is available from Maison Glass (see page 456 for the address).

SAUCIER This is the registered trademark name of a line of reduced stocks made from all natural ingredients. There are 4 frozen varieties on the market: *Beef with Tomatoes*, similar to our *demi-glace*; *Chicken; Fish with Lobster*, which can be used when we call for either a reduced fish stock or a reduced lobster stock; and *Bordelaise*. Note that the frozen variety is made without salt and will seem bland to you. Also note that these are not as reduced as stocks you would reduce at home. This product is available in gourmet food stores and some supermarkets.

SHALLOTS Shallots are used frequently in this book. Fortunately they are readily available in all areas of this country. Unfortunately no one as yet has invented a way to peel shallots quickly—you must remove the skins one at a time. However, shallots do keep very well when minced in a food processor (or by hand), placed in a small stainless steel or plastic bowl, and covered with enough white wine so that they are not exposed to the air. Shallots will keep in this manner for 2 to 3 days.

SHRIMP Unfortunately most of the shrimp available in this country is frozen. Considering the prices charged for shrimp today, you may not be getting your money's worth by purchasing the frozen variety. We suggest you seek out the fresh.

STAR ANISE This is a spice usually used in Chinese cooking. It is shaped like a starfish, is dried, and has a faint licorice flavor. Buy it in Oriental or gourmet food stores. Store it in a covered jar on your pantry shelf.

SUPERFINE SUGAR Refined sugar comes in numerous particle sizes. The ones commonly available on the market are granulated sugar, superfine, and confectioners'. Superfine is a very finely crystallized sugar that will dissolve almost completely when it comes in contact with moisture. It is therefore recommended for use in recipes that require no cooking.

TAMARIND PASTE The tamarind is the fruit of the tamarind tree, which grows in tropical climates. The fruit of the tree contains a juicy, slightly sour pulp which is frequently used in condiments, such as Worcestershire sauce. It has a lovely sour flavor and can be used in different ways. It is available in many Indian and gourmet food stores. It comes concentrated, packed in small plastic containers.

TOMATOES Unless you can get homegrown vine-ripened tomatoes, don't use them out of season (spring/summer)—they are tasteless. If you are doing a recipe which calls for tomatoes and none are available, we would recommend using canned imported Italian seeded plum tomatoes, and then only in recipes in which the tomatoes will require further cooking.

VANILLA BEAN When you can, use a fresh vanilla bean, since a great deal of vanilla extract today is made from a synthetic essence called vanilline. Vanilla beans are available in gourmet food stores. They come packed in thin glass tubes which keep them fresh. When buying beans, look for outside skins which are smooth and shiny. If the bean is shrivelled and looks dry, don't buy it. It should be flexible and you should be able to squeeze out the tiny black fleck-like seeds. They too should look shiny and moist.

VINEGARS Vinegars can be made from fermented fruit juice, the most common one being wine. The finest wine vinegars are made in Orléans, France, and we recommend you buy them from that region. The vinegars we use in this book are mainly red and white wine and tarragon vinegars. These, as well as the champagne, sherry, and cider vinegars are available in fancy food stores. Rice vinegar is available in Oriental food stores.

YOGURT "Dried" yogurt is a wonderful way to thicken sauce without the additional calories of cream or butter. To make it, put plain yogurt in a sieve lined with several layers of washed cheesecloth. Place this over a bowl, cover the sieve with plastic wrap, and put the bowl and sieve in the refrigerator for 48 hours. All excess water will seep to the bottom of the bowl leaving a dense, rich yogurt, ideal for thickening sauces. If you do use this to thicken a sauce, be sure you add the yogurt at the last minute, whisking it in off the heat to keep the sauce from separating.

Glossary of Equipment

BENCH SCRAPER (also referred to as a pastry scraper) A square metal blade with a wooden or stainless steel handle used either to cut dough or scrape dough off a work surface. It looks like a plasterer's spackler.

CAKE PANS In some of our recipes we call for false-bottomed cake pans. If you cannot find these then do the following: Line an ordinary cake pan, of dimensions specified in the recipe, with aluminum foil. Line the pan with enough foil so that an inch or so of it extends up and above the rim of your pan. When the cake is baked, you then can lift it out of the pan by lifting out the foil. When the cake is completely cool, you just peel off the foil. This is an easy way to prevent cakes from sticking to the pan.

CANDY THERMOMETER This is a thermometer registering the range of temperature in candy making. Used for all sugar work to determine when sugar is at soft, medium, hard ball, or crack stage. Taylor is a reliable brand to use.

CHEESECLOTH This refers to a loosely woven cloth which is useful for innumerable culinary preparations. It is important that you use 100 percent cotton cheesecloth because the synthetic kind smells and can impart an unpleasant taste to what you are cooking. Unfortunately, the cotton kind is increasingly difficult to find in ordinary housewares stores. As an alternative source, try art supply stores.

CHINA CAP This term refers to a conical-shaped sieve which comes in different mesh sizes. It is used to strain out solids from a liquid or to pass soft cooked matter into a purée. The advantage of the china cap over an ordinary round sieve is that all the liquid passes through at a single point. Thus you have to press down on the solids only at this single juncture.

DRUM SIEVE A round sieve, shaped like a drum. It is placed over a bowl which catches the purée as you push it through the mesh with a plastic scraper. This is one way to further refine a purée you have passed through a food mill. The end result, however, still has more texture than a purée made with a blender.

FOOD MILL An old-fashioned, hand operated metal or plastic puréeing device. It comes with 3 discs—one for grating, the others for puréeing to two degrees of fineness.

FOOD PROCESSOR This is one of the most extraordinary machines on the market today. Its mechanical action makes elaborate preparations possible in the home kitchen. If, however, you do not own one, here are some less costly gadgets and equipment you can substitute. For purées, a food mill and/or blender is all the equipment you need. The food mill comes with discs with 2 sizes of mesh to make coarse or fine purées. For grinding nuts, chocolate, and hard cheeses by hand, buy a small hand rotary grater called a Mouli. If you can't find one, use an old-fashioned stationary grater made, if possible, of stainless steel, to prevent rust and discoloration.

HAND GRATER A four-sided metal grater which stands on a counter. It has holes of varying sizes on 3 sides and a slicer for potatoes on the fourth side.

ICE CREAM MAKERS We have tested all kinds of ice cream makers. Without a doubt, the old-fashioned method of making ice cream in a bucket with crushed ice and rock salt makes ice cream second to none. If you are going to go to the trouble of making your own ice cream, then invest in the right machine. The kind that makes ice cream in your freezer is not as satisfactory.

LARDING NEEDLES The simplest kind of larding needle you can get is a hollowed-out metal tube with a pointed end and a handle end. Into this hollowed-out tube you put pieces of fat, or, as in our recipes, peppercorns. You insert the pointed end into the roast, and withdraw the tube, leaving the peppercorns inside the roast. If you do not have a larding needle you can instead make small incisions in the roast with a sharp knife and force the peppercorns in with your fingers, aided by the handle of a spoon.

MEAT THERMOMETER The only kind of meat thermometer we believe in is the kind you insert into the roast after it is cooked and then remove immediately. The temperature is "instantly" registered on this thermometer. Known as an "instant" thermometer, it has a range of 0 to 220 degrees and cannot be left in the roast as it cooks. Taylor is the brand to get.

MARBLE SLAB This is a square piece of marble used to provide a cold surface on which to roll or cut pastry. It comes in a variety of sizes and is available at kitchen supply houses.

NON-STICK PANS We do not recommend using the completely non-stick pans for two reasons—either they are coated with something which eventually will come off, or they are too thin. What we do recommend instead is a new semi-non-stick pan called Calphalon. This cookware is made from aluminum with a protective finish which has been applied by an electrochemical process making the finish an integral part of the aluminum. Thus, it does not come off. This finish protects the aluminum from reacting to, and thereby discoloring, certain foods. In addition, it is so well constructed that it comes in a heavy-weight gauge which conducts heat evenly. When you do burn something onto the pan just soak it in soapy water overnight and the burned-on matter literally lifts off without much scrubbing.

PARCHMENT PAPER There are two kinds of parchment paper. There is the ordinary kind used to wrap and bake food and there is a special silicone-treated paper called "kitchen parchment." This is used to line baking pans. It is excellent to use when baking sticky things such as meringue layers or sugary doughs. The paper comes in a dispenser. When you intend to use this paper for baking be sure to purchase the one which is specifically treated to be "non-stick."

PASTRY SCRAPER *See* **Bench Knife**

PLASTIC CUTTING BOARD This is a new portable cutting board made of hard plastic. Better than a wooden cutting board because it does not smell, it is washable and does not dull knife blades. It may be chilled in the refrigerator and used instead of a marble slab as a surface for rolling out pastry.

RAMEKINS Individual oven-proof baking dishes which come in small sizes ranging from ¼ cup to ½ cup.

SILICONE-TREATED BAKING PAPER *See* **Parchment Paper**

SAUTEUSE Also referred to as "sautoir" or "sauté pan." It is a pan which has straight sides, about 3 to 4 inches deep. This type of pan is usually used for dishes in which braising follows sautéing. Be sure to purchase sturdy heavy-duty ones, either tin-lined copper, stainless steel-lined heavy aluminum, or Calphalon.

SKILLET In many of our recipes, we recommend reducing sauces or heavy cream in skillets rather than in saucepans. This is recommended for the simple reason that skillets have a much wider surface area than saucepans. Therefore, any evaporation that takes place is done much more quickly and your sauce is more quickly reduced than it would be if reduced in an ordinary saucepan.

SPATULA This can refer either to the rubber utensil used to fold egg whites into souffles and mousses or the long thin blade used in icing cakes.

STEAMER When we refer to a steamer, we are referring to a stainless steel folding steamer with 3 legs which sits in the pot of your choice. You place the food inside the folding flaps of the steamer; the legs of the steamer keep it above water. This is a practical piece of equipment because the adjustable flaps permit it to be used in a small or large pot.

THERMOMETERS For all kitchen thermometers, whether candy, deep fry, or all-purpose, we recommend buying the Taylor brand. See **Candy Thermometer** and **Meat Thermometer.**

Glossary of Terms

BARDING This refers to covering meat, poultry, or game with pieces of fat before it is roasted. The fat is secured with string. The purpose is to keep the meat moist. Usually the fat is removed before serving.

BLANCHING This refers to dipping foods such as tomatoes or peaches into boiling water for a few seconds to loosen their skins for ease in peeling.

CARAMELIZED This refers to sugar cooked to the point at which it turns golden brown and smells of caramel. In our recipe for Caramelized Onions, we use the term when the natural sugar in the onions begins to turn brown, thus lending their color and flavor to the onion dish.

CHOP When we call for something to be chopped, it means to roughly cut the food into uneven, largish pieces.

DEGLAZING When you sauté or roast something, there are usually little brown particles of coagulated juices that adhere to the bottom of your pan. Once you have poured out the excess fat from your pan, you add liquid to these browned particles and scrape them into the liquid as it comes to the boil. The particles dissolve into the liquid.

DEGREASE This refers to one of two processes: After you have sautéed or roasted something, there might be an accumulation of fat on the bottom of the pan. To discard this fat is to degrease. To degrease also refers to removing the film of fat on the surface of a hot liquid, such as stock or a sauce.

DICING To dice is to cut food in small square shapes. Usually a dice is about ¼-inch square and "finely diced" refers to smaller cubes, somewhere between ⅛ and ¼ of an inch.

FELL This refers to the tough translucent skin which covers the fat layer on lamb. This should be removed because it is tough to carve through and causes the meat to curl when cooked.

GRATING *See* **Shredding**

GRATING FRUIT PEELS When you remove the peel of citrus fruit, whether orange, lemon, or grapefruit be sure to peel or grate only the skin. Leave the white pith on the fruit or discard as this has a bitter taste.

JULIENNE To cut food into matchstick pieces usually about ⅛- to ¼-inch wide and whatever length the recipe specifies. If it does not specify, cut it into 2-inch lengths.

LOOSELY PACKED When we refer to loosely packed, as in herbs for example, we mean for you to place your ingredients into a measuring utensil without tamping them down.

MINCE To chop foods into tiny irregular pieces.

PARBOIL This refers to precooking something, often in boiling water, which you are going to finish cooking later.

PLATES When you serve hot foods, be sure to heat the plates you are going to be serving on. If you do not have room in your oven to keep them warm, you can warm them on the "warm" cycle of your dishwasher, or keep them off the heat on top of the stove. In our book this is crucial, because food is presented on individual plates, which means that unless they are hot, the food can cool off by the time you are finished dishing it out. Chill plates in the refrigerator when serving cold salads or desserts and ices or ice creams.

POACHING This refers to a cooking process in which food is submerged in a liquid which is barely simmering. Bubbles should only occasionally break the surface of the liquid. This method is used for fragile foods, such as fish and shellfish.

REDUCE This refers to heating a stock, sauce or cream so that it begins to evaporate and thereby becomes more condensed and flavorful. If a recipe calls for you to "reduce a sauce by half," boil the liquid until its volume is half what it was when you began reducing. Watch out that the sauce doesn't get too hot and boil over the side. This is correctible by lowering or raising the heat maintaining a constant rolling motion on top of the liquid.

SAUTÉING This refers to cooking food in a skillet for a short period of time, in little fat, and over medium to very high heat. You usually are moving the food around constantly, either by shaking the skillet or by stirring with a spoon.

SEASON LIGHTLY Many times recipes will tell you to "season lightly." This means you must take a pinch of salt and dust the surface of the food to be seasoned. The same is true for pepper. However, we suggest you apply the pepper directly from a pepper mill. Since every portion of food to be "lightly seasoned" is a different size it would be impractical to list exact measurements for salt and pepper in each instance.

SHREDDING VEGETABLES This means to tear food such as lettuce into uneven pieces, or to grate food on the large holes of a grater to produce thin strands.

SIMMERING This refers to cooking food in a liquid in which bubbles gently break the surface. This cooking is slightly more active than poaching, but way under the boiling point. The temperature range is usually between 135 and 160 degrees.

Mail-Order Sources

NORTH:

Aphrodesia Products, Inc.
28 Carmine Street
New York, NY 10014

Stocks every conceivable herb and spice, including oriental ones.

Bazaar De La Cuisine
International, Inc.
1003 Second Avenue
New York, NY 10022

Carries imported gourmet foods, including foie gras and vinegars, and also stocks Smithfield hams.

Fraser Morris & Co., Inc.
931 Madison Avenue
New York, NY 10021

A good source for fresh venison, rabbit, wild rice, and foie gras.

Kitchen Bazaar
4455 Connecticut Avenue, NW
Washington, DC 20008

Stocks specialty kitchen equipment.

Lekvar By The Barrel
1577 First Avenue
New York, NY 10028

Good source for herbs and exotic spices, as well as specialty kitchen equipment.

Maison Glass
52 East 58th Street
New York, NY 10022

Carries luxury foods such as green peppercorns packed in water, imported chocolate, and foie gras, and is the only source we know of for praline paste.

Paul A. Urbani Truffles
PO Box 2054
Trenton, NJ 08650

Only source we know of in the United States which ships fresh black and white truffles, when in season.

The Vermont Country Store
Weston, VT 05161

Stocks exotic spices, herbs, and condiments, imported luxury foods, and specialty cooking equipment.

SOUTH:

Creole Delicacies Co., Inc.
533 Saint Ann Street
New Orleans, LA 70116

Carries native ingredients, such as Smithfield hams and some imported gourmet items.

Neiman-Marcus Epicure Shop Main and Ervay Streets Dallas, TX 75201	*Source for luxury imported canned goods, such as specialty vinegars and canned truffles.*
Teel Mountain Farms Box 201 Standardsville, VA 22973	*Excellent source for organically raised, milk-fed veal.*

MIDWEST:

B & B Food Products Route 1 Cadiz, KY 42111	*Excellent source for Kentucky hams, dry-cured and hickory-smoked.*
Maid of Scandinavia 3244 Raleigh Avenue South Minneapolis, MN 55416	*Stocks specialty kitchen equipment, especially baking equipment, and is a source for silicone-treated baking paper.*
Omaha Steaks International 4400 South 96th Street Omaha, NE 68127	*Good source for fresh meats, especially beef. Stocks saddle of lamb, pork tenderloin fillets, and boneless leg of spring lamb.*

WEST COAST:

Anzen Japanese Foods and Imports 736 NE Union Avenue Portland, OR 97232	*Carries oriental spices and condiments, as well as kitchen equipment.*
Jurgensen's Grocery Company 842 East California Boulevard Pasadena, CA 91106	*Stocks Smithfield hams, fresh prime meats, and some imported luxury canned foods.*
Williams-Sonoma PO Box 3792 San Francisco, CA 94119	*Source for specialty kitchen equipment, and·some imported luxury foods such as black olives from France and specialty vinegars.*

Index

C

Cakes, 370–387
  Chocolate Almond, 370–373
  Chocolate Sweetness, 373–375
  David's, 377–380
  Fine Orange, 382–385
  Lemon Almond, 380–382
  Penuche and Raisin Layer, 385–387
  Souffléed Chocolate 375–377
Calves Liver, 300–304
  with Currant Glaze, 302–304
  with Leek Purée, 300–302
Caper Sauce, Venison Steak with, 296–297
Capers, Veal Loin with, 223–224
Capon Stuffed with Wild Rice, 234–236
Caramelized Onions, 342–343
Carrots
  Onions, and Mushrooms, Baked Wild Rice with, 344–345
  and Onions, Roast Beef with, 166–167
  Shredded, with Orange Juice, 332–333
Cassis
  Frozen Mousse, 417–418
  and Whole Shallots, Sweetbreads with, 304–306
Cauliflower
  Purée with Celery, 331
Celery Julienne, Bay Scallops with, 145–146
Cheese, Goat, and Pears in Salad, 104–105
Cherries, Fresh, in Puff Pastry, 392–395
Chestnut Purée, Squabs on a Bed of, 288–290
Chicken, 237–265
  with Basil and Tarragon, 260–262
  Breasts, Pecan-Breaded with Mustard Sauce, 258–260
  Breasts, Sautéed, 247–248
  Breasts with Hot Tomato Vinaigrette, 262–263
  in Fresh Tomato and Vinegar Sauce, 245–247
  with Garlic Sauce, 237–239
  Legs, Stuffed, 254–256
  Liver, Piquant Salad with, 100–101
  and Sautéed Apples in Puff Pastry, 249–251

  in Spinach Broth with Fresh Vegetables, 240–242
  Terrine, 251–254
  with Vegetables, 242–244
  Wings with Tamarind and Garlic, 264–265
Chives, Sole with, 131–134
Chocolate
  Almond Cake, 370–373
  Chip Tartlets, 400–402
  Dark, Pink Pear with, 433–435
  -Dipped Strawberries, 435–436
  Mocha Cream, 415–416
  Souffléed Cake, 375–377
  Sweetness (Cake), 272–375
  Truffles, 408–410
Cider, Veal in, 217–219
Cold Bay Scallops with Cumin Vinaigrette, 147–149
Cold Beef Salad, 102–104
Cold Loin of Pork with Green Peppercorn Mayonnaise Sauce, 190–191
Cold Oyster and Tamarind Soup, 83–84
Cold Sweetbreads with Oranges, 307–309
Cookies, 407–412
  Butter, 407–408
  Chocolate Truffles, 408–410
  Palmiers, 410–412
Cooking in a restaurant, 21–24
Cornish Game Hen(s), 266–273
  in Cumin and Vinegar, 268–270
  with Plantains and Pine Nuts, 266–268
  Stew, 270–273
Crabs, Soft Shell, 160–163
  with Lime Sauce, 160–161
  with Lobster Sauce, 162–163
Cranberry(ies)
  Duck with, 280–281
  Soufflé, 413–415
    Cucumber, Shredded with Dill, 333–334
Cumin
  Vinaigrette, Cold Bay Scallops with, 147–149
  and Vinegar, Cornish Game Hens in, 268–270
Currant(s)
  Glaze, Calves Liver with, 302–304
  Raisin, and Red Wine Sauce, Rabbit with, 298–300
  and Spices, Salmon Fillet with, 116–118

J

Jerusalem Artichoke Soup, 81–83
Julienne of Winter Root Vegetables, 345–347

K

Kale Simmered in Cream, 340
Kohlrabi Soup, 74–75

L

Lamb, 200–216
    Boned Saddle of, Stuffed with Mushrooms, 206–208
    Boneless Steak with Yogurt and Mint, 209–210
    Herbed Leg of, with Anchovy Butter, 200–201
    Leg of, with Mustard and Fresh Pineapple Sauce, 202–204
    Medallions of, with Artichoke Sauce, 211–213
    Medallions, with Bordelaise and Port Sauce, 213–214
    Rack of, with Anise and Sweet Garlic, 204–206
    Sautéed Rib Chops with Rosemary and Thyme, 215–216
Leek Purée, 341–342
    Calves Liver with, 300–302
Leg of Lamb with Mustard and Fresh Pineapple Sauce, 202–204
Lemon
    Almond Cake, 380–382
    Sauce, Veal and, 224–226
Lettuce, Stuffed Sea Bass Steamed in, 121–123
Lime
    Ice, 315–316
    Sauce, Soft Shell Crabs with, 160–161
    Soufflé, 419–421
Liver
    Calves, with Currant Glaze, 302–304
    Calves, with Leek Purée, 300–302
    Chicken, Piquant Salad with, 100–101
Lobster, 135–140
    Baked, 135–137
    with Vegetables, 138–140

Lobster Sauce, Soft Shell Crabs with, 162–163

M

Mango Ice, 317–318
Mayonnaise, Green Peppercorn, Sauce, Cold Loin of Pork with, 190–191
Meat, 165–231
    Beef, 166–185
    Lamb, 200–216
    Pork, 186–199
    Veal, 217–231
    See also Game and Variety Meats
Medallions of Lamb with Artichoke Sauce, 211–213
Melon with Honey and Rum Sauce, 428–429
Menus, 25–43
    principles of composing, 25–27
    timetables for preparation of, 33–39, 42–43
    two examples of, 28–43
Mint and Yogurt, Boneless Lamb Steak with, 209–210
Mocha Cream, 415–416
Mousse Cassis, Frozen, 417–418
Mushrooms
    Boned Saddle of Lamb Stuffed with, 206–208
    Carrots, and Onions, Baked Wild Rice with, 344–345
Mussel(s)
    in Puff Pastry, 140–142
    and Saffron Soup, 85–87
Mustard Sauce
    and Fresh Pineapple, Leg of Lamb with, 202–204
    Pecan-Breaded Chicken Breasts with, 258–260

N

Nectarine and Plum Flan, 421–422
Nouvelle cuisine
    American interpretation of, 18–20
    composing and planning two menus, 28–43
    explanation of, 7–17
    history, 3–6
    principles of a menu, 25–27
    recipe format, 44–45
    in a restaurant kitchen, 21–24

W

Y